ECHOES OF VALOR

THE TIMELESS TRADITION OF MILITARY FUNERALS IN AMERICA

Benjamin A. Saunders

Echoes of Valor

The Timeless Tradition of Military Funerals in America

Benjamin A. Saunders

Library of Congress Cataloging-in-Publication Data

Saunders, Benjamin A.
Echoes of Valor: The Timeless Tradition of Military Funerals in America / Benjamin A. Saunders.
p. cm
Includes bibliographical references and index.
ISBN: 979-833-344310-6 (paperback) ISBN: 979-833-529148-4 (hardback)

Originally published in hardback by Benjamin A. Saunders, August 2024

1. Saunders, Benjamin A. 2. Military Funerals—United States—History. 3. Firing Three Volleys—United States History. 4. Funeral Service—United States—History. 5. Taps—United States—History. 6. Folding of the Flag—United States—History. I. Title.

Library of Congress Control Number: 2024917712

Cover art and design by Benjamin A. Saunders

First Printing

Dedicated to the men and women in the United States armed forces past, present, and future-who knowingly look death in the eyes, their families, and those that honor the dead.

And to my own family without which none of this would have been possible.

ACKNOWLEDGMENTS

"...he commanded our fathers, that they should make them known to
their children:
That the generation to come might know them,..."

Psalm 78:5-6, KJV

It has been said, "It takes a village to raise a child." I can tell you it takes a village to write and publish a book. I was reminded of the above Bible scripture listening to a sermon by pastor, teacher, and author Dr. Adrian Rogers titled, "Christian Faith and Values for the Coming Generation." In his sermon he said, "I want a nation that we can thank God for, one nation under God." With that being said, I'd like to thank God for answering my prayers and allowing this book to come to fruition. Secondly, like I did at my speech when I graduated number one in my class from mortuary school, I extend my deepest gratitude to my mother.

In this book I revisit stories of our American heritage as told in our history and civics classes in school. Some are well-known heroes, others a little lesser known, and some unknown. I have conducted numerous funerals and military funerals, and asked members of the honor guard, individually, if they could tell me the origins of which this book speaks. I have asked numerous veterans and active-duty military personnel about the origins of the draping of the flag on a casket, firing the three volleys over the grave, the sounding of Taps, and the folding and presentation of the flag, to this group of people I say thank you for your sacrifice and commitment to America, and for honoring the memory of your fallen comrades. A special acknowledgment goes to the unknown 82-year-old Vietnam veteran I encountered at the Kroger grocery store in Springfield, TN. Your readiness to serve your country once again exemplifies the fortitude that defines America. I am grateful for the authors and experts who lent their support: Marc Leepson for his invaluable direction on flag research, Bryan Davis for his insights

ACKNOWLEDGMENTS

on proofreading, formatting, and publishing, Erick Rheam for his marketing tips, and Terio for his guidance on editing. Special thanks to Laura Mosher, the Cadet Engagement Librarian at the United States Military Academy, for her assistance in research.

I am grateful to all of the families that I have served in funeral service, and to those who helped me become a licensed funeral director. I also want to thank Oakland City University for the countless hours spent in their library, which enriched my understanding and fueled my passion for this project. Last but certainly not least, I owe my deepest appreciation to my wife, Jeanill, and our children and grandchildren. Your words of encouragement and love inspire me every day. And for anyone that I missed, saying thank you just doesn't seem like enough, but you have my sincerest appreciation.

CONTENTS

Show me the manner in which a nation or a community cares for its dead, and I will measure with mathematical exactness the tender sympathies of its people, their respect for the law of the land, and their loyalty to high ideals.

-William Ewart Gladstone, 19-century British Prime Minister

PROLOGUE

An aerial bomb marks the opening of the gates on race day of Memorial Day weekend at the Indianapolis Motor Speedway. As crowds from around the country gather in for their own pre-race ceremonies of breakfast, tailgating, and beer drinking, the sound of the world's largest drum of the Purdue University Marching Band can be heard with its thud as it's being driven around the track. There is the playing of songs by the Purdue Marching Band of On the Banks of the Wabash, and Stars and Stripes Forever. There's a parade, with the display of the Borg-Warner Trophy adorning the faces of some seventy-five plus drivers who have won the Indy 500 since its inaugural event in 1911. Then there is the chaos of the open-wheel miniature airplane-looking cars brought to the grid behind the start finish line yard of bricks. Finally, driver introductions from the 11th row to the front row as they report to their vibrant-colored cars.

Traditions, memorials, and cemeteries all come out of sacrifice and death. Honoring our loved ones is never more evident than when the matriarch or patriarch of a family passes away. The ceremonies of a public funeral pay tribute and bring people closure, as if saying a final goodbye or see you later. Death comes to us all, but will we be remembered for how we lived or how we died? The men and women of the United States Armed Forces will. Their final salute will be on behalf of a grateful nation and the nation's debt owed for their service. Each year on the door steps of summer (Memorial Day) and winter (Veteran's Day), the nation pauses to recognize and pay tribute to the men and women serving and who have served in the United States armed forces, and those who gave their lives to preserve our democracy and freedoms. In town squares and military cemeteries, we bow our heads in silent homage and reverence for those fallen soldiers, airmen, sailors, marines, and for those lost for the cause of exploring outer space and gave their lives believing beyond the stars. In their service and death, we find a deeper appreciation for what it means to be an American, a deeper appreciation for the ultimate sacrifice.

On a weekend in May, America throws some of its grandest parties. None bigger than at the Indianapolis Motor Speedway where a celebration of speed and bravery is conducted in the vibrant colors of the "The Greatest Spectacle in Racing" and like no other sport. However, there could be no Memorial Day party such as this if it were not for the sacrifice of the men and women in uniform. Without sacrifice there is no party, and without the sacrifice of those in the Armed Forces, there is no America. Imagine what the country would be like if those who fought the Revolutionary War against the British had surrendered. Would there be an American dream? Would people pull themselves up by their bootstraps and, with raw determination, push forward until their cause is won? America was founded on sacrifice, which has developed into American traditions and customs. Traditions that have stood the test of time.

At Indianapolis that tradition has always been understood and has always stood in solidarity and gratitude with our military. Traditions dating back to 1911 when Ray Harroun won the Indianapolis 500 in a single-seat Marmon Wasp. Then called Decoration Day, where mourners honored the Civil War dead by decorating their graves with flowers, citizens continued that tradition passed down from generation to generation. Who would have thought racing and Memorial Day would be almost symbiotic? Besides the Indianapolis 500 there is also a NASCAR race in Charlotte, North Carolina called the Coca-Cola 600 that also has a similar tradition to that of Indianapolis, but the tradition of Indianapolis goes back more than a century pausing for World War I, when the track was used for aviation support. During World War II, the Indy 500 was postponed another four years, while the Speedway area became the production center for airplane engines to support the war effort. In the words of Tim Layden, "Most of all on a weekend of revelry and remembrance, the Indy 500 is a vital piece of connective tissue, an assembly of Americans that pointedly never forgets what Memorial Day means the most. That we are here for the roar, that we are here for speed, and that we are here because of them."[1]

Having been to the Indianapolis 500 on numerous occasions, the traditions are like none other. The Army paratrooper skydiving, with the American Flag attached, lands in the infield. The call from the public address announcer Dave Calabro, although I remember for years hearing the voice of Tom Carnegie who retired in 2006 and passed away in 2011, "Ladies and Gentlemen, please rise and remove your hats for the presentation of colors, invocation, and a moment of reflection for those who have given their lives unselfishly to defend our freedom."[2] Just writing about this race takes me back to my childhood days, where famous racers walked and the unknown became champions. As the public address announcer is speaking, the color guard marches to the stage with the colors of our country and flags representing each branch of service, including Space Force. Each flag represents not just a military branch, rather groups of volunteers that recognize the potential of looking death in the eyes and that their work is dangerous and are willing to give their lives for the purpose of furthering America.

The Archbishop of the Archdiocese of Indianapolis usually gives the invocation, but other members of the clergy have done so in the past. In 2024, it was Archbishop Charles C. Thompson who said, "Let us pray. Eternal God, in your wisdom and love. You call us to search always for that which is praiseworthy, excellent, and gracious. And so, as we commend to you the men and women who have died for our freedom. May we strive for whatever is true, honorable, and just in our lives. Bless these drivers, their teams, the officials, and all the fans. Make this gathering a time of gratitude for human achievement while we savor so many glimpses of your glory. God bless those who have died for our freedom. God bless all those gathered for this the greatest spectacle in racing! And God bless America!"[3]

In true military fashion the commander of the honor guard gives the order "Port arms. Forward march. Mark time, march. Firing party halt. (As seven members of the United States Army form the firing squad gather.) Port arms. Right face. Ready, aim, fire. Ready, aim, fire. Ready, aim, fire. Ready. Present arms." Then the bugler in the flag tower at the start finish line sounds the familiar and heartfelt notes we recognize as "Taps." The traditions of the Indianapolis Motor Speedway don't stop there but continue with American Idol Champion Philip Phillips singing God Bless America, and sometimes there is a rendition of America the Beautiful. Then Jordin Sparks, who was also a former American Idol winner, sang the National Anthem as the Air Force Thunderbirds flew overhead near the end of the song. Just before the Chairman of the Indianapolis Motor Speedway Roger Penske gave the command to start engines, Jim Cornelison sang Back Home Again in Indiana. Most of these traditions, particularly the military one, are familiar to us as Americans, unless you grew up as race fans or in Indiana. It is long-standing military customs like this and the wishes of the primary next of kin that are the foundation of the ceremonies mentioned to honor the dead. The military has rooted and expanded these traditions in their standing orders. My hope is to shed light on the origins of what I call the four parts of a military funeral, draping of the flag on a casket, firing of three volleys, the sounding of "Taps," and the folding and presentation of the flag to the primary next of kin. Although some origins may seem to be unknown, they are deeply woven into the fabric that built America. Just like a race that honors the men and the women and the first responders who keep our country safe and secure, we honor those who pass away deserving of our nation's highest honors, and we owe them our gratitude.

Chapter 1

Military Funerals

"You always hear all the statements like 'freedom isn't free.' You hear the president talking about all these people making sacrifices. But you never really know until you carry one of them in the casket. When you feel their body weight. When you feel them, that's when you know. That's when you understand."[1]
-Staff Sergeant Kevin Thomas, United States Marine Corps.

I n a book titled: Echoes of Valor: The Timeless Tradition of Military Funerals in America, the book you are reading, it is a good idea to begin with an overview of military funerals. According to the latest unclassified Army Regulations (AR 600-25) dated September 10, 2019, the Defense Department provides the blueprint for what constitutes a military funeral and how the ceremony should work. This chapter establishes the etiquette and protocol for how military funerals are conducted, as well as who conducts them. Although, as a funeral director, I use local retired veterans of the American Legion and Veterans of Foreign Wars, some funeral homes in metropolitan areas use these organizations and active-duty service members. I also believe that funerals should be tailored to the deceased's life or the life they shared with their family and friends. Funeral services are anything but routine because each family, and their dynamics are unique.

A military funeral provides a public service to the bereaved and is really a show of public support, showing a support system that says, "We are behind you and with you in your time of grief and mourning." Remember three days after planes flew into the World Trade Center in Manhattan on September 11, 2001, President George W. Bush echoed this saying, "Thank you all. I want you all to know -- it [bullhorn] can't go any louder -- I want you all to know that America today, America today is on bended knee, in prayer for the people whose lives were lost here, for the workers who work here, for the families who mourn. The nation stands with the good people of New York City, New Jersey, and Connecticut as we mourn the loss of thousands of our citizens. [Crowds says they can't hear the president.] I can hear you! I can hear you! The rest of the world hears you! And the people— and the people who knocked these buildings down—will hear all of us soon! The nation -- The nation sends its love and compassion to everybody who is here. Thank you for your hard work. Thank you for makin' the nation proud, and may God bless America."[2] Terrorists had struck America and Bush's speech at what we call "Ground Zero" was the rallying cry that would send our nation to war.

During these times, a member of the clergy or a designated officiant almost always oversees the funeral service or ceremony and provides religious support to those in mourning, all while expressing the same message. We are behind you. They are providing that rallying cry. As a funeral director, it sometimes seems inappropriate for some religious officiants to take advantage of a captive audience by saying come to Jesus as their alter call, when what they are essentially saying is that we are behind you, we are here for you in your time of mourning and grief, and that Jesus has the answer and offers you comfort and peace.

The military and religious ceremonies not only facilitate the honoring of the deceased, but also serve as a reminder that there are others who have experienced similar circumstances and stand alongside the family during their lowest moments of grief and mourning. **"I will NEVER leave a fallen comrade"**[3] is part of the Soldier's Creed. We revere those who have died and lay to rest those who have served our country with dignity, honor, and respect. Funeral directors and members of the clergy treat the families they serve with courtesy and compassion in hopes of giving the deceased's family a service worth remembering or a home going that is not just honorable but makes the Almighty God nod and smile with approval. Funerals reflect the value and worth of the individual, the life they lived, and the roles they served. In Star Trek terms, the needs of the one outweigh the needs of the many. However, we find many of today's traditions rooted in the past, codified into General Orders, or as discussed here, Army Regulations (AR). Most of what follows is from the Army Techniques Publication (ATP 1-05.02) dated November 27, 2018. Just know that like everything the military does, the Salutes, Honors, and Courtesy of AR 600-25 is very regimented, very formal, and very disciplined. As you read this book, you will discover how some of the history and customs we see today in the twenty-first century came about. It is my hope to give an explanation from a funeral directors' perspective and explore the potential origins of where these traditions derived, doing so with the utmost dignity, honor, and respect to those who are currently serving in our armed forces and those countless veterans who have honorably served.

It is incredibly important to establish the person authorized to direct the disposition of human remains (PADD) no matter what type of funeral service. Most states have such laws or codes in their laws establishing a hierarchy for the person authorized to direct disposition. As a funeral director in Indiana and Tennessee, for example, "The right to control disposition of a decedents body, to make arrangements for funeral services, and to make other ceremonial arrangements after an individual's death devolves on the following, in the priority listed:

(1) A person:

(A) granted the authority to serve in a funeral planning declaration executed by the decedent under this chapter; or

(B) named in a United States Department of Defense form "Record of Emergency Data" (DD Form 93) or a successor form adopted by the United States Department of Defense, if the decedent died while serving in any branch of the United States Armed Forces (as defined in 10 U.S.C. 1481) and completed the form. So, when you join the military today, if something happens in the line of duty it is clear who has the right of disposition.

(2) An individual specifically granted the authority in a power of attorney, or a health care power of attorney executed by the decedent, or a health care representative named by law. In Indiana and other states, there is what is called the Funeral Planning Declaration, which supersedes or acts as the power of attorney because it specifically names who is going to make the funeral arrangements and is signed by the deceased prior to their passing.

(3) The decedent's surviving spouse. You would think that the surviving spouse would be first, which is true in most cases. Every law is the result of a mistake made by one or more people, such as improper identification of the deceased or cremated human remains. The individual paying for the funeral is not necessarily the person authorized to direct the disposition. Additionally, there have been numerous cases where the deceased has had a mistress or girlfriend who thinks they are in charge, when in reality, it is the wife to whom he is still legally married. Laws exist to maintain order. Again, for every law to become important enough to maintain the order of things and become a law, someone had to commit a foolish act.

(4) The decedent's surviving adult child, or if more than one (1) adult child is surviving, the majority of the other surviving adult children. However, less than half of the surviving adult children have the rights if the adult children have used reasonable efforts to notify the other surviving adult children of their intentions and are not aware of any opposition to the final disposition instructions by more than half of the surviving adult children.

(5) The surviving parent or parents of the decedent. If one (1) of the parents is absent, the present parent has rights provided they have made reasonable efforts to notify the absent parent.

(6) The decedent's surviving sibling or, if more than one (1) sibling is surviving, the majority of the surviving siblings. However, if less than half of the surviving siblings have used reasonable efforts to notify the other surviving siblings of their intentions and are not aware of any opposition to the final disposition instructions by more than half of the surviving siblings, then they have the right.

(7) A guardian appointed by a court.

(8) The law grants an individual in the next degree of kinship the right to inherit the decedent's estate, or, if more than one (1) individual in the same degree survives, the majority of those in the same degree of kinship. But people with less than half of the same degree of kinship have rights if they have tried reasonably hard to let other people with the same degree of kinship know what they want and don't know of any opposition to the final disposition instructions from more than half of the people with the same degree of kinship.

(9) If none of the people described are available, or willing, to act and arrange for the final disposition of the decedent's remains, a stepchild (as defined by law) of the decedent. If more than one (1) stepchild survives the decedent, then a majority of the surviving stepchildren. However, less than half of the surviving stepchildren

have rights if they have used reasonable efforts to notify the other stepchildren of their intentions and are not aware of any opposition to the final disposition instructions by more than half of the stepchildren. All this essentially means is that no one can stonewall the process once notifications for the primary next of kin begins.

(10) The person appointed to administer the decedent's estate.

(11) If none of the persons described in sections (1) through (10) are available, any other person willing to act and arrange for the final disposition of the decedent's remains, including a funeral home that:

(A) has a valid prepaid funeral plan executed by legal statues that makes arrangements for the disposition of the decedent's remains; and

(B) attests in writing that a good faith effort has been made to contact any living individuals described in sections (1) through (10).[4]

As you peruse through the complexity of the person authorized to direct the disposition of human remains, just know that other states have something similar, and the military differs slightly in its regulations. I do like that they say," Only one person at a time can be the PADD, that gives you one person in charge, and to give a comparison I put Army Regulation 638-2 dated March 3, 2023, page 17 subsection 3-3 as follows which was briefly mentioned in point 1 subsection B:

On the DD Form 93, the individual designated by the deceased member is entitled to direct the disposition of the remains, including subsequent portions, or retained organs. If a member has failed to designate a PADD, or the designated PADD does not wish to exercise the responsibilities of the PADD and therefore requests to relinquish his/her rights to direct disposition of the remains, the hierarchy listed in paragraphs b. (1) through (9) will be utilized to determine who serves as the PADD, in order of precedence. If two or more people claim the right to direct disposition but are unable to provide documentary support, agreement may be reached either mutually or through legal adjudication in civil courts. The Army will comply with any civil court's decision regarding the authority to dispose of a fallen soldier's remains.

b. The following persons may be designated to direct the disposition of the remains of a decedent covered by this chapter:

(1) The PADD is the person designated by the decedent on the emergency data record (DD Form 93 or any successor to that form), irrespective of the relationship between the designee and the decedent.

(2) Surviving spouse.

(3) Children over 18 years of age, in order of age from oldest to youngest.

(4) If the decedent is not divorced, the custodial parent or legal guardian, whichever is older, will receive the right to direct the disposition. If divorced when the decedent was a minor, the custodial parent or legal guardian has the right to direct disposition. If the parents divorced after the decedent was of legal age, the eldest parent has the right to direct disposition.

(5) A blood relative who had legal custody by court decree or statutory provision.

(6) Brothers and sisters over 18 years old, in order of age from oldest to youngest.

(7) Grandparents, in order of age, from oldest to youngest.

(8) According to state laws, blood relatives over 18 years of age are listed in order of relationship to the deceased. Seniority by age, in equal degrees of relationship.

(9) Adoptive relatives of the decedent in order of relationship and age.

(10) A person standing in loco parentis to the decedent if no person in paragraphs b. (1) through (9) can be found.

c. When the person in the highest position in the order listed in paragraphs b. (1) through (10) declines in writing to direct the DOR, the authority will be offered to the next person in order of priority.

d. When no person in the order of priority can be identified or located, disposition of the remains will be made by the administrative determination of the CG (Commanding General), HRC (Human Rights Commission) (AHRC–PDC). In other words, a probate court or higher authority, depending on whether it is military or civilian.

The Department of Defense has developed guidelines through several centuries of legislation, primarily in the twentieth century, to provide military funeral honors for all present and former military personnel.

Some of those guidelines are as follows:

Medal of Honor recipients, active-duty Soldiers, and retirees are provided full Military Funeral Honors with a service detail consisting of a 9-member team.

- Veterans are entitled to Military Funeral Honors with a service detail consisting of at least 2 uniformed military members, at least 1 of whom will be from the veteran's parent service.
- Every effort will be made to obtain a live bugler to play "Taps."
- Local commanders determine the availability of their resources as they pertain to military funeral honors support, the composition of the burial honors details, and any restrictions relating to military honors.

The Army divides military funerals into two classes: chapel service, graveside service only, and movement to the grave or place of interment for final disposition with the prescribed escort. The word "chapel" is interpreted to include church, home, funeral parlor, or other place where services are held, other than the service at the grave.

There are three types of military funerals that may be performed. They include:

1. A full military funeral that normally consists of, or is supported by, a 9-person funeral detail has the following elements:

   Casualty assistance officer (CAO).

   Officer in charge (OIC) or noncommissioned officer in charge (NCOIC) (appropriate for the rank of the deceased).

   One bugler to play "Taps" (or an electronic recording).

   Six active-duty pallbearers and a firing party. (This is a dual function, as the pallbearers also serve as the firing party and will render these honors).

   Military clergy (if requested and available).

2. If resources permit, a larger funeral detail may be provided, which is composed of all the elements of the nine-person funeral detail, and may also include the following:

   - Colors.
   - A separate firing party, consisting of no more than 8 or less than 5 riflemen, is required.
   - Hearse (caisson).
   - Honorary pallbearers.
   - Personal colors (if appropriate).
   - Escort unit or units (appropriate for the rank of the deceased).

3. A two-man military funeral honors detail consists of the following elements:

   - An OIC or NCOIC (appropriate for the rank of the deceased).
   - An enlisted Soldier.
   - One bugler to play "Taps" (or an electronic recording).[5]

The Army provides burial honors for deceased Army personnel, including active duty and retired personnel, as well as eligible Reserve Components and authorized veterans, upon the family's request. The key words here are at the request of the family. The Marine Corp Casualty Assistance Center has a motto "Taking care of our own." A motto, if you ask this author, extends beyond providing funeral honors and is a tribute to always having one's back and taking care of family no matter what. As a funeral director, you see numerous family dynamics. You see families with life insurance, cash in hand, and those without money and in need of assistance trying to figure out how to cover the cost of a funeral service, cremation, celebration of life, or burial. When a family walks into a funeral home, they already have a fairly good idea of what they want or need. The main things they are looking for are compassionate individuals who can guide them through their time of need without imposing unnecessary charges or upgrades. People know what they want, but they may not always know how to communicate what they want or need in what can be an emotionally charged time, a difficult time. Additionally, they want to be guided through the funeral arrangements process by knowledgeable educated funeral directors.

If you take the time to read the Army Techniques Publication's Religious Support to Funerals and Memorial Events (ATP 1-05.02), you could almost replace the reference to the officiant with the term "funeral director." There is a whole section on funeral arrangements, but the key to making funeral arrangements is: What are the needs of the family? The family has the right to provide their input about the honors that are being given. If the deceased were Buddhist, Methodist, Baptist, Catholic, Lutheran, Muslim, Jewish, Latter-Day Saints (Mormon), etc., they have the right to have a member of the clergy representing the religion or denomination of the deceased. Depending on the deceased's religion, the family also has the right to ensure adherence to religious customs such as body washing, dressing, and funeral vestments. The funeral may also be conducted locally or at graveside. I'll give you the funeral director's perspective, but in the

Army, it is the responsibility of the chaplain or funeral director to be the action officers and prepare and conduct funerals. The assigned chaplain typically conducts funerals following the death of a soldier or family member from a unit. At other times, the installation or higher headquarters may task the chaplain to funeral duty in accordance with DA Form 6 (Duty Roster).

In chapter 2, Looking Death in the Eyes, I describe making funeral arrangements for a veteran who lives in Cincinnati, Ohio, who is a retired Army Ranger and works for the Department of Veterans Affairs in Cincinnati and is now being served by his local funeral home, where he grew up in southwest Indiana, and where he is now buried. What's crucial is the family's involvement and the details of who, what, when, and where the funeral will take place. Who will officiate the service? Where will the service be held? The service could take place at a funeral home, on a military base, in a church, mosque, synagogue, graveside, etc. What is the family's preference? Do they want retired veterans of the American Legion or Veterans of Foreign Wars, or active-duty servicemen and women? What is the date and time that the calling hours or visitation and funeral services begin, and when does the honor guard need to arrive and perform their duties? An even more important question comes when talking about military funerals: Who is going to receive the burial flag? In some cases, siblings squabble over who is going to receive the flag. As a funeral director, I only interject my opinion when we are not getting anywhere with the conversation. I make suggestions, but ultimately, the family must come to a consensus in the absence of a spouse. The decision is typically easy if there is only one child, grandchild, or next of kin, but it can be an interesting dynamic.

Author's side note, in my experience the eldest child and/or grandchild receives the flag as designated in the absence of a spouse, but the family always seems to work out who is to receive the flag.

For funeral directors and clergypersons, it is important to take care of the bereaved. When a family has a loved one pass away, it is an emotionally charged time. The funeral director serves as director, grief counselor, advocate, and friend. The family chooses their funeral home based on the family tradition of "Oh, we have always come here" or it was close to where I live, or because of the quality of service, and how the deceased looks in their casket or the small intricate details, and sometimes their decision is based on social media. I would have to say quality service is what is missing at most funeral homes. I am talking from the first impression of the phone call reporting the death (first call) to the committal service at the grave. Interestingly, on Flag Day, June 14, 2024, as I was heading to my home in Tennessee, I unexpectedly received a phone call as I pulled into the gas station to fill up my truck. I recognized the number and the person on the caller ID, and then I heard a familiar, friendly voice. The voice is of a gentleman, who is a licensed pilot and lives in sunny Florida. His aunt passed away in May 2023 and his uncle, an Army veteran who served from 1956 to 1959 just after the Korean War, passed away in July 2023. Coincidentally, this couple rests at Williams Cemetery in Winslow, Indiana, a short distance from the veteran I reference in the chapter "Looking Death in the Eyes." To be honest, my initial assumption was that the caller's father had passed away and he wanted him to be buried close to his aunt and uncle, but this was not the case. On the phone, he expressed gratitude for the quality of service provided in caring for his aunt and uncle, as well as their funeral services. He says, "I just had to call you tell you just how much I appreciated the service you provided for my aunt and uncle." He stated that he was attending a funeral for one of his pastors who had passed away where he went to church. He described a scene at the graveside, where the funeral tent covered the deceased pastor and his closed casket, leaving family and friends to stand and sit in the scorching Florida sun.

While not all funeral homes operate with the same etiquette and protocol, sounding like something from Star Wars, for providing quality customer service, it's important to note that when this isn't the case, it can reflect negatively on all of us as licensed professionals, a topic for another day. Just think, the customer service and portion sizes at McDonald's or Panda Express are not what they used to be, and neither is the quality of human interaction, if there is any. Families are paying for a service and expect to receive service. They want to be treated like royalty, well at least like they are the most important family, as they navigate their grief and mourning. The funeral director's role is to be empathetic, non-emotional, non-judgmental, and to go above and beyond to leave a lasting, hopefully positive, impression on the family.

The other piece that coincides with the funeral director is when the family decides on who is going to officiate the service. The clergy/officiant, in most cases, plays a large part in any funeral. The clergyperson assumes a multitude of duties and responsibilities when preparing for a military funeral. In most cases, if a member of their congregation has passed away, the pastor has visited or is at the bedside offering comfort and support at the time the deceased passes away. The clergy's role is to be a rock and provide a supportive spirit to the bereaved by offering comfort and compassion by "providing hope for the future in the face of death."[6] It's also crucial for the funeral director to brush up on some religious traditions, rites, and sacraments to better guide the family during the arrangement conference. The other part of that is coordinating with members of the clergy officiating the service to discuss the funeral service itself and establish an order of service and where music, videos, benediction, prayers, and if family and friends want to speak, etc., depending on the religious belief or denomination of the deceased.

Military Funerals

A full military funeral applies to all military funerals, with distinctions being made according to the rank of the deceased. When the funeral is held in a military chapel, the officiant will consult local Standard Operating Procedures (SOP) for guidance in arranging the funeral. A chapel funeral service varies in time from, in my experience, as little as 15 minutes to 2 and a half hours, while a funeral mass usually lasts between 45 minutes to an hour and fifteen minutes. Timing is crucial when coordinating with the honors team waiting at the graveside or if the chapel is needed for another funeral. The honor guard will typically perform a walk through and salute the deceased and may even stand guard changing out every 15 minutes during the visitation prior to the funeral service, depending on rank of the deceased or family request. This also happens with honor guards of first responders (fire and law enforcement officers). A procession to the grave or place of interment follows the funeral service. During graveside services, the funeral procession forms at an entrance or in a central location within a reasonable distance from the cemetery. The pastor or clergy officiating may accompany the family to the cemetery. Typically, the clergyperson rides in the hearse with the funeral director, or if they opt to drive to the cemetery, they will trail directly behind the hearse, march ahead of the caisson for a brief distance, or position themselves at the head of the deceased's grave. The officiant will stand next to the officer-in-charge or noncommissioned officer-in-charge, near the grave site, and salute the hearse as it passes. If the officiant's first personal contact with the family occurs at the cemetery, and I would sure hope it is not their first interaction, the officiant will go to the family car to meet them and then return to their original position. Then the graveside or committal service is conducted. In my experience, the officiant/clergy person always meets the funeral director and pallbearers at the back of the hearse, then leads the pallbearers to the grave site as they carry the casket to its final resting place.

If the deceased has been cremated, and the cremated human remains are interred with military honors, the funeral service is modified to make accommodations for the placement of the urn and the possible unfolding and refolding of the United States flag. When asked to share in a joint worship service with another member of the clergy, officiants are guided by policies set by their denomination or endorsing agent. Or they get together and have a conversation about who is going to do what and when. The military chaplain is involved and sensitive to the needs of the civilian clergy chosen by the family. When a funeral is held at a civilian church, synagogue, or funeral home, the military chaplain co-officiates. In such cases, the officiant presides when military honors are rendered. The deceased's family or representative may request that fraternal or patriotic organizations, of which the deceased was a member, take part in the funeral service. As was the case with President George Washington, the immediate family gave their approval for Alexanderia Masonic Lodge and the militia to conduct service activities prior to and at the gravesite. Today, the folding and presentation of the flag to the primary next of kin marks the conclusion of the military portion of the ceremony before departure from the cemetery.

When military services are conducted, there are other things to consider that are not part of a regular funeral service. Weapons, which are not normally part of a funeral service, are generally not carried into the funeral home, church, or military chapel. On-duty military and civilian law enforcement personnel, as well as concealed carry laws, may be exceptions to this general rule. At off-post locations and facilities, the OIC, NCOIC, or officiant will follow the lead representative's instructions regarding the presence of weapons. The use of a bagpiper is another consideration. In some cases, it is customary to use a bagpiper that plays Amazing Grace as the funeral is dismissed prior to the procession to the gravesite. It is impressive if you have never seen the bagpiper walking through the funeral home or standing outside piping away due to the loud volume and hum of the instrument. It is equally impressive to see a bagpiper in the open air or standing in the center of the cemetery and playing the bagpipes, but it's not as impressive as the sounding of Taps. When using a bagpiper, it's crucial to position them correctly to protect everyone's ears.

Some clergy members, depending upon religion or denomination, may wear some form of headdress on their heads as part of their official vestments. Unless a liturgical headdress is worn, the clergyperson uncovers (removing their head vestments) both inside and outside the chapel, unless there is a liturgical headdress worn. The officiant in uniform uncovers inside the chapel and covers outside the chapel (unless standing under a roof or canopy). All personnel, except active pallbearers, follow the example of the officiant in uniform. If vestments are required during the overall planning and rehearsal process, officiants will allocate time for a quick change, given the potential time constraints for the funeral, graveside service, and final honors for the service member. Officiants may consider wearing vestments to the graveside or incorporating the religious affairs specialist into the plan to help them quickly change at an appropriate moment following the funeral service. Failing to plan means planning to fail. When planning a military funeral, there are other factors to consider that the funeral director may discuss with the family, like the weather and any required clothing (including a jacket, raincoat, hat, or gloves) that must be removed (after entering the chapel) or put on (during movement to graveside). Officiants ensure that all participants (including the religious affairs specialist, OIC, NCOIC, CAO, and funeral director) understand the inclement weather plan and are briefed on any required changes to the sequence of events or delays. Military personnel and honorary pallbearers in uniform face the casket (which is draped with the flag) and execute the hand salute as follows:

- At the sound of honors.
- When moving the casket (except when they themselves are moving).
- During cannon salutes.

- During the firing of volleys.
- When "Taps" is being played.[7]

When conducting a military funeral, sometimes not all parties to the honor guard may be present. At the very least, there should be a two-man military funeral honors detail, or a three-person team if you include the bugler. The actual construction of the operations may vary and require necessary changes, depending on the layout and specific requirements of the cemetery or chapel facility, the Honor Guard's requirements, or the family's needs. Figures 1 through 5 provide diagrams for general planning purposes. In the military world, the chaplain will rehearse with their Honor Guard before funerals to finalize the funeral and graveside service scheme of maneuver, placement of the participants, and any specified cues required during the execution of the funeral or graveside service. For instance, during the chapel's entrance, as depicted in Figures 1 and 2, the Honor Guard rehearses. As a funeral director, I have seen the honor guard team of veterans from the American Legion and Veterans of Foreign Wars walk the area around the grave to determine the best placement for the colors and the firing squad that usually resembles Figures 4 and 5.

- The officiant will either be in position at the curb next to the OIC or NCOIC or at the chapel door.
- The officiant salutes as the caisson or hearse passes and the casket is removed.
- The officiant arrives with order arms and leads the procession into the chapel, up the aisle, and into position.

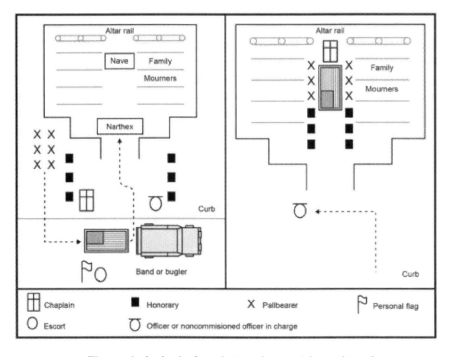

Figure 1. Arrival of casket and escort into chapel

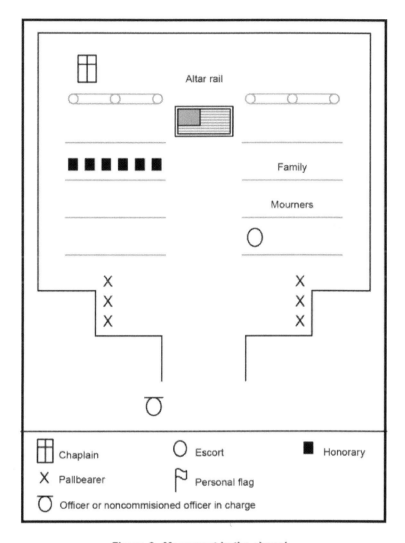

Figure 2 Movement in the chapel

After the service, the officiant/funeral director turns the casket and leads the procession out of the chapel (see figure 3). During the loading of the casket into the caisson or hearse, the officiant either returns to the curb next to the OIC or NCOIC or remains at the chapel door, stands at attention, and salutes.[8]

Military Funerals

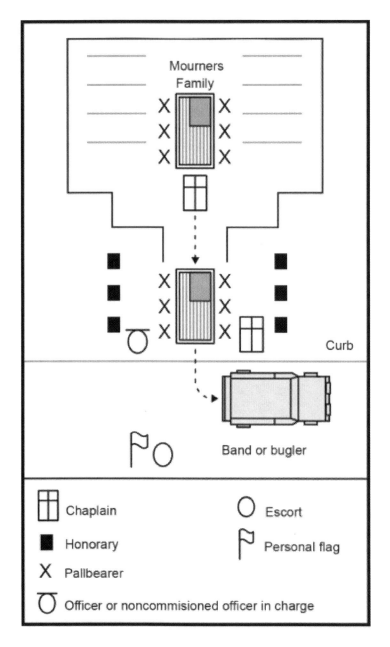

Figure 3 Procession out of chapel

For graveside services the dynamic is a little different. I've had graveside services last an hour or less, so in most cases the military honor guard performs their ceremony first in the event they have other commitments or funerals scheduled, then the officiant continues the graveside or committal service. The honor guard's committal service lasts approximately 15-20 minutes. For general planning purposes, a graveside service following a chapel service may contain the following activities, which are being explored in this book for their origins and what this author calls the four parts of a military funeral:

1. Graveside committal service, in which the flag is draped over the casket or folded for cremation and displayed.
2. Firing of volleys.
3. Playing of "Taps."
4. The U.S. flag is folded and presented.

The order of service is left to the discretion of the clergyperson officiating. During the service, a brief service of Scripture readings, prayer, and occasionally music or hymns may be used. For planning considerations, a graveside service—

- Can be denominational in nature (based on needs).

- This may include the appropriate desires of the family, such as a favorite poem or song.

- The officiant section or UMT coordinates with the cemetery or funeral director to use holy water, sand, or ashes during the ceremony.

- Will conclude with the committal.

At the words, "Let us pray," given by the chaplain/officiant, all personnel bow their heads. Everyone, being reverent and respectful, follows the lead of the officiating clergyperson in regard to headgear worn during the graveside service, except for pallbearers. When the officiating chaplain is military personnel and wears a biretta (a clerical headpiece) during the graveside or committal service, you will see military personnel, uncover (remove their hats), and everyone else follows. When the officiating clergyperson wears a yarmulke, all personnel remain covered.[9]

Standard honors at a graveside or committal service, as are all military services, very formal affairs. The funeral director and officiant dress in suits, while the Honor Guard wears uniforms. From the arrival of the casket to the pall bearers positioning. When the hearse or funeral coach arrives, the officiant positions themselves at the back of the hearse with the funeral director near the curb, if there is one, or where the funeral home I work for is located near the road because most of the cemeteries are in rural areas and don't have formal paved roads; some are gravel or dirt. As the funeral coach pulls up, the Honor Guard stands at attention and salutes as the hearse arrives. The Honor Guard commander summons order arms as the casket is removed from the caisson or hearse, and the officiant guides the casket to the gravesite. The funeral director guides the family and friends who trail behind the casket, or in some instances, they may have already taken their seats at the graveside. The officiant usually begins with prayer or thanking everyone for attending before reading appropriate Scripture verses as everyone settles in at the graveside. Until everyone reaches the graveside, the reverent journey with the casket and pallbearers remains silent, especially if the Honor Guard is serving as the pallbearers.

As shown in Figure 4, the pallbearers carry the casket and place it over the grave while the family and mourners take their seats. Depending on the branch of military service, the pallbearers may raise and hold the flag at a waist-high horizontal position through "Taps." On a side note: The Body Bearers of the United States Marine Corps carry the casket at shoulder level, then lower it from that position to waist level to place it on the bier or lowering device over the vault, where the casket is eventually lowered. The officiant proceeds to the head of the grave, waits for everyone to settle in, then receives a signal from the funeral director to commence the service. At the conclusion of the service, the officiant, and the Honor Guard commander exchange places at the head of the casket. The commander gives the order for the firing of three volleys followed by the sounding of "Taps." Under the supervision of the Honor Guard commander or NCOIC if active duty, the pallbearers fold the flag.[10] If it is not the six pallbearers folding the flag then a two-person team will fold the flag.

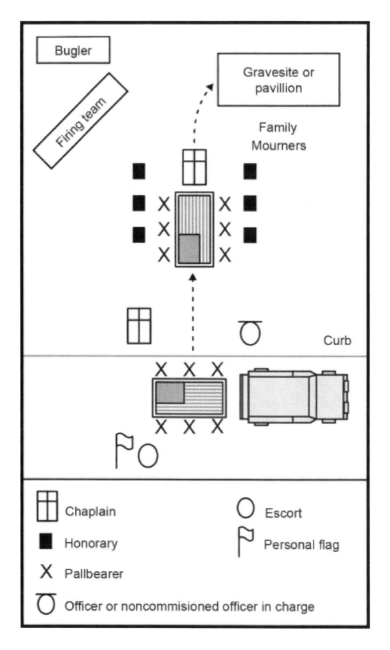

Figure 4 Arrival of casket and escort to gravesite

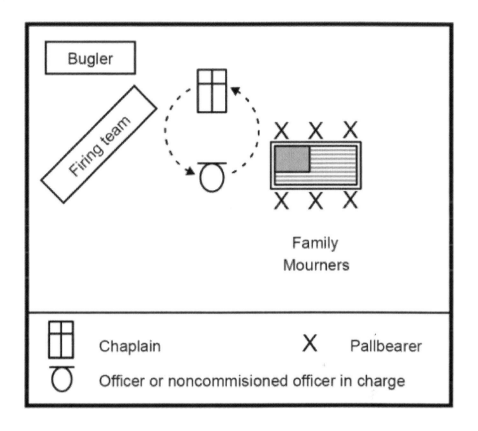

Figure 5 Graveside service

Figure 5 shows the positioning of the bugler and firing teams. After the flag is folded, the veteran designated senior pallbearer executes a right face and places the flag at chest level into the hands of the Casualty Assistance Officer (CAO). When I conduct military honors, the CAO in our county of residence is called the Veteran's Services Officer (VSO). The VSO salutes the flag for three seconds before accepting it from the senior pallbearer. The senior pallbearer salutes the flag for three seconds after presenting it to the VSO. The VSO then proceeds directly to the designated next of kin who is designated to receive the flag. The designated individual may not be the primary next of kin rather a child or grandchild who was designated. Upon presentation of the flag, the VSO will use verbiage in line with Department of Defense policy per the guidance from the Secretary of Defense— "On behalf of the President of the United States, (the United States Army; the United States Marine Corps; the United States Navy; or the United States Air Force), and a grateful nation, please accept this flag as a symbol of our appreciation for your loved one's honorable and faithful service."[11] After the flag is presented, the VSO returns to his/her original position. In some cases, the flag is presented by the officiant or the funeral director and is presented to the next of kin in a similar manner. It should also be noted that the flag that has been folded into a triangle has the point facing away from the next of kin and toward the VSO when presented as a form of flag etiquette. From the funeral director's perspective funerals are never routine or impersonal. It is important to honor and respect the wishes and desires of the family. A life well lived, and a well-prepared funeral extends religious support to those present and provides public support to the bereaved while honoring the deceased veteran or soldier. Army Regulations or standing orders continue to outline memorial services and other ceremonies.[12]

Some of you may be wondering about services for cremation or burial at sea. They are similar to those already outlined and usually involve a decorated table, with the urn containing the cremated human remains of the deceased, and the flag folded into a triangle or what some equate to a cocked hat honoring George Washington and the thirteen original colonies. Typically, one pallbearer carries the urn or receptacle containing the cremated human remains, while the other pallbearer carries the folded flag. The pallbearer carrying the flag is always to the right of the deceased's remains. When the urn/receptacle is carried from the hearse into the chapel, and from the chapel to the hearse, these two pallbearers are the only participants in the ceremony. The two pallbearers, followed by four additional pallbearers, carry the urn, receptacle, and flag during the procession to the gravesite. After placing the urn or receptacle containing the cremated human remains on the gravesite, all six pallbearers unfold the flag, hold it over the grave, and fold it similarly to a flag-draped casket. The only major difference for burial at sea is the fact that disposition of the urn containing holes or the casket containing twenty 2-inch holes is "at least three nautical miles from land and in ocean waters at least 600 feet deep."[13] The Environmental Protection Agency has other regulations for burial at sea, but the honor guard portion is very similar to that which takes place outside at the cemetery, except the committal takes place from a naval ship before the remains are deposited in the oceans depths.

There is a lot of work that goes into administering military honors or military rites for those who have honorably served. I mentioned the Body Bearers of the United States Marine Corps, but there are other regiments like the 3rd United States Infantry known as "The Old Guard" at Arlington National Cemetery. Lots of training, rehearsal, practice, and repetition go into the drill and ceremony of military funerals. Each regiment or branch of service strives for absolute perfection, aiming to perform flawlessly to honor the guardians of freedom and our American way of life.

Chapter 2

Looking Death in the Eyes

"We'd stared into the face of Death, and Death blinked first. You'd think that would make us feel brave and invincible. It didn't."[1]
-Rick Yancey, Author of The 5th Wave

I magine staring death in the eyes, and some of you reading this have done so by living a life, an adventurous life, one that may have included experiences such as bungee jumping, cliff diving, or jumping out of an airplane. Others may have even faced violence, combat, or other life altering things that brought them to look death in the eyes. Now, imagine that you are a soldier dedicated to a life of service and freedom. One who has left his or her family, friends, and home to serve a higher calling of duty, honor, and respect. People enlist in the United States Armed Forces for a variety of reasons, including financial, educational, skills or trade experience, housing, medical and dental insurance, pride, earning respect, and carrying on family traditions passed down from generation to generation, these are just a few of the reasons. Each service member undergoes 8 to 13 weeks of basic training, followed by additional training and drills in various specialty fields, depending on their assignment. For our purposes here, we are only focusing on the mortuary field, but we may mention some others. Following their training and unit assignment, soldiers are then unified by the identity of the person on their left and their right, and the support system of their brothers and sisters in arms. The very people you train with, drill with, and converse with on your mission as a soldier. You are them, and they are you. Then suddenly your unit is sent to some far-off place, and while there, defending the principles of freedom, there is a horrific blast striking one of your comrades next to you; you know it could have been you. You reach out to hold your comrade's dead body in your arms, feeling utterly helpless, and frozen by the shock that has just befallen your beloved comrade. As you contemplate what you perceive to be next, fear overwhelms you. Suddenly, the question of why you are here, and the meaning of life pierces your soul, revealing the possibility that there may be no purpose. And just like that, you snap back to reality with a range of emotions, embracing the body of your fellow soldier, a fallen soldier, and wanting to get them out and back to safety. As historian Mark Meigs noted, "Soldiers could view the task of picking up the dead of their own unit with a sense of duty and humanity."

We will all face death. We are dying to live and living to die. Frederick Walliser, founder of the House of Kim Tae Kwon Do School in Elwood, Indiana, retired Indiana State Trooper, and Army veteran once said, "If you make fear, pain, and death your friend, your life falls into place." Nothing prepares us for death, yet it is fear, pain, and death that drives our ever creative and destructive impulses. The more study and understand our fear, pain, and death, the closer we are to understanding ourselves and our society. Actions of honoring the fallen i.e., military funerals, monuments, and memorials either nationally or locally, holidays, and organizations like the Gold Star Mothers, American Legion, and Veterans of Foreign Wars, and others, have developed out of our collective fear, pain, and death, and because of those lost in war and those that so faithfully served their country with honor, come our veterans.

　　According to his memoir Surgeon with the Kaiser's Army and a subsequent interview recorded in 1963 as part of the BBC's Armistice Day coverage, the term armistice; means an agreement made by opposing sides in a war to stop fighting, and in this moment at the 11th hour of the 11th month and the 11th day of 1918, the end of World War I. This is also the day we in the United States recognize as the national holiday Veteran's Day. In the BBC interview, Dr. Stephan Westmann gives us the soldier's perspective of looking into the eyes of death during World War I. Stephan Westmann was a German soldier with the German 29th Infantry Division during World War I and later migrated to England in the 1930's to complete his education to become a physician. He served as a British medical officer during World War II.

"One day we got orders to storm a French position. We got in, and my comrades fell right and left of me. But then I was confronted by a French corporal. He with his bayonet at the ready, and I with my bayonet at the ready. For a moment I felt the fear of death. And in a fraction of a second, I realized that he was after my life exactly as I was after his. I was quicker than he was. I tossed his rifle away and I ran my bayonet through his chest. He fell, put his hand on the place where I had hit him, and then I thrust again. Blood came out of his mouth, and he died. I felt physically ill. I nearly vomited. My knees were shaking, and I was, quite frankly, ashamed of myself. My comrades – I was a corporal there and then, we were absolutely undisturbed by what had happened. One of them boasted that he killed a poilu with the butt of his rifle. Another one had strangled a French captain. A third one had hit somebody over the head with his spade. And they were ordinary men like me. One of them was a tram conductor, another one a commercial traveler, two were students, the rest were farm workers. Ordinary people who never would have thought to do any harm to anyone. How did it come about that they were so cruel?

I remembered then that we were told that the good soldier kills without thinking of his adversary as a human being. The very moment he sees in him a fellow man, he is not a good soldier anymore. But I had, in front of me, the...dead man, the dead French soldier...and how I would have like him to have raised his hand. I would have shaken his hand and we would have been the best of friends, because he was nothing, like me, but a poor boy who had to fight, who had to go in with the most cruel weapons against a man who had nothing against him personally, (**Author's side note**, this somehow reminds me of Muhammad Ali's speech in 1967 when he refused induction in the United States Army because he didn't want to kill other people of color, but is a discussion of another time.) who only wore the uniform of another nation, who spoke another language, but a man who had a father and mother, and a family perhaps, and so I felt. I woke up at night sometimes, drenched in sweat, because I saw the eyes of my fallen adversary, of the enemy, and I tried to convince myself, what would have happened to me if I wouldn't have been quicker than he? What would have happened to me if I wouldn't have thrust my bayonet first into his belly? What was it that we soldiers stabbed each other, strangled each other, went for each other like mad dogs? What was it that we, who had nothing against them personally, fought with them to the very end and death? We were civilized people after all. But I felt that the culture we boasted so much about is only a very thin lacquer which chips off the very moment we come in contact with cruel things like real war. To fire at each other from a distance, to drop bombs, is something impersonal. But to see each other's white in the eyes and then to run a bayonet against a man, it was against my conception and against my inner feeling."[2]

These two examples discussed are just a glimpse of looking death in the eyes. Thousands of soldiers and veterans, who have witnessed combat in every war or conflict the United States of America has engaged in, have recounted a horrific perspective, if not, a real one of someone who held their comrade's body in their hands during combat, while another is a real-life account from a World War I veteran, detailing his remorse and feelings. War is very personal and takes place for various reasons. It's been a part of humanity in just about every age of human history, if not every age. History teaches us that there is always something to fight for, such as changes in political ideology, land, or territory, preventing technological advances, riches, power, and even the most basic of rights, liberty, and freedom. Yet behind every battle, there is one thing that remains true. The strategies developed lead to potential death and the fallen. Soldiers who voluntarily left their family, friends, and loved ones to pursue something higher or greater than themselves, a life of service. Looking in the face of death not knowing if they are coming home, but knowing that those same people, they left will be safe under the protection of the freedom they provide. We pay tribute to the men and women in the United States Armed Forces. Those who have served and continue to serve, and to those that gave their lives for a cause greater than themselves to ensure our freedom. It is also a testament to the numerous veterans, wounded veterans, and warriors who are still dealing with the effects of war or military service, and how we honor them once they pass away.

From my point of view, we cannot talk about death enough. As a funeral director and embalmer, I recognize the importance of honoring the deceased, not just those who served in the military. I mean everyone who passes away. Everyone has a unique story to tell or a personal history that is worth honoring, yet our focus here is only on the echoes of valor. We so masterfully conceal death behind the locked doors of our prep or embalming rooms and rarely pull back the curtain as if to hide the secrets of a magic trick. These days you can Google just about anything and find an answer on the internet. In doing research for this project, I mainly want to discuss the history of the four parts of military services that I see on a consistent basis. What I have found is that you just cannot Google everything and get an answer. The tradition of draping the flag on a coffin dates back centuries, the folding of the flag has an unknown origin, or does it?, the firing of three volleys, commonly referred to as a 21-gun salute, has a rich history, and the sounding of Taps has been a part of the ceremony for only about 162 years. My purpose is to share the origins of these parts of what amounts to an honorable ceremony and shine light on other's service in dealing with our deceased veterans.

The writing of this book is an exercise in knowledge for the reader concerning historical writings and experiences with military funerals. Hopefully, it pulls back the veiled curtain and shines some light on how military funerals and traditions were developed. Funerals for the people we see in our local community having served in the United States Armed Forces and may not want to be recognized (because the deceased served in a time of "peace" and did not see combat) and yet they should be recognized for their honorable service. Some of these people are our grandparents, great-grandparents, our fathers, mothers, brothers and sisters, cousins, nieces and nephews, neighbors, friends, etc. Hopefully, this will assist someone in the future who is considering entering the military, the mortuary profession, or both, or maybe you just want to explore some military history concerning funeral rites. If you are a funeral director maybe you just want to go beyond the brief pages discussed on this topic in mortuary school. There are hundreds of funeral rites, and military rites are the most consistent and disciplined, which is what we are going to explore. The origin of these timeless traditions in our American culture evokes memories of the past and the valor for which those who have died and honorably served.

"There's nothing stronger than the heart of a volunteer."
Lt. Colonel James Doolittle, April 18, 1942

If you have never seen the 2001 film Pearl Harbor, it's worth seeing for a fictitious spin on the events that thrust the United States into World War II. The movie is loosely based on the history of those events with a Hollywood twist of drama. It stars Ben Affleck, who is currently married to Jennifer Lopez, Kate Beckinsale, Josh Harnett, Alec Baldwin, and others. Alec Baldwin plays the role of Lt. Colonel James Doolittle, who is an American hero. James Doolittle, at the time, was a lieutenant colonel in the United States Army Air Corps. On April 18, 1942, he, and his squadron of 16 stripped down B-25B Mitchell medium bombers launched from the aircraft carrier the USS Hornet on their way to bomb Japan, almost four months after the bombing of Pearl Harbor, the event that thrust America into World War II. Doolittle's Raid was a huge success, and of course we know how the war ended. History has brought about death and the need for strategies, but what about the strategies to bring home our deceased, to honor them, and to honor those who came back or served in so-called times of peace? It should be noted that there are differences in the way a military service is conducted for active-duty members and veterans that are retired and have been honorably discharged, yet the four parts of the actual military service remain the same.

If it were up to this author, the United States government would bury every military veteran of honorable discharge. The government would offer a stipend that would pay in full for a veteran's funeral to their funeral home of choice, in addition to what the Department of Veterans Affairs offers with burial flags, headstones, medallions, pension benefits, etc. The average cost of funerals today, just guessing and without running actual numbers, is probably between $9,000 and $14,000 for a full same day traditional burial depending upon where you live in the United States. So, a stipend of $20,000 would be enough to cover someone who served their country. Of course, this is just my opinion. I feel the United States government falls short in its support for our veterans, and burial should be the least of their worries when that time comes for the family. Burial should be provided in addition to what was previously mentioned and benefits for their health, mental health, physical therapy, and rehabilitation.

I see it all the time when a family comes to the funeral home at their time of need to make arrangements. Families may not mention the deceased's veteran status either because of the length of their service, or in some cases, the veteran's status is not disclosed because the deceased had served in combat and the family didn't want to equate his or her war experience as part of their identity, yet it is part of the identity of America. Then there comes the other side. Families want a military funeral and the traditional ceremonies because their deceased loved one identified as a patriot or lived a life of service. Some, after leaving the military, went to work for Veterans Affairs or other affiliated groups that help veterans. Veterans like the gentleman I'm about to describe who devoted his life to the United States Army. Let me tell you the story of his funeral throughout this writing, changing the names of the deceased and his family for anonymity. A man that most definitely looked death in the eyes.

The phone rings at the funeral home and I answer it. The person on the other end of the call identifies themself as a nurse at a hospital in Cincinnati, Ohio, who has recently had a patient pass away. The family has requested your funeral home. Well, I am currently employed at a funeral home in southwest Indiana, where I proceed to gather the deceased's information on a form known as a first call sheet. This sheet lists several things that have to be filled-in: the date, name of the deceased, location of the deceased, the doctor or medical examiner signing the death certificate, if there is an autopsy going to be done, permission to embalm, does the deceased need to be clean shaven?, the informant relationship, in this case the nurse, next of kin information, the appointment time, and contact phone number for the primary next of kin, is the deceased a veteran, and who the call is taken by? I received the information, and it is for Mr. James Bryant. Mr. Bryant passed away at Mercy West Hospital in Cincinnati, Ohio. I was given his wife's contact information as the primary next of kin (NOK), then asked for some of the other information listed on the first call form. Mr. Bryant is a United States Army veteran, who held the rank of Command Sergeant Major. He was once part of the 23rd Chemical Battalion, an Army Ranger and jump master with the 82nd Air Borne Division earning him the nickname "Ranger Bryant." CSGTM Bryant was also a highly decorated noncommissioned officer, earning numerous medals and meritorious service awards, including, 2-bronze stars, the National Defense Medal, the Southwest Asia Service Medal, and a Purple Heart for being wounded during the Persian Gulf War. Again, a man who looked death in the eyes. The funeral home in Southwest Indiana, where he grew up, will now serve this decorated soldier who had a distinguished 30-year military career.

Shortly after my conversation with the hospital nurse, the primary next-of-kin, Mrs. Bryant, was contacted. We set up an arrangement conference for a few days out because she had to travel from Ohio to Indiana. During our brief phone conversation, she told me that the family is going to have a two-day traditional service, meaning four hours of visitation the night before the funeral service and a few hours of visitation the next morning. She was informed that embalming in Indiana is not State Law, and she says, "Oh, yes he'll be embalmed because we are having a public viewing." Typically, I recommend embalming if there is going to be a public viewing of a significant amount of time such as a few days or, in this case, a week away from the funeral. The law in Indiana states something to the effect that there is no embalming requirements, though there is a definition, but arrangements for final disposition must be made within "a reasonable time after death."[3] And for those wondering, the definition of embalming is the temporary preservation and disinfection of human remains by the internal or external application of chemicals or by other methods in preparation for disposition. Well, that's the Indiana definition of embalming. As a licensed funeral director and embalmer in Indiana and Tennessee, it is my responsibility to make sure each family is informed of their rights and responsibilities. It is also my responsibility to the state as a licensed practitioner to maintain public safety and for the purposes of infectious disease control and other reasons as the funeral industry is highly regulated by the Federal Trade Commission.

Most people, when they come to the funeral home, know what they want or need, and things are just a matter of semantics. The funeral director bears the responsibility of ensuring the funeral service runs smoothly, alleviating the family's burden, and initiating the healing process through grief and mourning, even though the family is paying for the service. Mr. Byrant passed away on a Thursday, so I met with Mrs. Byrant the following Monday. Mrs. Bryant arrived at the funeral home with Mr. Bryant's clothing for burial. In this case, his Army dress uniform with all of his service ribbons and medals, black boots, black belt, and undergarments, including socks. She also brought in his maroon beret with a patch representing the 82nd Airborne Division.

After formal greetings were exchanged, Mrs. Bryant, her daughter (who is also an active-duty Army soldier and was in from Colorado before being stationed in Hawaii), her mother-in-law, and sister-in-law were shown into the conference room where the funeral arrangements would be made. The family was offered something to drink before we started the formal conference. There are essentially three parts to an arrangement conference. The funeral service itself, (which includes the statement of funeral goods and services (finances), selecting of the burial vault, casket, and guest book, memorial cards, dates and times for the service and visitation, minister, music, etc.), vital statistics, and the obituary information. I like to start by asking the family to tell me about their loved one and ask questions from there about the deceased. It is a therapeutic story from the family that also allows for the grief and mourning processes to begin and helps reduce some of the emotionally charged feelings that come with someone we love dying. I am also jotting down notes on my at-need form (at-need meaning at the time of death) or checklist, so I don't have to ask a lot of questions when needing information for the obituary.

The process of a general conversation leads to the collection of vital statistics and demographic information the state requires for the death certificate. Mrs. Bryant is asked all of these personal things: the formal government name of the deceased, his date of birth, social security number, where he was born, his highest level of education, legal address, parents names, including their mother's maiden name, marital status (because the person you are talking to may not be the legal next of kin because they are divorced or legally separated, or the deceased has a mistress or girlfriend that feels they are the wifey, and sometimes you run into people that claim they are a common law spouse), occupation and type of business, and the informant's information, which is usually the primary next of kin, and in this case Mrs. Bryant. Mrs. Bryant also presents two rings, and I jotted down in my notes two yellow rings, one with a white stone and an inscription on the sides. It is evident that the first ring was Mr. Bryant's wedding band, and the other was a class ring of sorts from his time in the Army, but it is written down as color, color of stone and etching, or plain yellow ring. A funeral director is not a gemologist or a jeweler and has no real idea if the stone is a diamond, or a cubic zirconia, or even if the ring is made of gold. So, your assets are covered by making generalizations in the event an item goes missing and must be replaced. If you wrote the latter, you run the risk of incurring thousands of dollars in potential punitive damages, so good documentation and descriptions of what is received from a family is a must. I also inquire and record any requests from the family for the return of items following the funeral and prior to the permanent closure of the casket. Next, we discuss the obituary after deciding on a date and time for the visitation and funeral service, as well as who will officiate it.

If you have read an obituary, it is like reading the "CliffsNotes" of a person's life, well at least the highlights. You have when the person passed away and may have the location where they died, and sometimes even may list the illness, where they graduated from high school or college, and what year, if they served in the military, as Mr. Bryant clearly did until he retired after 30 years, the story of love and marriage, who he married and for how long, their hobbies and interests, memberships in clubs and organizations, religious affiliations, who is surviving, i.e., parents, children, grandchildren, etc., then those who preceded him in death. These are the notes that are being taken while the family is telling their loved one's life story and when they offer the small details of their loved one's life. **Author's side note:** I typically tell people this, we do obituaries for two reasons, lineage, and to give a snap shot of the deceased's legacy in life.

Just before typing up the obituary, I was given a picture to be used for CSGTM Bryant's obituary in his uniform. Prior to the obituary being typed up or while it is being typed by someone else, the family is shown into the selection room where they can look at caskets, burial vaults, and other funeral merchandise, or what the funeral industry calls sundry items. These are the various items that the funeral home sells: keepsakes, monuments, jewelry, flag cases, etc. Upon entering the selection room, families can view and touch a variety of caskets, vaults, urns, and other sundry items. They can also examine the various fabrics of the caskets and make their choice. In Mr. Bryant's case, he chose a 20-gauge steel M39 Neapolitan Blue casket from Batesville Casket Company. The casket features a removable Army logo on two corners, affixed to a magnetic adapter at the head of the casket, and two eagles with a flag on the corners at the foot of the casket. The vault, a Wilbert Veteran Triune, was painted Navy blue and silver to match the casket. It featured corrosion-resistant stainless steel and high impact plastic on the interior, a stainless-steel lid featuring the army logo, and a plaque featuring the United States flag, the deceased's name, year of birth, and year of passing.

Author's side note: Now, I don't know about you, but I always root for the Army during the Army Navy football game, but recognize the military academies are all on the same team when we talk about our country.

The guestbook package selected includes thank you cards, memorial folders (this is what people who come to the viewing or visitation hours take as a keepsake), and a bookmark, and of course the guestbook itself. The package is a gold box housing all of these things called, "Old Glory," which is the theme of the package. Next, the family reviews the obituary to ensure accuracy of all information, correct spelling of names, and inclusion of all family members. We then discuss the dynamics of the service, including the music, the possibility of family members speaking, the pastor's message, the eulogy, the invocation, the benediction, and so on. In the case of CSGTM Bryant, his battalion commander, who is a full-bird Colonel in Fort Leonard Wood, Missouri, came to speak about their time in Ranger School together. We also discussed active-duty military versus retired veterans of the American Legion or Veterans of Foreign Wars. Mrs. Bryant wanted both. I contacted the Office of Veteran Affairs in Evansville, Indiana, to make a requisition for active-duty United States Army soldiers to conduct the funeral rites for CSGTM Bryant. I also contacted the local retired veteran's groups (American Legion and Veterans of Foreign Wars) to assist with the active-duty soldiers. The funeral home hosted the visitation from 4 p.m. to 8 p.m. on Friday of that same week, and after meeting with Mrs. Bryant, we scheduled the funeral service for 10 a.m. on Saturday morning.

I mentioned earlier going the extra mile. Here is where I went the extra mile for this military family. After the times and dates were set, Mr. Bryant's mother says she wants to show me where she wants James to be buried. I asked if she already had a burial plot, and she said she thought she did but wasn't sure. I reached out to the cemetery overseer or sexton, Bud Bolin, and together with Mrs. Bryant, her daughter, her mother-in-law, and her sister-in-law, we piled into our escort vehicle, a 2018 Black Cadillac, and drove the five miles from the funeral home to Williams Cemetery in Winslow, Indiana. We walked to the cemetery, and just across the small gravel road from Patoka Grove United Methodist Church, Mr. Bryant's mother told Mr. Bolin that she wanted James buried on top of the hill next to his dad. All agreed that it was a great spot. Before departing from the cemetery, Mr. Byrant's mother, due to her visual impairment, grasped my arm and guided me back to the car. During this journey, she imparted the history of the church, detailing its relocation from its previous location several miles away to its current location, surrounded by Williams Cemetery. The church was moved onto logs and rolled down the street to its present location.

Having visited the cemetery briefly and finalized the funeral arrangements, I, as the licensed funeral director, proceeded to follow a checklist, reaching out to various entities such as the grave digger, the cemetery, the Office of Veterans Affairs, casket and vault companies, the flower shop, and the American Legion. I secure a United States burial flag that is to be draped on the casket from the United States Post Office using VA Form 27-2008 Application for United States Flag for Burial Purposes. One may ask, "who is eligible for a burial flag?" Well, according to the United States Department of Veteran Affairs instructions that come with VA Form 27-2008, "veterans with an other than dishonorable discharge. Note: This includes veterans who served in the Philippine military forces while such forces were in the service of the U.S. armed forces under the President's Order of July 26, 1941, and died on or after April 25, 1951, and veterans who served in the Philippine military services are eligible for burial in a national cemetery. Veterans who were entitled to retired pay for service in the reserves, or would have been entitled to such pay but not for being under 60 years of age. Members or former members of the Selected Reserve (Army, Air Force, Coast Guard, Marine Corps, or Naval Reserve; Air National Guard; or Army National Guard) who served at least one enlistment or, in the case of an officer, the period of initial obligation, or were discharged for disability incurred or aggravated in line of duty, or died while a member of the Selected Reserve." Other parts of the instruction sheet will be discussed in the chapters about the draping of the flag and the folding of the flag.[4]

After going through the checklist, it is now time to embalm, dress, casket, and cosmetize the deceased in preparation for his funeral. In Mr. Bryant's case, we utilized the Greater Cincinnati Trade Service. As the funeral director who handled the initial call from Mercy West Hospital in Cincinnati, Ohio, as previously discussed, my next step was to consult the Yellow Pages. Yes, the Yellow Pages. At the funeral home we have a Funeral Home and Crematory Directory produced by NOMIS Publications, Inc. The directory is broken down by state and within each state lists funeral homes alphabetically in each city in that state. I came across a phone number and called Greater Cincinnati Funeral Trade Company, Inc. I also used Google Chrome and Googled, for those in this century, the trade service. I then initiated a conversation a gentleman who answered the phone at the trade service, clarifying that I required the retrieval of a deceased individual from Mercy West Hospital in Cincinnati, Ohio, and the preparation of his corpse for transportation to Southwest Indiana. The gentleman asked for the name of the deceased, Mr. James Bryant. Contact information for our funeral home was given, and then I was asked if we would be picking him up, or did I need to schedule a flight? I settled on sending someone to Cincinnati to pick him up and transport him back to the funeral home in Indiana, which was a cost saving measure. We were given a date and time that Mr. Bryant would be ready, and the funeral home staff arrived about thirty minutes early and transported him back to the family's funeral home of preference, Lamb Basham Memorial Chapel in the small coal mining town of Oakland City, Indiana.

Once back at the funeral home and having received clothing from his wife, in this case Mr. Bryant's Army Service Uniform (ASU). The Army Service Uniform, what has been called the "dress uniform" is the most formal type of uniform used by the United States Army.

Official ceremonies, receptions, and other formal social functions, like state dinners, utilize this impressive uniform. It consists of a single breasted dark blue jacket with a stand-up collar, epaulets, and four buttons on the front, a white dress shirt, a black necktie, and dark blue trousers made of a wool blend with a gold stripe down the side, and a black belt. Command Sergeant Major Bryant would now wear it for his funeral and burial, displaying his burgundy beret with the 82nd Airborne logo at the left-hand corner of his casket near his head. Just as the funeral director and mortuary student finished dressing Mr. Bryant, the M39 Neapolitan Blue arrived. We inspected the casket to ensure it was free from flaws, chips, dents, or scratches, and to confirm the security of the handles and swing bars.

Next, the casket was unsealed to reveal an ivory velvet pillow and the interior of the same. The Army logo was displayed on the cap (head) of the casket's inner panel. The head and foot of the casket bed was cranked up into their appropriate positions to make sure that CSGTM Bryant rested comfortably. A mortuary lift was used to place CSGTM Bryant comfortably in his casket. The funeral director applied very little cosmetics to the deceased's face and hands in order to give the appearance of being alive and at rest. The casket was placed upon a bier, a moveable frame or stand on which the casket of the deceased rests or is transported in a church or crematorium, or before burial in a cemetery. Magnetic adapters were put on the corners with colored Army logos at each corner of the head of the casket and an eagle with the flag on each corner of the foot. The casket was arranged on the bier in the main chapel under the lights, with torchières near the head and foot of the casket. Mr. Bryant appeared to be peacefully resting. Depending upon the region or local area, the casket is a half couch or perfection cut, which is what most people are accustomed to seeing at a funeral. The next twenty or thirty minutes of the funeral director's time are spent addressing the burial flag and how it is to be situated on the casket, which introduces us to the first custom of a military funeral service: draping the flag. You will find several sections of In Memoriam or the obituary, written or abridged today, throughout the book. In some instances, the In Memoriam may list descendants, but it is pretty redundant to say who survived and who preceded them in death. It may list some descendants to give us a better understanding of various points in United States history.

Chapter 3

Flag an American Symbol

Resolved, That the flag of the United States be thirteen stripes, alternate red and white: that the union be thirteen stars, white in a blue field representing a new Constellation.[1]
-Resolution adopted by the Second Continental Congress, June 14, 1777

In 1982 there was a television special called "I Love Liberty," where actor and comedian the late great Robin Williams dressed like and provided the voice of the American flag. Created by writer Norman Lear and sponsored by the organization he founded, People for the American Way, Williams' performance was aired to commemorate the 250th anniversary of George Washington's birthday. He so masterfully switches between voices and embodies a proud, yet brave, and bold American flag. A video of his performance can be watched on YouTube. Just go to YouTube and type Robin Williams as the American flag.

He begins, "Thank you very much. I'm the one that they're singing about. Yeah, I'm the Stars and Stripes Forever, Star-Spangled Banner. You can call me "Old Glory" but let's just keep it simple. I'll just call me, flag. Oh, say can you see? Ok, well, a little flag humor. Well, you probably don't recognize me. Say, who is that, Evel Knievel? No way. Yeah, you see you can't recognize me because I'm in my birthday suit (as he switches to a higher pitched voice.) Yes. I'm wearing the original 13 here. Yeah, I remember Miss Betsey sitting there going, 'oh this could be the start of something big' (as he again changes voices) Tom, don't be a pain. Yes. I was born on June 14, 1777, that makes me a Gemini. That makes me unpredictable more crazy. Yes. I like the outdoors and I'm the life of any party whether it be Republican, Democrat, Independent, Socialist anything Libertarian I'll be there. You know I'm 204 years old. People say, "Flag, how do you stay so young?" Is it jogging? No. Is it tennis? (as he makes like he is swinging a tennis racket and connecting with a ball) No! It's waving. (as he waves his hand around). You know we're talking about billowing, furling, and unfurling. Richard Simmons eat your heart out. Now, it hasn't always been easy for me though. I had a tough puberty. Yeah, war, famine, invasion, and 1861 well I had a little skin problem that broke out into 34 stars. But now, well, a little patience and look what we got. Now look at this, here hold on here Ha, Ha! All fifty. (as he removes his right sleeve of thirteen stars exposing all fifty stars).

Everybody is on here, look at this Alaska (as he makes seal noises). Hawaii (as he hula dances and sings in Swahili). We got to Tennessee, 'how are ye doin today' (as he changes voices) here's Vermont, 'you can't get there from here' (as he changes voices again), and there's California, 'For sure, totally' (as he acts like a surfer). You know I had a tough time for a while. I've been in a lot of wars. They fired missiles and muskets at me, but you know come the dawn's early light I'm still there. You know I've been made in everything from designer jeans to T-shirts and I've even been a cape for Mick Jagger. 'Well alright, the rockets red glare, well all right,' (as he impersonates Mick Jagger). But people haven't always been respectful to me. Sometimes it's been tough. Then when some people try and spit on me, trample me, burn me foreigners and occasionally some Americans to, but I don't let it get me down because I'm not a stay-at-home kind of flag. You know I've been to Europe. I've been to both the North and South Pole. I was at Iwo Jima (trying to impersonate the Iwo Jima monument). Recently, I've even been to the moon (as he impersonates Neal Armstrong and the communication of his words on the moon.) Now, my friends, you see me in all sorts of different postures. When I'm like this that means everything is okay (as he sticks his arm out) I'm upside down here put on your Mae West and hit the deck. But when I'm like this well that's not my favorite position because that's half-mast (as he goes to one knee). I don't mean to bum you out. I didn't come here to depress you, but I got to tell you something honestly. I haven't been getting out much lately. I guess it's not very chic to put up the flag anymore, you know. Muffin and I have a flag, but we haven't found it for very long. Hey, but look at it this way don't look at it as saluting me, look at it as saluting yourselves. You know hey, I'm just a flag, a symbol. You're the people. If I may say so from here (as he points to his heart) long, may you wave you." Robin Williams then salutes and exits the stage to thunderous applause. What a great, yet brief tribute to the flag of our country, a symbol that belongs to all loyal Americans.[2]

Our country's flag, the United States of America, is steeped in tradition and myth dating back to the Revolutionary War. The United States flag is probably the most recognized symbol of liberty and freedom in the world. Loved by some and hated by those who are against for which it stands. Some burn it to make a political statement, and others kneel opposed to saluting it or to make a political statement. No matter how you feel about it, it is a symbol of America. There is much that could be said about the flag of our country, but to understand the draping of the flag's origins, we must look at the flag's history, and in doing so, I hope that those opposed to the flag can understand and respect those that served under it and what it took to secure our freedom as a nation. Blood has been shed for numerous reasons as mentioned earlier, and most feel that to disrespect the flag is to disrespect America, and those who fought so gallantly in its defense or under its banner. Seeing the flag disrespected is somewhat disheartening, especially considering how many people sacrificed their lives to defend it. Again, some were political reasons, maybe the wrong reasons, but when you are a soldier, you answer the call and serve, no questions asked. During the Vietnam era, people disrespected and called soldiers "baby killers" because they disagreed with the defense of a deep seaport, the desire to unify Vietnam, or the prevention of communism's spread. I'm not a historian, but I heard all those arguments as justifications for fighting in the Vietnam War or conflict. Those people didn't have a choice as many were drafted, some volunteered, yet all were following orders. Well, they had a choice of not enlisting, dodging the draft, or going AWOL (absent without leave or permission). The point is that the flag is America, defended by Americans no matter the reason, sometimes backed by the entire government, and sometimes, according to the war powers resolution, just the President in a unilateral move as Commander-in-Chief of the military.

Francis Scott Key wrote our national anthem The Star-Spangled Banner after witnessing the  British bombardment of Fort McHenry during the War of 1812. Numerous books have been written documenting the flags' history. People have referred to it by various names, including the Stars and Stripes, Old Glory, and our beloved Star-Spangled Banner, among others. A new constellation for a fledgling new country. Imagine the bells and overwhelming joy of beginning something new and opposing those in power by declaring yourself free and independent. Well, that's what happened on July 2, 1776, when the Second Continental Congress approved the resolution declaring that the colonies "are, and of right ought to be, free and independent States." Free and independent states yet no matter how independent and governed by their laws created what we know now as the Federal Government. With the Declaration of Independence approved in the late afternoon of July 4, 1776, at Independence Hall in Philadelphia, Pennsylvania, it was realized that a new symbol would need to be created to represent the newly independent states. Interestingly, unlike most government operations, no action took place until nearly a full year later. Up until that point, George Washington utilized the Continental Colors as that symbol. The Continental Colors like our "Old Glory" has numerous names, The Grand Union Flag, the Cambridge Flag, First Navy Ensign, and Congress Flag, yet similar to the flag of the East India Company. The

Grand Union Flag was first raised on December 3, 1775, on the USS Alfred by Captain John Paul Jones, and I might add a gangster name for a pirate like something out of Pirates of the Caribbean, also recognized as the "Father of the American Navy." At or near his Cambridge headquarters, General George Washington declared in his general orders for New Year's Day 1776 the commencement of a "new army,"[3] where all the colonies fought for everything valuable and dear to being free men was at stake. He was referring to a unified Continental Army not just one from New England, and to rally the troops, raise morale, and demonstrate their commitment to patriotism, Washington, "with the crash of a 13-gun salute, raised a new flag in honor of the birthday of the new army-a flag of thirteen red and white stripes, with the British colors (the crosses of St. George and St. Andrew) represented in the upper corner. When the British in Boston saw it flying from Prospect Hill, they at first mistook it for a flag of surrender."[4]

In Memoriam: Francis Scott Key
(August 1, 1779 – January 11, 1843)

Author of the National Anthem

Frederick, Maryland — Francis Scott Key, 63, the celebrated poet and author, passed away on January 11, 1843, at his daughter, Elizabeth Howard's, home in Baltimore, Maryland, leaving behind a legacy that will forever resonate in the hearts of Americans. Born on August 1, 1779, in Frederick, Maryland to the late John Ross Key and Ann Phoebe Penn Dagworthy Charlton. Key's life was marked by his unwavering commitment to justice, patriotism, and the written word. He married Mary Tayloe Lloyd in 1802 and together they raised their eleven children.[1]

"The Star-Spangled Banner," Key's most enduring contribution, emerged from the tumultuous War of 1812. As he witnessed the relentless British bombardment of **Fort McHenry** in 1814, Key's eyes were fixed on the American flag fluttering defiantly against the dawn sky. Inspired by this stirring sight, he penned the poem **"Defense of Fort McHenry,"** which would later be set to music and become our national anthem. The anthem's powerful verses evoke the resilience and pride of a young nation, standing firm in the face of adversity.

Beyond his poetic prowess, Key was a distinguished lawyer. He argued before the **Supreme Court** and served as the **District Attorney for the District of Columbia** during President Andrew Jackson's administration. His legal acumen was evident in cases such as the **Burr conspiracy trial**, where he defended the rule of law and upheld justice.

Key's complex relationship with slavery reflects the contradictions of his time. He owned slaves during his lifetime, a fact that underscores the complexities of his character. He held eight human beings in bondage at the time of his death. While he publicly criticized the institution and provided legal aid to enslaved individuals seeking freedom, he also represented slave owners. His legacy is a reminder that history is rarely black and white—often shaded in nuanced grays.

Key, an Episcopalian, found solace in faith, and his spiritual convictions guided his actions. He helped found and financially supported several parishes in our nation's capital, including St. John's Episcopal Church in Georgetown, Trinity Episcopal Church in present-day Judiciary Square, and Christ Church in Alexandria, Virginia.

Today, we honor Francis Scott Key not only for his poetic eloquence but also for his role in shaping the American narrative. His words, immortalized in our anthem, continue to echo across generations, reminding us of our shared heritage and the enduring quest for liberty. Initially interred in the vault of John Eager Howard at Old St. Paul's Cemetery in 1843, his mortal remains now rest in the family plot at Mount Olivet Cemetery in Frederick, Maryland. His cause of death was pleurisy, an inflammation of the thin layer of tissue that lines the lungs and chest walls caused by a virus, bacteria, or other disease or illness.

Rest in peace, Francis Scott Key. Your words still ripple through time, inspiring us to seek the light even in the darkest hours.

In Memoriam: John Paul Jones
(July 6, 1747 – July 18, 1792)

The Father of the U.S. Navy

John Paul Jones, 45, of Arbigland Estate, located in Kirkcudbrightshire, Scotland, a name etched in the annals of maritime history, breathed his last on July 18, 1792, in Paris, France, leaving behind a legacy that would forever shape the course of naval warfare. He was born, the fourth child out of seven, to the late John Paul, Sr., and Jean McDuff on July 6, 1747. He embarked on a seafaring journey that would propel him into the heart of the American Revolution.

At the age of 13, he was placed aboard the ship Friendship as a sea apprentice to learn the art of seamanship. At 21, he received his first command. After several successful years as a merchant skipper in the West Indies, John Paul migrated to the colonies. He added the last name Jones in 1773 and escaped to America, fearing he would not receive a fair trial for killing a mutinous sailor on Tobago Island in self-defense.

As the tempest of rebellion swept across the colonies, Jones found himself drawn to the cause. His unwavering commitment led him to join the fledgling Continental Navy, where he would carve his name into the very fabric of freedom. With sails billowing and cannons roaring, he danced upon the treacherous waves, challenging the mighty British Empire.

His defining moment would be the **Battle of Flamborough Head**, a fateful crash in the North Sea. Aboard the Bon Homme Richard, he faced the formidable HMS Serapis—a ship that outgunned and outmanned him. Yet, Jones, with fire in his eyes and courage in his heart, uttered those immortal words: **"I have not yet begun to fight!"**[1] And fight he did, with unmatched valor. The sea bore witness to their deadly embrace, as wood splintered, smoke engulfed, and blood stained the salted decks. Victory was hard-won, but it was his.

Beyond the cannon smoke and salt spray, Jones was more than a naval commander. He was a visionary—a man who understood that liberty's safeguard lay in the strength of the fleet. His vision extended beyond borders, and he secured the first-ever foreign salute for the American flag when French Admiral La Motte Piquet honored the **USS Ranger** in France.

With the revolution won, Thomas Jefferson advised Jones to accept an offer from Empress Catherine II of Russia to serve in the Russian Navy. He took part in one naval campaign against the Turks. Russian Naval officers plotted against him, impeding his efforts until his recall to St. Petersburg, where Jones was relegated to duty-free. Naval officers continued to plot against him, fearing the foreigner would become a rival. Frustrated, he resigned after a year of service.

Yet, fate is a capricious mistress. In Paris, far from the rolling tides, and with a grateful America appointing him U.S. Consul to Algiers, a commission he never saw, Jones succumbed to the relentless march of time. His final breaths whispered tales of courage, sacrifice, and unyielding determination. The father of the U.S. Navy had sailed his last voyage, succumbing to interstitial nephritis (renal failure). Later clinical studies suggested that his condition was exacerbated by heart arrhythmia. His body was placed in a lead coffin filled with preservatives and buried in the Protestant Cemetery near the Hospital St. Louis. Over time, the cemetery became forgotten, recycled, and used by squatters who constructed shacks over the property. John Paul Jones remains were lost.

A century after his death, President Teddy Roosevelt launched an intensive search to find his body. That day came in 1905, when investigators hired by General Horace Porter, the American ambassador to France, discovered his body and, amid great ceremony, brought John Paul Jones back to America aboard the USS Brooklyn accompanied by three other cruisers. Seven battleships met them off the American coast, and, in a single column, sailed into Chesapeake Bay. The escorting battleships fired a 15-gun salute as the Brooklyn sailed into Annapolis. The coffin rested on trestles in Bancroft Hall at the United States Naval Academy for seven years.   Today, as the stars and stripes flutter over azure seas, we remember John Paul Jones—the mariner, the sea snake warrior, the legend. His mortal remains rest within the hallowed halls of the U.S. Naval Academy Chapel in Annapolis, Maryland, in a magnificent marble sarcophagus below the chapel, modeled after the tomb of Napoleon. A naval midshipman stands at attention beside the sarcophagus on days when the tomb is opened to the public.[2] "Non sibi sed patriae" meaning "Not self, but country." This defined John Paul Jones.

Fair winds and following seas, Commodore Jones. Your legacy sails on.

Francis G. Mayer/Corbis/Vcg/Getty Images

Many may not know the story of Captain John Paul Jones, but if you grew up and went to school in the United States, you've probably heard the Betsy Ross story. A charming tale of how Elizabeth Griscom Ross, a.k.a. Betsy Ross, a renowned upholsterer, sewed and created the first flag. Legend has it that one day in 1776, George Washington, Commander-in-Chief of the Continental Army, Robert Morris, Chairman of the "Secret Committee,"[1] a renowned senator from Pennsylvania and signer of the Declaration of Independence, and George Ross, also a signer of the Declaration of Independence, member of the Continental Congress, and uncle to John Ross, Elizabeth Griscom's husband, identified themselves as members of a congressional committee while visiting Mrs. Ross. During the visit to her upholstery shop located at her house, Washington reached into his coat pocket, producing a folded piece of paper with a crude sketch of his vision for the flag. The initial design had thirteen red and white stripes and thirteen six-pointed stars, each representing the thirteen colonies soon to become the United States of America. This flag's stars would be similar to General Washington's Commander-in-Chief standard, which marked his presence on the battlefield during the Revolutionary War and also had thirteen six-pointed stars. The white stars were also on a blue field representing a "new constellation" and later adopted on June 14, 1777. Looking at the design, Betsy Ross convinced George Washington to make one important alteration as seamstresses do, i.e., change the six-pointed stars to five-pointed stars, demonstrating they would be easier to cut out than the original six-pointed stars. After the men visiting agreed to the alteration and much debate about it being easily recognizable, Besty was asked if she could make the flag. She famously replied, "I don't know, but I will try.,"[2] then set out working on the first American flag. Now, that's a pretty convincing legend when you consider the historical figures mentioned. This was taught as an actual fact when I was in elementary school, and for those older than me, grade, or grammar school, but it is just that a fable, a myth, a legend.

How did the legend come about, as there is no archival evidence or transcriptions to corroborate this story or the verbal tradition of the first American flag? To answer our question, we'll have to skip March 1870 when her grandson, William Canby, the son of Jane Claypoole Canby (Betsy Ross' daughter) and Mr. Caleb Canby, publicized the Besty Ross story in a speech he gave to the Historical Society of Pennsylvania for a paper he wrote titled, "The History of the Flag of the United States."[3] From what I have read he offers no concrete evidence that he heard the story directly from his grandmother or his mother, Jane Claypoole Canby. He does claim, however, that he did hear the story straight from the source, his grandmother, yet the congressional record of the day remains inconclusive and evidenced by his brother George Canby and Lloyd Balderston, George's nephew, in their book "The Evolution of the American Flag."[4]

In Memoriam: Elizabeth Griscom Claypoole
"Betsy Ross" (January 1, 1752 – January 30, 1836)

American Upholsterer, designer of the Betsy Ross Flag

Elizabeth Griscom Claypoole, 84, of Philadelphia, Pennsylvania, is a remarkable woman whose legacy is woven into the very fabric of American history. She departed this world peacefully in her sleep on January 30, 1836, in Philadelphia, Pennsylvania. She was born on January 1, 1752, in Gloucester City, New Jersey to the late Samuel and Rebecca James Griscom (both of whom died in 1793 in the Philadelphia yellow fever epidemic). She was the eighth child out of eleven. She leaves behind a trail of courage, creativity, and patriotism.

Elizabeth, also known as Betsy Ross, was an American upholsterer. Her needlework skills were legendary, and she left an indelible mark on the nation. Coming from a long line of craftsmen, Betsy learned to sew at a young age, being taught by her great aunt, Sarah Elizabeth Griscom. She attended a Quaker school and was the apprentice to William Webster, an upholsterer. It was in Webster's shop that she learned to sew mattresses, chair covers, and blinds.

Betsy's nimble fingers wove tales of courage and creativity. As an **American upholsterer**, she transformed fabric into symbols of freedom. Her needlework prowess was legendary.

Betsy Ross's impact extended far beyond her needle and thread. Her unwavering commitment to the American cause during the Revolutionary War and her role in shaping the nation's symbols make her a true hero.

While some historians debate its authenticity, family tradition, as told by Betsy's grandson William Jackson Canby (son of Caleb Henry Canby and Jane Claypoole Canby) in March 1870 before the Historical Society of Pennsylvania, holds that **General George Washington**, along with **Congressman Robert Morris**, and **George Ross**, visited Betsy in 1776. She convinced Washington to alter the stars on the flag from six-pointed to five-pointed, showing that it was easier to cut the latter. Although archival evidence is scarce, the tale persists, and Betsy is credited by some with creating the first or second official U.S. flag— the beloved **Betsy Ross flag**.

During the American Revolution, Betsy stitched flags for the Pennsylvanian navy. Her work extended beyond the war, as she continued to create U.S. flags for over fifty years. Notably, she crafted fifty garrison flags for the U.S. Arsenal on the Schuylkill River in 1811.

Betsy, no stranger to tragedy, faced widowhood three times as well as the deaths of some of her children. Her first husband, whom she married in 1773, **John Ross**, passed away at the outset of the Revolutionary War in 1775. John's uncle is George Ross, mentioned in the legend, and who was a signer of the Declaration of Independence. Later, she married **Joseph Ashburn** on June 15, 1777, with whom she had two daughters, Zilla, who died at age nine, and Eliza. Ashburn died in a British jail in 1780. She then married **John Claypoole** in May 1783, with whom she had five children Clarissa, Susanna, Jane, Rachel, and Harriet (who died in infancy). John Claypoole died in 1817.

As we bid farewell to Betsy Ross, let us remember her as more than a seamstress—she was a beacon of courage, creativity, and love for her country. May her memory continue to inspire us all. Besty Ross was initially interred at the Free Quaker Burial Grounds on North 5th Street in Philadelphia, Pennsylvania, alongside her husband, John Ross. She has been buried two (maybe 3) more times after her initial interment: at Mt. Moriah Cemetery, and perhaps under the great oak tree on July 4, 1876, in Basking Ridge, New Jersey, but currently on Arch Street in the courtyard adjacent to the Betsy Ross House next to her husband John Claypoole.[1]

So, who designed the American flag? After all, everything made has a maker, right? Enter Francis Hopkinson. If you have never heard of him, you are probably asking, Who is this guy? Francis Hopkinson was an inventor, musician, poet, lawyer, and signer of the Declaration of Independence. In 1774, he was appointed to the New Jersey Governor's Council, later represented New Jersey in the Continental Congress, and was mentored by Benjamin Franklin. He was a friend of Thomas Jefferson and George Washington. Hopkinson was very connected to our country's founding fathers. On June 14, 1777, the Second Continental Congress adopted the Stars and Stripes as the first official national flag of the newly independent United States. Today we celebrate this on our calendars as Flag Day, and thanks to a proclamation made on this day officially establishing it as Flag Day in 1916 by President Woodrow Wilson and again as National Flag Day by an act of Congress in August of 1949, Flag Day is not recognized as an official national holiday. However, you will find various veterans' groups, such as the American Legion, Veterans of Foreign Wars, 40/8, Patriot Guard Riders, Amvets, etc., celebrating Flag Day by performing various ceremonies, parades, and dedications. June 14th is also the day the United States Army was founded just a few years earlier, in 1775. The resolution creating the flag came out of the Continental Marine Committee, of which Hopkinson was a member, in 1776. At the time of the flag's adoption, he was the chairman of the Navy Board, which was under the Marine Committee. The duties of the Marine Committee today are assigned to or have been transferred to the Secretary of the United States Navy.[1]

According to his book titled "So Proudly We Hail: The History of the United States Flag," co-authors William Furlong and Byron McCandless write, "On May 25, 1780, Hopkinson asserted in a letter to the Board of Admiralty that he had designed "the flag of the United States of America" as well as several other ornaments, devices, and checks appearing on bills of exchange, ship papers, the seals of the boards of Admiralty and Treasury, and the Great Seal of the United States."[2] On a field of blue, the Board of Admiralty seal contained a shield with seven red stripes and six white stripes. In his letter Hopkinson noted that he didn't seek compensation for his work or designs and was now seeking restitution for his work in the form of "a Quarter Cask of the public wine" claiming it would be "a reasonable and proper reward for his labors."[3]

Forwarding his letter to Congress, the Board receives another letter on June 24, 1780, containing a bill for his "drawings and devices." Hopkinson makes no mention of designing the flag of the United States in this second letter, rather, the first item listed is "the great Naval Flag of the United States" along with the other contributions previously mentioned. The flag with its red outer stripes was designed to show up well on ships at sea. A similar flag for the national flag was most likely intended by Hopkinson with white outer stripes as on the Great Seal of the United States and on the Bennington flag, which commemorated the 50th anniversary of the founding of the United States in 1826.[4]

Bennington Flag
National Archives

The Bennington flag also featured thirteen six-pointed stars on a blue canton with two stars in the upper corners and eleven making a semi-circle over the number 76, the year of independence.

Ironically, Hopkinson's Navy flag was the preferred choice as the national flag. The first design of the blue canton is reminiscent of George Washington's Commander-in-Chief Standard, with thirteen six pointed stars on a blue background with the stars alternating in a 3,2,3,2,3 pattern.

George Washington's Commander-in-Chief Standard
Museum of the American Revolution

There are no known sketches of a Hopkinson flag, either U.S. or naval, in existence today.[5] However, history has recorded that Hopkinson incorporated elements of the two flags he designed in his rough sketches of the Great Seal of the United States and his design for the Admiralty Board Seal.[6] The rough sketch of his second Great Seal proposal has seven white stripes and six red stripes. If you look closely enough at the impression of Hopkinson's Admiralty Board Seal, you will notice it has a chevron with seven shaded stripes and six white stripes. Hopkinson's designs for a naval flag and a governmental flag are represented by the Great Seal and the Admiralty Board Seal, respectively. Thirteen stripes were supposed to be on both flags. Hopkinson's U.S. flag may have been intended to use six-pointed stars, as the original stars used in the Great Seal had six points. His original design for the Great Seal, which included a starry U.S. flag with six-pointed asterisks for stars, supports this once more.[7] The flag of the

Continental Colors, which features seven alternating red stripes and six alternating white stripes with the crosses of St. George and St. Andrew, may also be a tribute to it, but instead of using those crosses in the canton, the Great Seal used the stars from Washington's Commander-in-Chief Standard.

For his various designs, Hopkinson asked for cash in the amount of twenty-seven hundred pounds. James Milligan, the Auditor General, commissioned an evaluation of the request for payment. The report from the commissioner of the Chamber of Accounts said that the bill was reasonable and ought to be paid. Congress asked for an itemized bill  for payment in cash. Hopkinson demanded nine pounds for the naval flag. A committee investigated Hopkinson's charges that his payment was being delayed for arbitrary reasons. The Treasury Board turned down the request in an October 27, 1780, report to Congress. The Board gave various justifications for its decision, mostly political, one of which was that Hopkinson "could not claim the sole merit of these and is not entitled in this respect to the full sum charged, as he was not the only person consulted on those exhibitions of Fancy that were incidental to the Board (among them, the U.S. flag, the Navy flag, the Admiralty seal, and the Great Seal with a reverse)."[8]

The reference to other people's work is most likely a reference to his work on the Great Seal.[9] Afterall, there were at least three committees assigned to work on the Great Seal. "Hopkinson's account remained unsettled until August 23, 1781, when Congress passed a resolution "That the report relative to the fancy-work of Francis Hopkinson ought not to be acted on." Writers on both the flag and the currency have pointed out, however, that no one had challenged Hopkinson's assertion that he had designed most of the items for which he asked for compensation, and the action of Congress may have been based principally on the fact that Hopkinson had been a government official when he did the work. Whether because of this experience or for other reasons, Hopkinson took no further part in the work of the second committee; and the committee made no further serious effort to produce an acceptable seal design."[10] What is clear is that Francis Hopkinson would not be paid for The Great Seal of the United States based on "collaboration with others" and that he would no longer work on it, so it was still a work in progress. Secondly, to my knowledge and during research for this book, I was unable to find a known committee of the Continental Congress where an assignment was given to design the national flag or naval flag. As a result, I came to the logical conclusion that there is no evidence of collaboration with others on his design for the flag of our nation.

However, politics played a part in Hopkinson not being paid, but isn't that usually the case? Again, Willilam Furlong and Byron McCandless put it this way, "Hopkinson's enemies blocked all attempts to have him paid for his services, but they never denied that he made the designs. The journals of the Continental Congress clearly show that he designed the flag. In the minds of the authors of this volume, there is no question that he designed the flag of the United States."[11]

In Memoriam: Francis Hopkinson (1737–1791)

Creator of the United States Flag

Francis Hopkinson's flag for the U.S with 13 six-pointed stars arranged in five rows[1]

Hopkinson Flag for the U.S. Navy[2]

Francis Hopkinson, 53, of Philadelphia Pennsylvania, In the quietude of May 9, 1791, the world bid farewell to a polymath, a patriot, and a visionary. His multifaceted life wove together threads of creativity, legal acumen, and unwavering commitment to the birth of a new nation.

A Renaissance man, Francis Hopkinson was born on October 2, 1737, in Philadelphia, Pennsylvania to the late Thomas and Mary Johnson Hopkinson. Hopkinson's intellectual pursuits knew no bounds. His alma mater, the **College of Philadelphia** (now the **University of Pennsylvania**), witnessed his scholarly journey. **Artium Baccalaureus** in 1757, and **Artium Magister** in 1760, laid the groundwork for a life of remarkable achievements. On September 1, 1768, he married the love of his life, Ann Borden, and they raised their five children.

In the sweltering heat of July 1776, Hopkinson's quill danced across parchment, etching his name into history. As a delegate from New Jersey, he lent his signature to the **Declaration of Independence**. His conviction echoed through the hallowed halls, shaping the destiny of a fledgling nation.

Hopkinson's creativity knew no bounds. He wove symbols and colors into the very fabric of America. From the **United States flag** to the ensign of the fledgling **United States Navy**, Hopkinson's designs fluttered in the winds of change. His artistic hand graced the design of **Continental paper money**, a tangible expression of a nation's promise. He was also consulted as a designer for the **Great Seal of the United States.**

Beyond the courtroom, Hopkinson's soul resonated with music. In 1759, he composed a secular song, becoming the **first native American composer** to do so. His legal prowess found expression in the **Second Continental Congress**, where he shaped the laws of a nascent nation.

His life was interwoven with greatness. Across the Atlantic, England beckoned, and Hopkinson sailed its waters. His quest for the position of **commissioner of customs for North America** remained unfulfilled, but the journey enriched his spirit. His conversations with Lord North, kinship with Cousin James Johnson, and artistic camaraderie with painter Benjamin West painted the canvas of his life. Fabrics and port wines flowed through his hands, bridging commerce and culture.

As the sun dipped below the horizon on that fateful May Day, Francis Hopkinson's legacy transcended mere mortal existence. His name echoed in courtrooms, on paper currency, and in the hearts of those who dared to dream of liberty. Francis Hopkinson is interred at Christ Church Burial Ground in Philadelphia. Note:- This is also the burial place of Benjamin Franklin and three other signers of the Declaration of Independence (George Ross, Joseph Hewes, and Benjamin Rush).

In Memoriam

Hopkinson's cause of death was a sudden apoplectic seizure associated with a stroke or other vascular event.

Rest well, Francis Hopkinson. Your symphony lives on in the very soul of America.

Draping the Casket with Old Glory

The flag-draped casket bearing the remains of the late Senator John McCain lies in state at the U.S. Capitol Rotunda| Jim Watson/AFP via Getty Images

In his book A Walk-Through Time: A History of Funeral Service Ralph and Joan Klicker write, "This custom (referring to the draping of the flag on a coffin) began during the Napoleonic Wars (1796 – 1815). The dead carried from the field of battle on a caisson were covered with a flag."[1] On www.ushistory.org, it says the same thing about funeral flags.

Chapter 4

Masons and the Militia

"His example is now complete, and it will teach wisdom and virtue to magistrates, citizens, and men not only in the present age, but in future generations as long as our history shall be read."
- President John Adams, upon hearing of George Washington's death

So, what is a burial flag and how do I obtain one? What documentation is required in order to receive a burial flag? According to the United States Department of Veteran Affairs instruction forms that accompany VA Form 27-2008, "Provide a copy of the veteran's discharge documents that shows service dates and the character of service, such as DD Form 214, or verification of service from the veteran's service department or VA. Various information requested, is considered essential to the proper processing of the application. Ensure these areas are completed as fully as possible. Note: If the claimant is unable to provide documentary proof, a flag may be issued when a statement is made by a person of established character and reputation that he/she personally knows the deceased to have been a veteran who meets the eligibility criteria."[1]

Walking to the United States Post Office with VA Form-2008 Application for United States Flag for Burial Purposes and a copy of Mr. Bryant's Certificate of Release or Discharge from Active Duty, referred to as Form DD-214, I hand the paperwork with the appropriate signatures to the postal clerk and receive back a box containing a five-foot wide by nine and a half foot-long burial flag. Working in the funeral chapel and having Mr. Byrant already dressed and in his casket and set up on the bier in the funeral chapel, I open the box containing the burial flag. The flag is made of cotton and am proud to say, "Made in the USA." It is unfolded and ironed to remove the folds creases and wrinkles. After ironing the flag, issued on behalf of the Department of Veterans Affairs to honor the memory of one who has served our country, I draped the flag on Mr. Bryant's casket. If we were having a closed casket, the flag would be draped the full length of the casket, with the blue canton placed at the head over the left shoulder of the deceased. But since Mrs. Bryant requested a half couch with an open casket, the flag is draped by placing three layers to cover the closed half of the casket in such a manner that the blue field will be the top fold, next to the open portion of the casket on the deceased's left.

According to the American Legion, "When a casket is fully open (full couch), common sense suggests that the flag be folded in the traditional triangular method, placed in the casket cap above the left shoulder of the deceased.

On a half open (half couch) casket, the flag is arranged in three layers of ten-inch folds to cover the closed half of the casket. The blue field will be the top layer on the deceased's left.

Accepted patriotic practice suggests that when the military service includes cremated remains that the flag be folded in the traditional triangular method and be placed next to the urn."[2]

John M. Hartvigsen wrote in his article Draping a Casket with the Flag, "This tradition began in the United States around the U.S. Civil War. When the nation was founded decades earlier, it was common to place a black cloth covering, called a pall, over a coffin."[3] The Civil War was a time when there was mass carnage and little concern for individual soldiers, who were typically buried in mass graves before the fighting began again. Grieving families sought ways to honor and remember those who fought, some soldiers were embalmed, as this is around the time embalming began in America and returned to their families for a "proper burial." One of those honors was to have the Union canton of stars placed at the head and over the left shoulder of the deceased. During a military funeral at the funeral home, if a person is viewing a flag draped casket from the foot of the deceased, the flag looks as if it is reporting death because it presents the illusion of looking like it is backwards, whereas if you are standing at the front of the casket it appears as it should. The tradition of draping the flag is one derived from royalty, when the flag or pall with the family crest was displayed in a similar manner causing the same illusion.

Looking back at history and our topic of the timeless tradition of military funerals in the United States of America, it's likely impossible to pinpoint the exact origin of some of these traditions, but it's a mystery we are striving to unravel. After all, the United States was a fledgling country born out of the American Revolution with then General George Washington at the helm of the army. Many soldiers have died on the field of battle, resulting in these traditions. Every day, Arlington National Cemetery, and its honor guards bear witness to the draping of the United States flag as soldiers receive the honors we are discussing. To give us a better perspective on where our country's military funeral customs possibly originated concerning the draping of a flag or pall, we must explore the death and funeral of an American hero and our first officially elected President of the United States of America, General George Washington. Washington was a man of many firsts, but not the first to have a general mourning period declared by the nation. That honor belongs to Benjamin Franklin, who died in Philadelphia, Pennsylvania, of pleurisy (inflammation of the membrane of the lungs) on April 17, 1790. This makes George Washington the second declaration of a grief and mourning period for the nation in a span of nine years. Despite his desire for a simple burial, hundreds of people attended his funeral, marking the beginning of more formal military honors: the caparisoned horse, the firing of three volleys at sea answered by those fired from the lawn at Mount Vernon, and a U.S.

flag carried in the procession. It was also attended by hundreds of Master Masons of Virginia from numerous masonic lodges, of which George Washington was a member. Hence the title, Masons and the Militia.

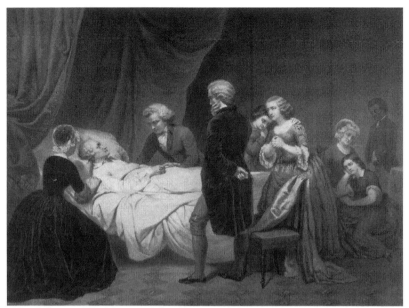

Life of George Washington: The Christian, lithograph by Claude Regnier, after Junius Brutus Stearns,1853. Gift of Mr. and Mrs. Robert B. Gibby, 1984 [WB-55/A1], Mount Vernon Ladies' Association, Mount Vernon, VA.

It was Thursday, December 12, 1799, and the 67-year-old George Washington rose before dawn, probably starting his day with a meal of three small cornmeal cakes (Hoe Cakes) and three cups of tea without cream. According to his step-granddaughter, Nelly Custis Lewis, the small mush cakes would be swimming in butter and honey. She also mentioned that he always wrote or read until seven in the summer and half past seven in the winter.[4] So why should this day be any different as most people have some sort of daily routine? As is often the case on the East Coast and other regions, the weather patterns on this day unexpectedly shifted from light snow to hail, and as the temperature increased, rain and sleet started to fall. Out on horseback supervising the farming activities of his beloved Mount Vernon, George Washington was out in it. Upon his return home around dinner time, it was suggested by one of his servants that he change out of his damp riding clothes. Washington, known for his punctuality, meaning you could almost set your watch by his daily routine, decided to remain in his wet clothes.[5]

As wintery bliss slowly approaches and persists, as it is not yet officially winter but close enough, old man winter creeps in making his wintery presence felt dumping heavy snow throughout the night. By morning, Friday, December 13, 1799, Mount Vernon, and the east coast were covered in at least three to four inches of snow and the day found George Washington feeling unwell and with a sore throat. Despite his aliment, Washington set out on his daily routine. After the weather cleared, he went to the hanging wood area on the east side of his mansion to select trees he wanted removed by his enslaved workers. As the day progressed, Washington's servants noted that his voice was becoming raspier. Most evenings and this Friday evening was like most others, Washington read the newspapers and correspondence of the day with his personal assistant or secretary, Tobias Lear, and his wife Martha. Washington tried to clear his throat and at some point, stopped reading aloud asking Lear to complete the reading, then retired for the night.[6]

After retiring for the night, Washington awoke in his bed in the master bedroom of the mansion around two o'clock the morning of Saturday, December 14, 1799, in terrible pain and discomfort. He had a high fever, an extremely sore throat, and labored breathing. Martha, who had just recovered from a cold herself and concerned for his well-being, wanted to seek help for her ailing husband. Despite his agony, still hoarse and with a sore throat, and showing care and concern for her recent illness, Washington refused to allow his wife to leave the comfort of their bedroom. At daybreak, an enslaved handmaiden named Caroline Branham came to the house, as she did on most days, to light the fire in the fireplace and begin the day's affairs. Upon hearing her, Mrs. Washington sent her to retrieve Tobias Lear, who rushed to Washington's bedside. Upon entering his bedroom, Lear found Washington lying in bed wheezing and with difficulty breathing, as his throat had now developed some form of infection. Lear immediately sent for George Rawlins, an overseer at Mount Vernon. In today's terms, he would be called a yard foreman, ranch hand, or ranch supervisor, a trusted overseer by George Washington, nonetheless. Once he arrived in his room, Washington requested that Rawlins, who appeared agitated, to bleed him telling Rawlins, "Don't be afraid."[7] Unfortunately, in the late eighteenth century, bloodletting was still considered an acceptable medical practice. For those who don't know bloodletting is the withdrawal of blood to prevent, or, in eighteenth century thinking, cure illness or disease. Today, donating blood could be considered a form of bloodletting. Anyhow, George Rawlins removed about a half-pint of blood from George Washington. When Tobias Lear summoned George Rawlins, he also sent word to Alexandria, roughly ten miles away, summoning Washington's trusted friend of forty years and physician, Dr. James Craik, so the bloodletting took place prior to Dr. Craik's arrival. Unfortunately for Washington, bloodletting was his preferred treatment, and despite his wife's objections, he believed that it could cure him of his ailment as it had done in the past. In fact, when Rawlins made the incision in his arm, Washington told him, "The orifice is not large enough" despite blood running pretty freely.[8]

While waiting for Dr. Craik, Washington was given a tincture of molasses, butter, and vinegar to soothe his throat. Now if one has a sore throat, you will think vinegar would burn the throat on the way down and would most certainly be the last thing you would want to drink. As a result of this sage tea gargle, Washington nearly suffocated. Martha Washington, concerned that her husband's condition was not improving, asked that Tobias Lear summon a second doctor. As the morning progressed, Washington, not feeling any relief, agreed with his wife, Martha, and Lear sent for Dr. Gustavus Brown of Port Tobacco, Maryland, some thirty-three miles away. Dr. Craik felt that Dr. Brown had an excellent reputation for diagnosing and treating conditions such as that of George Washington as reported later by Tobias Lear. By nine in the morning, Dr. James Craik arrived and began his examination of his friend. During the examination Dr. Craik "produced a blister on his throat in an attempt to balance the fluids in Washington's body." Then Dr. Craik in his medical opinion felt it necessary to bleed Washington a second time and ordered another solution this time concocted of vinegar and sage tea, which Washington gargled.[9]

Noticing that Dr. Brown had not arrived yet and the lateness of the morning, Dr. Craik summoned for a third physician, Dr. Elisha Dick, around eleven o'clock feeling that Washington's ailment was more serious than he realized. At noon, our beloved George Washington was administered an enema, resulting in no improvement in his condition, and he was bled a third time. Could you imagine a needle, lancet, or a sharp piece of wood with a drain tube inserted into a vein in your arm and blood let out with the only means of stopping the bleeding being a turnicate or some other measure of the day? In some cases, leeches were used instead of the crude instruments of the eighteenth century. Despite Dr. Elisha Dick's objections, George Washington's physician, James Craik, arrived at the mansion around two o'clock in the afternoon and decided to perform a fourth and final blood transfusion, extracting approximately 32 ounces of blood. Now, this author is not a mathematician or a doctor; however, if one were to Google how much blood were in the human body, you would find somewhere between nine and a half to twelve pints of blood, or around 5 liters, which is roughly around 170 ounces, and the geniuses of Washington's day blood let 32 ounces? That's almost a full liter of blood. A total of 2.365 liters of blood is reported to have been removed from Washington's body, or some 40% of his total blood volume taken in a twelve-hour period.

From our twenty first century perspective, the torture continues, and Washington is awake through all of this. After Washington's doctors consulted each other as to the next course of treatment, Dr. Craik gives him an emetic, a medicine to induce vomiting, and surprisingly has no "beneficial results." Despite their best efforts to relieve his symptoms, provide him comfort, and improve his overall condition, George Washington's condition worsened. Now we know Washington had at least three physicians, his beloved wife, Martha, and enslaved servants present while the doctors were planning their course of treatment. There may have been others in the home checking on him as well such as friends and other family members. Feeling himself getting worse and around four-thirty in the afternoon, George asked Martha, who came to his bedside, to retrieve his two wills from his study. After careful examination of both, he kept ahold of one and discarded the other, which Martha burned.[10]

Feeling the end was near he told Lear, "I find I am going, my breath cannot last long. I believed from the first that the disorder would prove fatal. Do you arrange and record all my late military letters and papers? Arrange my accounts and settle my books, as you know more about them than anyone else, and let Mr. Rawlins finish recording my other letters which he has begun."[11] George Washington got out of bed at five in the afternoon, got dressed, and went to his chair. However, he felt uncomfortable, so he returned to bed after about thirty minutes or so. Washington said to Dr. Craik when he went to check on him. "Doctor, I die hard; but I am not afraid to go; I believed from my first attack that I should not survive it; my breath cannot last long,"[12] Washington thanked the three doctors for their services not long afterward. Dr. Craik stayed inside the chamber. More blisters and cataplasms were applied to Washington's legs and feet at eight o'clock at night. At ten at night, George Washington spoke, requesting to be "decently buried" and because he so feared being buried alive told Tobias Lear to "not let my body be put into the Vault in less than three days after I am dead."[13]

On December 14, 1799, at around 10:20 PM, George Washington passed away with his wife Martha sitting in mourning at the foot of the bed. He passed without a struggle or a sigh according to Tobias Lear. A seemingly innocent throat infection that his doctors described as inflammatory quinsy ultimately defeated the battle hardened general. The most recent historical and medical accounts have narrowed the cause of death to acute epiglottitis, a virulent throat infection that essentially closed his windpipe. Yet, as painful as his death must have been, Washington faced it with courage and was surrounded by the people who were closest to him including his friends Dr. Craik, and Tobias Lear, the enslaved housemaids Caroline, Molly, Charlotte, and even his enslaved valet, Christopher Sheels, who stood in the room throughout the day. His last words were "Tis well."[14] Dr. Elisha Dick stopped Washington's bed chamber clock at the time of the general's death.[15]

Funeral preparations began almost at once. According to his wishes, Washington was not buried for three days. Around midnight on Sunday, December 15, 1799, servants carried his body to the large dining room and Dr. Elisha Dick, one of Washington's attending physicians, measured his frame for the coffin 6'3 ½ inches in exact length, one foot nine inches exact across the shoulders, and two feet exact across the elbows.[16] As it was freezing cold outside, the windows in the large dining room were opened to help slow decomposition and preserve Washington's body. Tobias Lear immediately dispatched letters to family and friends informing them of Washington's death and requesting that they attend the funeral at the request of Mrs. Washington. He sent a hasty correspondence to President John Adams, who was in Philadelphia, but it did not arrive until the afternoon of the 18th of December, the same day as the funeral.[17] Because the deceased's body was not shown laid out in their caskets in funeral homes as they are today, and undertakers or funeral directors as we know them today did not exist, Tobias Lear had to rely on numerous professions to meet Mrs. Washington's demands.

During the eighteenth century, various individuals contracted out all supporting services for a funeral based on their specific skills and/or advertised professions. On Sunday, December 15, 1799, Tobias Lear "Engaged Mr. Ingles (sic) and Mr. McMunn to have a Mahogany Coffin made, lined with lead, in which the body was to be deposited." Both Mr. Joseph and Henry Ingle were brothers and cabinet makers. Joseph ran the Mahogany Plank, while Henry called his place a "Hardware Store."[18] Mr. George McMunn was a coppersmith and plumber sought by the Ingle brothers to provide the lead liner for

Washington's coffin. Washington's estate accounts identify Michael and Margaret Gretter of Alexandria as the individuals who provided the burial shroud and the black pall cloth that was draped over Washington's coffin with a white masonic apron and two of his military sabers on top of the pall.[19]

On Monday, December 16, 1799, Tobias Lear notes, that Washington's farm Manager, Mr. James Anderson, traveled to Alexandria "to get a number of things prepared for the funeral." Mourning clothes were ordered for the Family Domestics and Overseers. After learning from Alexandria that the Militia, Freemasons, and other groups were resolved to honor the General's memory by attending his body to the Grave, Lear directed provision be prepared for a large number of people, as some refreshment would be expected by them."[20] Lear sent James Anderson to hire John and James Scott at "Taylors/Habit Makers"[21] in Alexandria, Virgina to make the mourning clothes for the funeral. The Scott's were unable to fill the entire order due to having similar issues today, i.e., manpower and supply issues. The remainder of James' order was filled by tailor William Bowie whose shop was a few doors down from the Scott's establishment.[22]

On Tuesday, December 17, 1799, Mr. Lear writes in his journal, "About one o'clock the coffin was brought from Alexandria on a stagecoach. Mr. Ingle and Mr. McMunn accompanied it."[23] The lead-lined mahogany casket bore the inscription: Surge Ad Judicium (Fly to Justice) and, in the middle, the words Gloria Deo (Glory Be to God). Inscribed on a silver name plate was "General George Washington departed this life on the 14th of December 1799 aged 67."[24]

On Wednesday, December 18, 1799, the day of the funeral, Lear journals, "About 3 o'clock the procession began to move...[it]...proceeded round in front of the lawn, & down to the vault...The body born by the Free Masons & Officers...the Revd. Mr. Davis read the service...The Masons performed their ceremonies, & the Body was deposited in the Vault...After the ceremony the Company returned to the house where they took some refreshment, & retired in good order."[25]

Tobias Lear was tasked with making all the arrangements, as noted in his memoir asked, for a mahogany coffin, mourning clothes, post burial refreshments, a graveside service, and other details including the cutting of a lock of the general's hair for his wife Martha to keep before the coffin was sealed. Despite Washington's request that "my corpse may be interred in a private manner without parade or funeral orations."[26] His funeral was grand and most notably against his wishes to have such fanfare. Washington wanted a simple funeral, but others had different plans and for good reason as Major General Henry Lee said in his funeral oration of George Washington, "First in war, first in peace, and first in the hearts of his countrymen."[27] Even though other militia and military members preceded Washington in death, his funeral gives us our first look into not just the dominant masonic funeral rites of the day, but the establishment of a more formal military ceremony that would be refined with each passing generation of servicemen.

In the late eighteenth century, and even through the mid-nineteenth century, buildings went into mourning and on this occasion, Mount Vernon, and the mansion itself were adjourned with mourning vestments. A painted hatchment, bearing the arms of Washington and Dandridge crest, hung above the mansion door. The doorway was further embellished with black crepe, and the window shudders were tightly closed and tied together with black ribbon. Inside the mansion, all the mirrors and many of the pictures were covered in white cloth to hide one's reflections, which were considered to be a distraction during the period of mourning. The belief in covering the mirrors and pictures was to prevent the deceased's spirit from getting trapped in the looking glass. Washington's shrouded body was placed inside the coffin in the large dining room, where more than one hundred candles were burned during the family's three-day vigil. The use of candles not only provided light but also helped mask the unpleasant odors in the room. Finally, a small group of masons, all officers of Alexandria Lodge No. 22 led by Dr. Elisha Dick, master of the lodge, performed a private ceremony opening the lodge of sorrow around Washington's coffin in the large dining room.

Washington was a mason for nearly fifty years, joining the masonic lodge in November 4, 1752, at the age of 20 when he received his Entered Apprentice Degree, his Fellowcraft on March 3, 1753, and raised as a Master Mason on August 4, 1753,[28] so it surprised no one that his fellow masons arrived in full force. In fact, masons representing three local lodges gathered at Mount Vernon the day of the funeral, each wearing a ceremonial apron symbolic of a master mason. Historically speaking, the burial of General Washington on December 18, 1799, is arguably the one of the most significant events in which the Masonic Lodge has ever taken part and is unquestionably the most significant of its kind in the history of the American Fraternity. Few people realize how extremely simple and truly Masonic the obsequies of this great man were. Washington's illness, which would be his last and prove to be fatal, was sudden and severe, lasting nearly twenty-four hours. There were four men at his bedside when he died: Doctors Dick, Craik, Brown, and Washington's Secretary, Tobias Lear. Three of these were members of the Craft; Doctors Dick and Craik were members of his own Lodge, Dick being the Master; and Dr. Brown was the fifth Grand Master of Masons in the State of Maryland, while Tobias Lear joined the Lodge in 1803.[29]

A committee from the lodge, including Dr. Elisha Dick, the Worshipful Master, Colonel George Deneale, the Junior Warden, and members, Colonels Simms and Little, arranged the funeral ceremonies. The body was borne from the death chamber at "low twelve" and deposited in the main room on the first floor, and the funeral appointed for "high twelve" on the 18th. Five of the six pall bearers, Colonels Little, Payne, Gilpin, Ramsay, and Simms, were members of Alexandria Lodge No. 22, as were three of the four ministers present, one of them being the Chaplain Colonel George Deneale, who also commanded the military organizations in attendance. Several of his subordinate officers were also members of the Masonic Lodge, as previously noted. The

Alexandria contingent, composed of the Masons, militia, and a large concourse of citizens, arrived late at Mount Vernon, causing the funeral cortege to start at three o'clock instead of the scheduled high noon. However, they carried the body from its resting place in the State Dining Room to the front veranda at Meridian, where the assembled throng took a final view of the remains.[30]

Important guests arrived at Mount Vernon by carriage, on horseback, and some on foot. Christopher Sheels, one of the many house servants and Washington's personal valet, stood at the door to the mansion to receive the guests. Four days earlier, he was found standing silently by Washington's bed as the master of Mount Vernon lay struggling with his final illness.[31] Throughout the day, Christopher never left Washington's side maintaining his vigilante post for twelve hours even though Washington himself asked the young man to sit. Two prominent neighbors, Lord Bryan Fairfax, who dined with the Washington's only seven days prior to his death,[32] and his son, Ferdinando Fairfax, who is the general's godson, arrived by coach. Washington has been friends with the Fairfax family since he was a young boy. He spent much of his childhood at their nearby Belvoir Plantation, which burned in 1783 and was completely destroyed during the War of 1812. The Belvoir Plantation is also where Washington learned surveying from the Fairfax's as a young man in the Virginia back country.[33]

As the Fairfax's entered the mansion, a stable hand named Wilson walked General Washington's horse up from the stables. Cyrus, a groom, and carpenter went to the study retrieving Washington's boots and pistol holsters. During the funeral procession, Cyrus and Wilson escorted Washington's horse equipped with his saddle, pistol holsters, and boots reversed in their stirrups. This horse, one of many at Mount Vernon faithfully transported Washington across his eight-thousand-acre estate many, many times, but on this occasion, he will be a caparisoned horse (riderless).[34] The fine black mourning suits that Cyrus and Wilson wore were purchased in Alexandria just two days prior to the funeral, along with mourning clothes for other family members and workers at Mount Vernon.

The kitchen staff was hard at work the morning of the funeral making preparations for refreshments for guests following the funeral. Mrs. Forbes, the family housekeeper and cook, and Caroline, a house servant, were busy preparing refreshments for the unusually large number of guests, and they would occasionally leave their kitchen duties to check on the arrival of guests and deliveries. One of whom was George Edick who arrived with forty pounds of cake from Alexandria. Large bowls of punch and cider were also prepared for after the funeral. Farm manager James Anderson, who works at the nearby distillery next to Washington's gristmill on Dogue Creek, about two miles from the mansion, brought twenty-nine gallons of whiskey from the Mount Vernon Distillery to the mansion, accompanied by two servants, Ben, and Frank. John Ladd, a Mount Vernon neighbor, offered three large wheels of cheese, weighing sixty-one pounds, that he took to the kitchen.[35] Coming up the south lane from the stables were members of the municipal government of Alexandria, led by Mayor Francis Payton. This small group included a reporter for the Alexandria Gazette, who would write about the funeral by the end of the day. For the majority of his life, Washington frequently dined at Gadsby's Tavern in Alexandria or resided in the townhouse he and Martha owned at the corner of Pitt and Cameron Street. He also owned shares in the Bank of Alexandria and was a benefactor of the Alexandria Academy.

Thomas Law and Thomas Peter shared a quiet moment outside the study. Thomas Law is the husband of Eliza (Elizabeth) Parke Custis Law, who is Martha Dandridge Washington's eldest granddaughter. Eliza and her mother, Eleanor Calvert Custis Stuart, are inside the mansion comforting Mrs. Washington. Law is talking over the funeral preparations with Thomas Peter, who's the husband of Martha's second granddaughter, Martha Parke Custis Peter. Martha Parke was unable to attend the funeral with her husband due to the severe illness of their daughter, Martha Eliza Eleanor Peter, who passed away at age 4 on August 31, 1800. Arriving late were the four members of the clergy that presided at the funeral. The Reverend Thomas Davis, rector of Christ Church in Alexandria, The Reverend Dr. James Muir, pastor of the Presbyterian Church in Alexandria, Virginia and chaplain of Alexandria Masonic Lodge No. 22, assisted Dr. Dick at the family vault when he administered the final masonic rites including the placing of a sprig of evergreen atop the coffin, The Reverend Mr. William Maffatt, a Presbyterian minister at Alexandria Academy, and rounding out the foursome is The Reverend Mr. Walter Dulany Addison, rector of the Episcopal Church in Oxon Hill, Maryland. Dr. James Craik and Tobias Lear greeted the clergymen on the steps at the mansion's front door.[36]

Tobias Lear was not just sad, but weary. He worked tirelessly for three days conducting Mrs. Washington's instructions in preparation for the funeral and meeting with family and friends to share the unhappy news. He greeted Colonel George Deneale and his large military contingent that participated in the funeral. The funeral was delayed for three hours while waiting for his militia to arrive. Close behind Colonel Deneale were several officers of the 106th Virginia Militia in Alexandria. Captain Robert Young commanded a detail of dragoons. Captain William Harper commanded the artillery. Captain Henry Piercy commanded the light infantry troops, followed by a band of musicians set to play special funeral dirges written in memory of George Washington. In all, at least one hundred soldiers attended the funeral to escort the coffin to the family vault. Tobias Lear reminded Colonel Deneal that the schooner, captained by Robert Hamilton, is anchored on the banks of the Potomac River, and prepared to fire its guns in answer to the artillery volleys from the lawn.

Lear greeted the ten men who were the coffin carriers, what we call today pall bearers, and the honorary pallbearers who will bear Washington's coffin to the family vault. Four young lieutenants of Virginia's 106th Regiment-James Turner, Lawrence Hoof, Jr., George

Wise, and William Moss- will shoulder the coffin on its bier.[37] The four young lieutenants were undoubtedly selected for their physical strength to lift the three-part coffin, which consists of a lead liner, a mahogany casket, and an oak outer case. The total weight of the coffin, including Washington's two-hundred-pound body inside, is approximately seven hundred pounds. However, it was Lt. Moss, who "broke down under the weight of the casket in removing the bier from the mansion to the tomb."[38]

Following the Lieutenants were six honorary pallbearers all Colonels in the militia: Charles Little, Charles Simms, William Payne, George Gilpin, Dennis Ramsay, and Phillip Marstellar, who will all march alongside the coffin, holding the edges of the black pall covering the coffin.[39] All six served with Washington during the Revolutionary War. All morning, family, neighbors, and slaves gathered on the Mount Vernon lawn and along the funeral procession route. Among the crowd is George Coryell, an Alexandrian merchant, joined the crowd as a coffin bearer after Lt. Moss unexpectedly collapsed during the procession. As the procession assembled, parishioners noticed one absentee, the grieving and newly widowed Martha Washington, still recovering from an illness herself, was not among the family members who would walk in the cold to the vault. The grieving widow remained indoors awaiting the funeral's conclusion. History notes that Mrs. Washington never reenters the master bedroom which she shared with her husband for a quarter of a century. She instead moved to a third-floor garret chamber which she used until her death at Mount Vernon in 1802. She may have watched the mournful procession from the third floor or elsewhere in the mansion.

As the music and muffled drums began to play, the procession made its way from the mansion's piazza to the family vault. The procession moved first north to the "Ha-ha Wall,"[40] which borders the lawn (and which has been recently restored), then east to the walk-in front of the mansion, then, by this walk, in a southerly direction, to the old tomb; the militia leading the way, followed by the Masons, the family, and other mourners bringing up the rear. On arriving at the tomb, the procession divided, forming columns, facing inward; Reversing the marching order of the procession, the family and relatives passed through the separated lines, forming an inner circle around the tomb; Next came the Masons, who arranged themselves in an outer circle around the family, while the militia filed back to the crest of the hill, forming a column facing east toward the river. "The ministers performed their divine services, the Masons their mystic rites and the militia closed the ceremonies with resounding volleys over the bier of the fallen chieftain."[41] Upon completion of the service, the attending masonic brothers filed past the coffin and placed evergreens upon it. The apron and two sabers were removed from the coffin just prior to interment. Alexandria-Washington Lodge No. 22 still owns the swords and displays them at the George Washington Masonic National Memorial in Alexandria, Virginia.[42]

The evening was far advanced when deep shadows fell upon Mount Vernon's landscape. The beloved home of George Washington was still in mourning as the Lodge, with its military and civic escort, started its lonely march over the snow-clad hills of Virginia back to the little town of Alexandria, nine miles away. How distant these scenes now appear under the later splendor of man's achievement. These devoted craftsmen spent several hours in their solemn march through the gathering twilight from Mount Vernon to Alexandria, whereas in our day of rapid transit, tourists board a trolley car at Mount Vernon gates and make the trip in thirty minutes, almost paralleling the road the funeral cortege wound its way over.[43]

With the descriptions of George Washington's funeral now over and some eighteenth-century funeral customs explained, we still haven't really discovered the origin of draping the flag over a casket. If you have ever attended a Christian funeral, especially those celebrated in the Catholic Church, you might have seen a large cloth that covers the casket during the liturgy. This cloth is called a pall, or mortuary cloth. In Catholicism, it is draped over the casket at the very beginning of the liturgy when the deceased's body is received or welcomed into the church. This is also where we get the word pallbearers, designating those people who assist in carrying the casket during the funeral, but unlike the funeral of George Washington, the pallbearers held the edge of the black pall as they marched to his final resting place, as the casket bearers carried his coffin at shoulder height.

Burial flags, as we know them today, were not necessarily used to adorn the casket of a fallen soldier or veteran. The custom of draping the flag, according to the American Legion, began during the Napoleonic Wars (1796-1815) where the dead were covered with flags and carried from the field of battle on a caisson to aid fellow soldiers in identifying the fallen. One could argue that this tradition originated in America during the American Civil War, given the limited availability of flags during George Washington's time. This author would argue that tradition of draping the flag on a casket began with George Washington, even though there were others who had a pall draped over their casket for religious reasons. The pall used at a funeral is a symbol of unity and of the hope for eternal life,; however, while it is unclear exactly when Christians started placing a large cloth over the casket, the tradition may have begun during the Middle Ages. Originally, the pall served various purposes, including serving as priestly vestments during the funeral mass celebration. These palls were quite elaborate and came in a variety of colors depending on the situation or ritual being performed. Since most priestly vestments were black, the selection of a black pall not only matched the officiant's attire but also symbolized the grief and mourning experienced by those who have lost a loved one. Yet, it could have been just as easy to adorn Washington's coffin with his personal Commander-in-Chief Standard or the Continental Colors. One report read that the American flag carried in Washington's procession was furled and twisted around the flagstaff to show it in mourning as it could not move freely.[44] An interesting point of history that the author discovered was the draping of a Confederate flag on the casket of General Thomas Jonathan Jackson. History records him as Stonewall Jackson, who died in 1863, and urban legend has it that Jackson requested his body be shrouded with the flag of the United States before being placed in his casket, showing respect and loyalty for both under which he served. **Author's side note**, history records

President Andrew Johnson as having been shrouded in a silk American flag, placed in his coffin with a copy of the United States Constitution under his head, and buried at the Andrew Johnson National Cemetery in Greenville, Tennessee, in 1875.[45]

The pall also gives us insight into the meaning of a draped flag. Changes within the Catholic Church ordered the pall to primarily be white in color, symbolizing everyone's equality in God's eyes and serving as a reminder of the spotless baptismal garment of the deceased, cleansed by the blood of the Lamb. At my own baptism, I wore a white robe or garment, which symbolized purity, and after declaring my faith as a follower of Jesus Christ in front of the church congregation, my pastor said a special prayer that linked this garment to my future death. The white pall is intent on reminding those present at the funeral of this reality, and the prayers said during the funeral reflect the hope that the deceased is bringing the purity of that white garment before the judgment seat of God. You may be asking; how does this relate to the flag?

Many symbols used at a funeral are designed to help those grieving understand the great mystery surrounding death and encourage them to reform their lives so that they can join their relative or friend in the heavenly embrace of God. One such symbol is the draping of the flag of our nation over the casket of a veteran, fallen soldier, or patriot. It stands for the bereaved as an important way to honor their loved one's sacrifice, their legacy, their life, and their service. It is a symbol of unity that we are, no matter our race, religion, creed, or national origin, Americans. Even though the flag tells only a portion of the story of the deceased, it serves as a reminder to the family and those in attendance at the funeral that this person answered the call to arms and unselfishly sacrificed themself for the greater good and the cause of honorably serving their nation. Some of you may be thinking that the person didn't volunteer and was voluntold to gain discipline, honor, and respect. Death, despite our best efforts to avoid it, comes to us all, and we will find ourselves standing before God, giving an account of our life, presenting to him our own baptismal vestments, burial, or service flag, and laying out our choices, which may be unstained or in need of some extra washing before being admitted into His eternal presence.

For many years paramilitary organizations or first responders, i.e., firefighters, law enforcement agencies, EMS personnel, doctors and nurses, hospice centers, funeral homes, and others that remove the dead have followed standards set forth by the United States military. In doing research for this book, I contacted the United States Air Force Academy about the traditions covered in this book and was told to contact the Army or the Navy because they were not founded officially until August 14, 1954. The United States Military Academy at Westpoint was helpful in providing leads and allowing me to track down some of these customs. Alice Morse Earle described the rule of two in her 1893 book Customs and Fashions in Old New England. The rule of two may sound similar to the Sith rule in Star Wars, but in this instance, it refers to two distinct sets of bearers who have no connection to Star Wars. She writes, "There were as a rule, two sets of bearers appointed; underbearers, usually young men, who carried the coffin on a bier; and pall bearers, men of age, dignity, or consanguinity, who held the corners of the pall which was spread over the coffin and hung down over the heads and bodies of the under-bearers. As the coffin was sometimes carried for a long distance, there were frequently appointed a double set of underbearers to share the burden."[46]

She is writing about funeral and burial customs of the late seventeenth and early eighteenth centuries. To give a historical point of reference, Alice Earle specifically mentions Judge Samuel Sewall (March 28, 1652 – January 1, 1730, who was judge in the Salem Witch Trials. Later on, in 1953, Arthur Miller would write a fictional play based on those events in Salem called The Crucible. Ms. Earle goes on to talk about the pall and how it is owned by the town and was of heavy purple or black broadcloth, or velvet, all similar to what we find at the funeral of George Washington, but as evidenced here the draping of the flag may have come from religious rites that predate the Napoleonic Wars.

Firing Party

A firing party from the Marine Barracks, Washington, D.C. (8th and I) fires 3-rifle volleys as part of military funeral honors with a funeral escort

(U.S. Army photo by Elizabeth Fraser / Arlington National Cemetery / May 10, 2019)

The Firing of Three Volleys

Chapter 5

Honor Our Fallen Comrade

(U.S. Army photo by Elizabeth Fraser / Arlington National Cemetery / May 10, 2019)

"Our nation owes a debt to its fallen heroes that we can never fully repay. But we can honor their sacrifice, and we must. We must honor it in our own lives by holding their memories close to our hearts, and heeding the example they set."
Barack Obama, 44th President of the United States of America

The retired veterans of the American Legion and Veterans of Foreign Wars show up at the funeral home in their dress uniforms to honor Command Sergeant Major James Bryant. For a two o'clock service, they show up about thirty minutes early and begin forming up for their final walk-through. The funeral director greets the commander and identifies Mrs. Bryant, who will receive the folded flag of our nation. These former service men and women show up about forty-one deep, along with active-duty members of his brigade, when he was stationed in North Carolina. The military walk through begins once the funeral director and staff have everyone seated. An instrumental version of America the Beautiful plays, some like Lee Greenwood's God Bless the U.S.A., as each member of the honor guard makes their way to the far side of the chapel and up the aisle to the casket, where each member of the honor guard stands at attention and salutes their fellow veteran before making an exit out the side of the chapel. The Honor Guard then reports to Williams Cemetery, where six of the members will function as pallbearers before taking their positions in the ceremony and firing party.

As the ruckus of the honor guard fades and silence falls upon those in attendance, the funeral director walks into the chapel with the pastor checking the microphone at the pulpit as Wings of a Dove is played overhead by Ferlin Husky. Then you hear, "Good afternoon" as the pastor greets everyone in attendance and thanking those who served for their service. The obituary is then read, followed by an opening prayer. Onward Christian Soldiers is played on the overhead sound system by the Franklin Chrisitan Singers after the prayer, and then the floor is opened up to anyone looking to speak about the life of Mr. Bryant. There was Colonel Fredrick Parker, 3rd Chemical Brigade Commander out of Fort Leonard Wood, Missouri, who explained how Mr. Bryant got the nickname, "Ranger Bryant." Mrs. Bryant spoke as did his mother and sister and several others, each telling their fondest endearing memories of their beloved career soldier. There were also the tales of his labrador retriever named "Ranger Buddy" and how he loved and followed college sports, then there were the not so embarrassing yet funny stories of his hunting and fishing trips. Next, played Elvis Presley singing In the Garden, a message from the pastor, a closing prayer, and Vince Gill's Go Rest High. The funeral director and staff dismissed the funeral, passing each row of people by the casket for a final farewell and to express their grief and love to the family. The funeral chapel had a sweet smell as numerous flowers were loaded up in a van and taken to Williams Cemetery as the funeral director and Mrs. Bryant had a conversation, then each family member took their time to privately say goodbye. When Mrs. Bryant was finished at the casket, she turned to the funeral director, asking for the casket to be closed, as she observed from the foot end of her husband's casket.

The funeral director took great care, moving very slowly and methodically like a cat waiting patiently and quietly moving to trap their prey. First a casket crank was used to lower Mr. Bryant's head, then his feet to the bottom of the casket. The linen extend over was tucked inside the casket and folded very neatly. The funeral director moved as if tucking one of his kids in bed for the night. The overlay was neatly folded and used as a blanket to cover Mr. Bryant's legs. As the funeral director reached for the cap panel, he turned to Mrs. Bryant, asking if there was anything that she wanted to come out of the casket. Her previous answers were no everything goes with him, except this time she said, "wait." "Take out his burgundy beret and his service medals and I'll place them in a shadow box." The funeral director complied, then slowly closed the casket. A casket crank was used at the foot, and it turned slowly as the casket was sealed. Mrs. Bryant thanked the funeral director, then she and the rest of her family reported to their vehicles, as did their friends, to make the trip to the cemetery. Six of the veterans in their dress uniforms stayed behind and assisted with placing Mr. Bryant in the funeral coach (hearse) after fully draping the interment flag over his casket.

The procession was underway with local law enforcement leading the procession, followed by the lead car, hearse, pastor, family, and friends. A procession that stretched for more than a mile. It was a short, slow ride the five miles to Williams Cemetery, where the veteran honor guard was waiting surrounded by United States flags placed around the gravesite by the Wilbert Vault Company. As the funeral coach approached, the honor guard and active-duty military personnel came to attention, saluting as the hearse rolled by their position along the gravel cemetery road. Upon stopping, the pallbearers gathered at the back of the funeral coach, standing at attention until the funeral director got out of the coach and opened the back door. The funeral director gave instructions and inquired if any of the pallbearers had any foot, hand, ankle, or shoulder issues, allowing them to position themselves on the side of the casket that would provide the most comfort for the carry to the grave. The funeral director opened the back door of the hearse and reached in grabbing the handle of the casket, then directed the pallbearers to reached in grabbing the handle and passing it to the next, as Mr. Bryant's casket was carried up the hill and placed feet first onto the lowering device over the grave. Family and friends followed behind the casket before taking their seats underneath the tent, with the pastor and funeral director at the head of the casket and surrounded by men and women in uniform.

The funerals of veterans and soldiers, more than any other ceremony, have followed an age-old pattern of the living honoring the dead. America is the land of the free and home of the brave, and none braver than those who serve in our armed forces. Military funeral honors reflect the highest regard for duty, honor, and respect. These honors are how soldiers, sailors, and leaders of our great nation show their gratitude for those who faithfully defended this country, during times of both war and peace. They also demonstrate military professionalism to the world. The entire military ceremony is impressive and none more impactful than the firing of the three volleys at the graveside and what followed on this cold Wednesday, January 4, 2023.

My mentor and fellow Funeral Director, Jerry Lee Basham, begins, "As family and friends, we have gathered here today to pay homage and tribute to Command Sergeant Major James Bryant and a very significant part of his life as a bachelor. In 1973, despite being in college, James got called by the United States Government to go forth and serve. As all proud and devoted Americans who love their country so often do, for the American soldier does so for various reasons a sense of duty, honor, and country. They enlisted to preserve what America stands for, i.e., the right of the people to govern themselves and choose their leaders by a vote of the majority, in a government of the people by the people, and for the people. The U.S. soldier preserves our freedom and liberty and also fights to preserve the symbol of America, the flag, and the red, white, and blue of Old Glory. Today we have gathered here to give him honor and tribute for his service to the United States of America as a soldier in the United States Army. When you look around here today, you will see some fellows that are gathered here to pay homage and perform the last military rites or tribute for James, who richly deserves them on behalf of the United States Government, and we thank this veteran and his comrades, active-duty and inactive, for their service to our great nation. The service today consists of four different major significant parts. The first, being the flag issued by the United States Government; second, between the place of service and the place of final disposition, the casket is fully draped. Most of all, the 3rd and 4th are the folding presentation of the colors, volleying of the rifles, and the blowing of the Taps. To most of us in the military world, Taps is not goodbye but my departed comrade or departed brother till we see you again. It is my honor and privilege to introduce the retired veterans of the American Legion and Veterans of Foreign Wars, who have so graciously come to pay honor and tribute to James's service. "Commander."

The chaplain of the honor guard or officer in charge speaks next. "We, the veterans of the American Legion and the Veterans of Foreign Wars of these United States, have assembled here today to pay our final respects to our departed comrade, Command Sergeant Major James Bryant, United States Army, serving from the end of the Vietnam era through the Persian Gulf War, thirty years of service. A man who served his country. Commander, order the honors."

Commander: "Sergeant of the guard, honor our fallen comrade."

Sergeant of the Guard: "Detail, Attention! Prepare to fire three volleys. Port Arms. Aim, Fire. Aim, Fire. Aim, Fire. Cease Fire. Present Arms."

The firing of three volleys commenced with seven rifles blasting out in unison for three rounds each: the first to signify a truce of battle of life, the second volley to clear and bury the dead, and the third to return to fight another day. Each time this portion of the ceremony is performed, you see people get startled, children and infants cry, and some people are just like stone. The firing of three volleys is often confused with that of the twenty-one-gun salute. There is not much to say or write on this particular topic because it is such a short yet important part of the Honor Guard's duty. The firing of three volleys and a twenty-one-gun salute are not synonymous; they are two very different things. If anything, they are similar in the fact that you have the thunderous clap of guns, the smell of gun powder, and yes, what can be some very big guns if fired from a ship, cannon, artillery, or anti-aircraft gun. What follows are similar accounts with the words of the Army followed by the origins of the Navy. Despite slight differences in their histories, the twenty-one-gun salute and the firing of three volleys have a rich history that dates back centuries before the United States became a nation.

According to the U.S. Army Center of Military History, "the use of gun salutes for military occasions is traced to early warriors who demonstrated their peaceful intentions by placing their weapons in a position that rendered them ineffective. Apparently, this custom was universal, with the specific act varying with time and place, depending on the weapons being used. A North African tribe, for example, trailed the points of their spears on the ground to indicate that they did not mean to be hostile. The tradition of rendering a salute by cannon originated in the 14th century when firearms and cannons came into use. Since these early devices contained only one projectile, discharging them once rendered them ineffective. Originally, warships fired seven-gun salutes, likely selecting the number seven due to its astrological and biblical significance. Scientists had identified seven planets, and the moon's phases shifted every seven days. The Bible states that God rested on the seventh day after Creation, that every seventh year was sabbatical and that the seven times seventh year ushered in the Jubilee year.

Land batteries, having a greater supply of gunpowder, were able to fire three guns for every shot fired afloat, hence the salute by shore batteries was 21 guns. The multiple of three was probably chosen because of the mystical significance of the number three in many ancient civilizations. Early gunpowder, composed mainly of sodium nitrate, spoiled easily at sea, but could be kept cooler and drier in land magazines. When potassium nitrate improved the quality of gunpowder, ships at sea adopted the salute of 21 guns. It became the highest honor a nation rendered. Varying customs among the maritime powers led to confusion in the saluting and return of salutes. Great Britain, the world's preeminent sea power in the 18th and 19th centuries, compelled weaker nations to salute first, and for a time monarchies received more guns than did republics. Eventually, by agreement, the international salute was established at twenty-one guns, although the United States did not agree on this procedure until August 1875. The gun salute system in the United States has changed considerably over the years. In 1810, the "national salute" was defined by the War Department as equal to the number of states in the Union--at that time seventeen. On Independence Day, all U.S. military installations fired this salute at 1:00 p.m. (later at noon). Whenever he visited a military installation, the President also received a salute equal to the number of states.

In 1842, the presidential salute was formally established at 21 guns. In 1890, regulations designated the "national salute" as 21 guns and redesignated the traditional Independence Day salute, the "Salute to the Union," equal to the number of states. Fifty guns are also fired on all military installations equipped to do so at the close of the day of the funeral of a president, ex-president, or president-elect. Today, we fire the national salute of 21 guns in honor of a national flag, the sovereign or chief of state of a foreign nation, a member of a reigning royal family, and the President, ex-President, and President-elect of the United States. On the day of a president's, ex-president's, or president-elect's funeral, the national salute also takes place at noon. Gun salutes are also given to other military and civilian leaders from this and other nations. The number of guns is based on their protocol rank. These salutes are always in odd numbers."[1]

By comparison, the firing of gun salutes is a centuries-old tradition, according to Naval History and Heritage Command. The way early warriors aimed their weapons to be useless was a sign of their peaceful intentions or a ruse to attack. When single-projectile weapons and cannons were introduced in the fourteenth century, their unloading was indicated by the projectile's discharge just before it reached a friendly port. The superstition that odd numbers were lucky can be linked to the rendering of gun salutes in odd numbers. For example, early civilizations thought that the number seven had magical mystical powers, like the Force in Star Wars. There were occasions when forts on land could fire three shots for every shot fired at sea because they could store gunpowder more easily and in larger quantities than on board a ship. An even number of guns in a salute was thought to indicate the death of the ship's master or captain during the voyage. For a long time, different nations fired different numbers of guns for different reasons. Britain's Royal Navy's use of twenty-one guns, was required by Parliament and began in 1730 on specific anniversary dates, though this was not required as a salute to the royal family until later in the eighteenth century.

The American Revolution saw a number of notorious well-known incidents of gun salutes. When the Continental Navy brigantine Andrew Doria, captained by Captain Isaiah Robinson, entered the harbor of St. Eustatius in the West Indies on November 16, 1776, she fired a 13-gun salute (some accounts give 11). The Dutch governor of the island issued an order a few minutes later for nine (or eleven) guns to return the salute. The standard salute given to a republic at the time was nine guns; a thirteen-gun salute would have represented the thirteen newly formed United States at that time. This has been called the "first salute" to the American flag. About three weeks earlier, on the Danish Island of St. Croix, an American schooner had her colors saluted. The American schooner flag flown in 1776 by Andrew Doria did not fly the Stars and Stripes, as it had not yet been ratified. Instead, it was the Grand Union flag, which has the British Jack in the center of thirteen alternating red and white stripes.

On February 14, 1778, the French fleet anchored in Quiberon Bay, France, returned fire with nine guns in response to the Continental Navy ship Ranger, Captain John Paul Jones, firing thirteen. This marked the first official salute to the Stars and Stripes by a foreign power. Although gun salutes were in use before the regulations were written down, the regulations for the United States Navy in 1818 were the first to prescribe a specific manner for rendering gun salutes. Those regulations required that when the President visits a ship of the United States' Navy, he is to be saluted with 21 guns. It may be noted that twenty-one was the number of states in the Union at that time. For a time thereafter it became customary to offer a salute of one gun for each state in the Union, although in practice there was a great deal of variation in the number of guns that were actually used in the salute.

In addition to salutes offered to the President and heads of state, it was also mandated that the Navy render a "national salute" on February 22nd (Washington's Birthday) and July 4th (the anniversary of the Declaration of Independence). These traditions became the standard for the United States Navy with the issuance of new regulations on May 24, 1842. They laid out the specifics:

"When the President of the United States shall visit a vessel of the navy, he shall be received with the following honors: The yards shall be manned, all the officers shall be on deck in full uniform, the full guard shall be paraded and present arms, the music shall play a march, and a salute of twenty-one guns shall be fired. He shall receive the same honors when he leaves the ship. Upon the anniversary of the Declaration of Independence of the United States, the colors shall be hoisted at sunrise, and all the vessels of the navy shall, when in port, be dressed, and so continue until the colors are hauled down at sunset, if the state of the weather and other circumstances will allow it. At sunrise, at meridian, and at sunset, a salute of twenty-one guns shall be fired from every vessel in commission mounting six guns and upwards. On the twenty-second day of February, the anniversary of the birth of Washington, a salute of twenty-one guns shall be fired at meridian from every vessel of the navy in commission mounting six guns and upwards."[2]

Although sometimes mistaken for a 21-gun salute, the three volleys fired at funerals by a firing party do not constitute a 21-gun salute. The custom of firing volleys at a funeral is thought by some to have originated in ancient times in the practice of making loud noises to scare off evil spirits. By the late nineteenth century the custom of firing volleys included the entire escort (of squad, platoon, company, or battalion strength). That was eventually reduced down to the front rank of the escort, a standard squad of 13 personnel. With the release of the Navy Landing Party Manual of 1960, the firing party was broken off from the escort formation and the size was reduced down to seven personnel. Currently, at funerals where military honors are rendered and a firing party is present, the team composition may consist of three, five, or seven members to fire three volleys.[3]

The practice of firing 21 shots in salute was formally adopted by the United States Congress in 1875 to match the international salute. Today, it's used in ceremonies honoring the national flag, visiting dignitaries, and the president. It is also fired at noon of the day of the funeral for a president, former president, or president-elect, on Washington's birthday, Presidents Day, and the

Fourth of July. On Memorial Day, a salute of twenty-one-minute guns is fired at noon while the flag is flown at half-mast. "As soon as the larger cities began to accrue wealth, the parentations of men and women of high station were celebrated with much pomp and dignity, if not with religious exercises. Volleys were fired over the freshly made grave-even of a woman. A barrel and a half of powder was consumed to do proper honor to Puritan John Winthrop (January 12, 1588 – March 26, 1649), the chief founder of Massachusetts. At the funeral of Deputy-Governor Francis Willoughby (October 13, 1615 – April 10, 1671) eleven companies of militia were in attendance and "with doleful noise of trumpets and drums, in their mourning posture, three thundering volleys were discharged, answered with the loud roaring of great guns rending the heavens with noise at the loss of so great a man."[4]

Volleys for men and women in the 1600's imagine that. The customary three volleys fired over a grave today, as mentioned at Ranger Bryant's funeral, originated as far back as the Roman Empire. If you recall, George Washington's funeral, had cannons fired from a schooner on the Potomac River, only to be answered by volleys from the lawn at Mount Vernon. The Roman funeral custom of casting dirt three times on the coffin constituted a "burial." When a Roman died, it was customary to call the name of the deceased three times, which ended the funeral ceremony, after which the friends and relatives of the deceased pronounced the word "vale" (farewell) three times as they departed from the tomb.[5] The current practice stems from a 17th-century European cease-fire tradition. When both sides of a battle paused to bury the dead and tend to their wounded, soldiers would fire three musket volleys to signal that the burial party was ready to resume battle. The 7-man firing party honored Mr. Bryant with three volleys for his service to our country on this day, January 4, 2023, as they have done for countless other veterans both here at home and abroad.

The origins of the firing of three volleys at military funerals are embedded in history dating to the Roman Empire. Colonel James A. Moss wrote in his book Officers Manual, originally written in 1911 and reprinted and copyrighted in 1915, 1916, and 1917. What follows are his words from the publication concerning customs of the service:

"In funeral rites of the Romans the casting of the earth THREE times upon the coffin constituted "the burial." It was customary among the Romans to call the dead THREE times by name, which ended the funeral ceremony, after which the friends and relatives of the deceased pronounced the word "Vale" (farewell) THREE times as they departed from the tomb. So that today, when a squad of soldiers' fires THREE volleys over a grave, they are, in accordance with this old Roman custom, bidding their dead comrade "Farewell," THREE times.

The number THREE was doubtless selected by the Romans because of its symbolic and mystical significance, 3, 5, and 7 being so considered in all recorded history. We have, for instance, the Holy Trinity, in Three Graces, the frequent recurrence of THREE in the Masonic ritual, etc. In the old Army it was customary in some regiments when a soldier was absent from roll call for the first sergeant to call the absentee's name again THREE times at the end of the roll. It is really interesting to note to what extent the number THREE enters our daily lives: Boys start their races by "One, two, THREE-Go!;" the baseball fan says, "THREE strikes-and out!;" a ship before leaving the same number whistles as a salute when passing another ship at sea; the enthusiast gives his "THREE cheers!" etc."[6]

In some cultures, the number three is associated with life and vitality, or stages of life: birth, marriage, and death (infancy, adolescence, and adulthood.) No matter what its significance, the firing of three volleys is a fitting tribute to a fallen comrade. If you think about it, the number three is significant. How many sides to a triangle? A folded flag has how many sides?

The 156th National Memorial Day Observance at Arlington National Cemetery

A bugler from the U.S. Army Band, "Pershing's Own" plays "Taps" during a Presidential Armed Forces Full Honors Wreath-Laying Ceremony at the Tomb of the Unknown Soldier at Arlington National Cemetery, Arlington, Va., May 27, 2024.

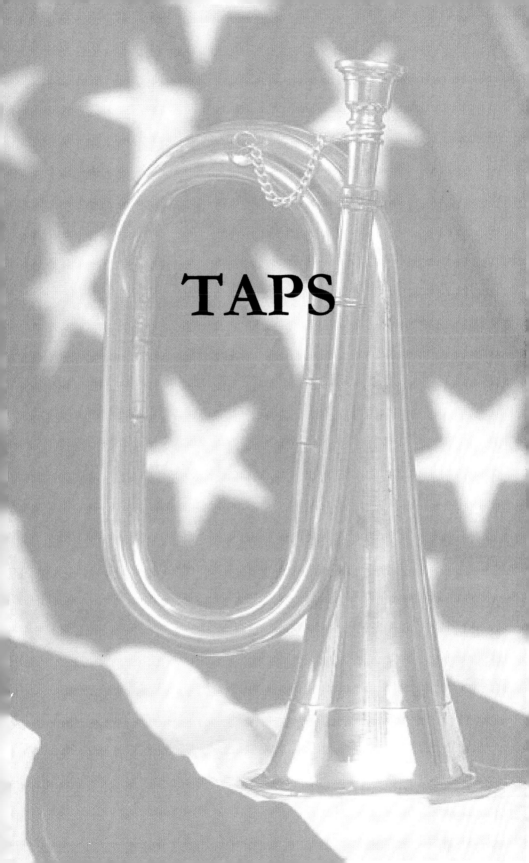

Chapter 6

You've Heard the Bugle

"The brilliantly simple melody brings to the moment a soulful reminder of service offered, sacrifices rendered, and a final salute to the fallen."[1]
Melanie Hoggan

Music has been an integral part of the military since the drum marches of the American Revolution. There are bugle calls or the rumbling of drums to communicate positions and orders, the signals of daybreak, cease fire, or lights out. Then, there are required pieces of music, such as the National Anthem, Reville, Retreat, and Taps. Depending upon branch of service a particular hymn may be played, the Navy Hymn-Eternal Father Strong to Save, the Army Hymn-The Army Goes Rolling Along (originally called The Caison Song as written by Edmund Gruber in 1908, and transformed to a march by John Phillip Sousa called "The US Field March" in 1917, or the Marine's Hymn, and finally the Air Force hymn referred to as "Wild Blue Yonder." In the military world all of these hymns have a tender significance, but to this author none more solemn and impactful than the bugle sounding "Taps" or "Echo Taps." On a quick aside here,

Echo Taps is when two buglers stand some distance apart with one bugler sounding Taps, while the other off in the distance plays to give an echo effect. When I first became a funeral director, there was a Navy veteran who sounded Taps at all the military funerals in my local area. It just so happened that his grandson had just been discharged from the Marine Corps after six years of service and was his grandfather's echo until his grandfather went to be with the Lord. I arranged his funeral and burial in April 2023, and the Honor Guard administered his last rites and sounded Taps. Even though the sounding of "Echo Taps" is not official protocol, the duo was impressive to hear, nonetheless.

As Command Sergeant Major Bryant's Honor Guard continues to salute after the firing of three volleys, came the notes we know as the sounding of Taps, as Taps Historian and Air Force veteran Jari Villanueva calls them "24 Notes that Tap Deep Emotions." And tap deep emotions they do. The commander gives the order, "Bugler sound Taps."

Several months after Ranger Bryant's funeral, I found myself working, writing, and doing research for this project. My cell phone rang startling me as I was in deep thought sitting at the computer typing away. When I answered the phone, I heard a familiar voice saying they need my services once again asking if I would be available. I set up an arrangement conference for a young lady who had passed away suddenly at her home. It just so happened that I served this family a year prior (2022) when I arranged the funeral and burial of her father. This time around, I met with the young lady's grandfather, who belongs to the Masonic lodge, and by the time this book is published, he could be the current or will be the past Grand Master of Masons in Indiana (2024-2025), his wife (grandmother), daughter (mother of the deceased), and her stepfather. After meeting with the family, and during the visitation of this young lady on September 10, 2023, the stepfather disclosed that he had served in the United States Army for several years, and had been deployed to Afghanistan, and he was honorably discharged after serving his enlistment. I was in the lounge of the funeral home having a cup of coffee and discussing with his father-in-law how George Washington's funeral was masonic and very military, as both played a dominant part in his funeral and burial. I mentioned I was authoring a book about the four parts of a military funeral. Almost immediately before I could finish my sentence, the stepfather says, "I know the origins of Taps." He then began to tell me and the group now listening, at the visitation of his stepdaughter, that he learned about Taps in the Army during his advanced individual training (AIT) at Fort Campbell, Kentucky. AIT is the training done after basic training for the job a person selected when they enlisted. I was completely astounded when this veteran said that he was taught that Taps was created by a Captain Robert Ellicombe, a Union officer, during the Civil War. This was while he was in AIT training at Fort Campbell.

The Army veteran begins, "While with his men at Harrison's Landing in Virginia in July 1862 and with the Confederate Army nearby on the other side of Harrison's landing separated by a narrow strip of land, Captain Ellicombe heard the moaning of a wounded soldier who lay severely wounded on the field of battle. Under the cover of darkness, not knowing if the soldier was friend or foe or some form of trickery to find their position, he decided to risk his life and bring the soldier to camp for medical attention. Crawling on his stomach through gunfire, Captain Ellicombe reached the wounded soldier and began the slow process of getting him back to camp to get him some much-needed medical attention. When the captain finally reached his encampment, he discovered he had rescued a dead Confederate soldier. Captain Ellicombe lit a lantern, caught his breath, and began looking more closely at the soldier. He went numb with shock as he looked upon the young soldier's face. Recognizing it was his son and consumed with grief, he held his son close. The captain's son had been studying music in the South at the outbreak of the Civil War and had enlisted in the Confederate Army without his father's knowledge. The following morning, heartbroken, and shaken, Captain Ellicombe requested permission from his superiors to give his son a full military burial despite his rebel status. He requested for the Army band to play a funeral dirge at his son's funeral but was denied the request by his superiors because they viewed his son as a traitor. However, out of respect for Captain Ellicombe as a father, his superiors did say that they could supply one musician. Captain Ellicombe opted for a bugler. He asked the bugler to play a series of musical notes that he had found on a piece of paper in his son's pocket."[2] The bugler played, but I'm sorry to say that what was played is not the solemn tune we know today.

Now that I have been conducting research on the subject of Taps, I can say with all certainty that this story of Captain Ellicombe is just a myth, yet I am standing in front of an Army veteran who is regaling myself, his father-in-law, and others with this story that he learned at Fort Campbell, Kentucky, while doing AIT training. Other than this event taking place at Harrison's Landing in July 1862, everything else is a falsehood. There is no proof that Captain Robert Ellicombe even existed, let alone enlisted in the Union Army. The questions that I asked were: What unit did he serve in? When was he discharged?, and is there discharge paperwork associated with him? Where did he enlist?, and when and how was he promoted to the rank of captain? Where is the son's service records and place of burial? There are none. So where did the myth come from?

Taps bugler and twenty-three-year Air Force veteran, Jari Villanueva, traced it to Robert Ripley, who created the story for his short lived-television program in 1949. If memory serves, as I read this somewhere because 1949 was before my time, Ripley had a heart attack while on stage discussing this military funeral dirge but recovered long enough to finish the show before checking himself into the hospital. He died three days later. "Believe It or Not!" On a side note, I do remember the show Ripley's Believe It or Not in the 1980's hosted by Jack Palance, and his winning an Oscar for Best Supporting Actor in 1992 for the movie City Slickers. There are other myths out there, and I can assure you that they are not the story of Captain Ellicombe as told to me by an Army veteran. Even though he told it with such heart and conviction, I had to agree with his father-in-law as he rolled his eyes and walked away telling me as we walked up the hallway to the funeral chapel, "That guy is a know it all." I responded, "Yet he's married to your daughter." We had a good laugh, nonetheless.

So, what are the origins of Taps? The Mexican American War (1846-1848), the war President Ulysses S. Grant said, "I do not think there was ever a more wicked war than that waged by the United States on Mexico. I thought so at the time, when I was a youngster, only I had not moral courage enough to resign."[3] This war was the result of Texas independence from Mexico in 1836 and its annexation by the United States in 1845. Mexico invaded Texas, killing dozens of soldiers under the command of General Zachary Taylor. As a result of President James K. Polk's words to Congress, "the cup of forbearance has been exhausted, even before Mexico passed the boundary of the United States, invaded our territory, and shed American blood upon American soil"[4] war was declared on May 13, 1846. So, concerning Taps here is the account of Colonel James A. Moss as written in Officer's Manual, "it is known that the custom of sounding Taps at military funerals obtained in some regiments during the Mexican War, and there is an impression in some quarters that the practice existed prior to that time, it having been formally inaugurated at West Point about 1840. However, be that as it may, it is evident that the custom in its present form did not become general until after the Civil War, as the following from the regimental history of the old 2nd Artillery shows:

"During the Peninsular Campaign in 1862 a soldier of Tidball's battery- "A" of the 2nd Artillery-was buried at a time when the battery occupied advanced positions, concealed in the woods. It was unsafe to fire the customary three rounds over the grave, on account of the proximity of the enemy, and it occurred to Captain Tidball that the sounding of Taps would be the most appropriate ceremony that could be substituted. The custom thus originated was taken up throughout the Army of the Potomac, and finally confirmed by orders."[5]

(U.S. Army photo/ Arlington National Cemetery A bugler from the U.S. Army Band, "Pershing's Own", plays "Taps"

The practice of sounding Taps is one of deeply felt sentiment to "rest in peace." Played today on most military and air bases around nine o'clock P.M. Taps is an announcement to soldiers, airmen, sailors, and marines that the day has ended. Taps is a command signifying "Lights out." And as sure as Taps ends the day, it's lingering notes at a funeral signify the end of life (Lights out) and to rest in peace. There is no such call as so beautiful and so moving that lights up the deep-seated emotions of the soul as the sounding of Taps.

Jari Villanueva writes, "Of all the military bugle calls, none is so easily recognized or more apt to evoke emotion than the call Taps. The melody is both eloquent and haunting, and the history of its origin is interesting and somewhat clouded in controversy. In the British Army, a similar type of call known as The Last Post has been sounded over soldiers' graves since 1885, but the use of Taps is unique to the United States military, since the call is sounded at funerals, wreath-laying and memorial services."[6] But who actually wrote it, and would you believe there is a tie to American Express? Yes, American Express the credit card or bank holding company.

Taps originated as an update for the Extinguish Lights (Lights Out) signal to end the day. The infantry call to extinguish lights was printed in manuals such as Silas Casey's Infantry Tactics (1801–1882) and other publications up until the Civil War. The music for this call was taken from French sources. In July 1862, Union General Daniel Butterfield adapted the music for Taps for his brigade (Third Brigade, First Division, Fifth Army Corps, Army of the Potomac).

Daniel Adams Butterfield was a New York businessman, law student, Union General in the American Civil War, author, member of Metropolitan Masonic Lodge No. 273 in New York City,[7] and a former Assistant U.S. Treasurer. He is credited with writing, rewriting, or composing the bugle call we now know as "Taps." He was other things too like a banker, real estate broker, and President of the National Bank of Cold Spring.

Born to the late John Butterfield and Malinda Harriett Baker Butterfield on Halloween (October 31, 1831) in Utica, New York. Young Daniel attended Union College in Schenectady, New York graduating in 1849 at the young age of eighteen, then began studying law. He became a member of the Sigma Phi Society worked for a number of companies in the South and New York, including the American Express Company, which his father, John Warren Butterfield, co-founded along with the Overland Mail Company, stagecoaches, steamships, and telegraph lines.[8] Only days after the fall of Fort Sumter, despite having little military background beyond part-time militia activities, he joined the Army as a first sergeant in Washington, D.C., on April 16, 1861. Within two weeks he was commissioned Colonel of the 12th Regiment of the New York State Militia, which later became the 12th New York Infantry. By July he commanded a brigade and by September he was a brigadier general.

Butterfield joined Major General. George B. McClellan's Army of the Potomac for the Peninsula Campaign in the V Corps (Fifth Corp) commanded by Major General Fitz John Porter. During the Seven Days Battles (June 25, 1862 – July 1, 1862, which included Battles at Oak Grove, Beaver Dam Creek (Mechanicsville), Gaines's Mill, Garnett's and Golding Farm, Savage's Station, Glendale or Frayser's Farm, and Poindexter's Farm (Malvern Hill). It was at Gaines' Mill on June 27, 1862, that Butterfield was wounded and despite his injury, he managed to seize the colors of the 83rd Pennsylvania and rallied the troops turning the tide in battle. This battle is also where he demonstrated bravery that eventually was recognized on September 26, 1892, with the Medal of Honor. The medal citation reads: "Seized the colors of the 83rd Pennsylvania Volunteers at a critical moment and, under a galling fire of the enemy, encouraged the depleted ranks to renewed exertion."[9] The night of June 27 after the Battle at Gaine's Mill is when General McClellan ordered the Army of the Potomac to seek respite at their secure base at Harrison's Landing on the James River.

It is here at Harrison's Landing, Virginia, while the Army recuperated from its grueling withdrawal during the Seven Days, Butterfield experimented with bugle calls and is credited with the composition of "Taps," probably the most famous bugle call ever written. If you recall it was Colonel James A. Moss who said Taps was first played in July 1862 at the funeral of a deceased soldier in Captain Tidball's 2nd Artillery, and he alluded to Taps being formally inaugurated at the United States Military Academy at West Point around 1940. Moss may have been referring to the bugle call "Scott's Tattoo," named after General Winfield Scott, to signal the end of the day and to prepare for bedtime roll call. Scott's Tattoo was found in the Army Drill Manual of the day and revised in 1835, 1836, and 1861, so what Moss is referring to may have been this earlier bugle call.

Personally, I don't see how a wounded man who just fought in multiple battles could find time to compose music. It is said that Butterfield wrote "Taps" to replace the customary firing of three rifle volleys at the end of burials during battle. "Taps" also replaced Tattoo, the French bugle call to signal "lights out." Although there is some doubt about the origin of Taps, let me clear it up. About three years prior to his death in 1901 an article came out in the August 1898 issue of Century Magazine called "The Trumpet in Camp and Battle," by Gustav Kobbe, (1857-1918) a music historian and critic. Kobbe was writing about the origin of bugle calls in the military and in reference to Taps, wrote:

"In speaking of our trumpet calls I purposely omitted one with which it seemed most appropriate to close this article, for it is the call which closes the soldier's day... Lights Out. I have not been able to trace this call to any other service. If as seems probable, it was original with Major Seymour, he has given our army the most beautiful of all trumpet-calls."

THE TRUMPET IN CAMP AND BATTLE.

BY GUSTAV KOBBÉ.

ONCE again the nation thrills to the call of the trumpet and the roll of the drum. The trumpet is the clock of the camp, but on the battle-field notes of command ring from its brazen throat. In camp it awakens the soldier, summons him to drill, invites him to mess, and bids him go to rest. In the face of the enemy it calls him to arms and to the charge. Over the soldier's grave it sings the last song—"lights out."

Considering the antiquity of the trumpet and the drum, and their obvious adaptability to sounding signals, it would seem as if field music must have originated simultaneously with these instruments. That soldiers marched and fought to their martial strains

Vol. LVI.—68.

in the most ancient times we know from passages in the Bible and the classics. But there is a difference between military and field music. The former is played by the regimental bands, and consists chiefly of marches and inspiring airs, the latter is played on the field of battle, to fire the soldier's heart. Field music is "sounded" by the bugle, the trumpet, the drum, or the drum and fife, and consists of a system of signals by which, instead of by word of mouth, commands are conveyed to the troops. It is impossible to discover when the first system of this kind originated. Probably it developed gradually. The fact that a trumpet or a drum can be heard much more distinctly on

Pictured left Norton later in life. 1ˢᵗ Lt. Oliver Wilcox Norton, on the right

According to Jari Villanueva, Kobbe was using as an authority the Army drill manual on infantry tactics prepared by Major General Emory Upton in 1867 (revised in 1874). The bugle calls in the manual were compiled by Major (later General) Truman Seymour of the 5th U.S. Artillery. Taps was called Extinguish Lights in those manuals since it replaced the "Lights Out" call disliked by General Butterfield. The majority of soldiers knew the call as Taps, so other manuals began referring to it by that name even though the call's title was changed later. Kobbe assumed that Seymour had written the call since he was in charge of the music in the Army manual. Oliver W. Norton wrote Kobbe a letter from Chicago claiming he knew how the call came about and was first to perform it. Kobbe was unable to determine the origins of Taps until he received Norton's correspondence.[10]

Norton wrote:

"Chicago, August 8, 1898

I was much interested in reading the article by Mr. Gustav Kobbe, on the Trumpet and Bugle Calls, in the August Century. Mr. Kobbe says that he has been unable to trace the origin of the call now used for Taps, or the Go to Sleep, as it is generally called by the soldiers. As I am unable to give the origin of this call, I think the following statement may be of interest to Mr. Kobbe and your readers… During the early part of the Civil War, I was a bugler at the Headquarters of Butterfield's Brigade, Morell's Division, Fitz-John Porter's Corps, Army of the Potomac. Up to July 1862, the Infantry call for Taps was that set down in Casey's Tactics, which Mr. Kobbe says was borrowed from the French.[11]

One day, soon after the seven days battles on the Peninsula, when the Army of the Potomac was lying in camp at Harrison's Landing, General Daniel Butterfield, then commanding our Brigade, sent for me, and showing me some notes on a staff written in pencil on the back of an envelope, asked me to sound them on my bugle. I did this several times, playing the music as written. He changed it somewhat, lengthening some notes and shortening others, but retaining the melody as he first gave it to me. After getting it to his satisfaction, he directed me to sound that call for Taps thereafter in place of the regulation call. The music was beautiful on that still summer night, and was heard far beyond the limits of our Brigade. The next day I was visited by several buglers from neighboring Brigades, asking for copies of the music which I gladly furnished. I think no general order was issued from army headquarters authorizing the substitution of this for the regulation call, but as each brigade commander exercised his own discretion in such minor matters, the call was gradually taken up through the Army of the Potomac. I have been told that it was carried to the Western Armies by the 11th and 12th Corps, when they went to Chattanooga in the fall of 1863, and rapidly made its way through those armies. I did not presume to question General Butterfield at the time, but from the manner in which the call was given to me, I have no doubt he composed it in his tent at Harrison's Landing. I think General Butterfield is living at Cold Spring, New York. If you think the matter of sufficient interest, and care to write him on the subject, I have no doubt he will confirm my statement." -Oliver W. Norton[12]

As suggested by Norton, the editor did write to Butterfield. In answer to the inquiry from the editor of the Century, General Butterfield writing from his Cragside estate in Cold Spring, New York on August 31, 1898, wrote:

"I recall, in my dim memory, the substantial truth of the statement made by Norton, of the 83rd Pa., about bugle calls. His letter gives the impression that I personally wrote the notes for the call. The facts are, that, at the time, I could sound calls on the bugle as a necessary part of military knowledge and instruction for an officer commanding a regiment or brigade. I had acquired this as a regimental commander. I had composed a call for my brigade, to precede any calls, indicating that such were calls, or orders, for my brigade alone. This was of very great use and effect on the march and in battle. It enabled me to cause my whole command, at times, in march, covering over a mile on the road, all to halt instantly, and lie down, and all arise and start at the same moment; to forward in line of battle, simultaneously, in action and charge etc. It saves fatigue. The men rather liked their call and began to sing my name to it. It was three notes and a catch. I cannot write a note of music, but have gotten my wife to write it from my whistling it to her, and enclose it. The men would sing, "Dan, Dan, Dan, Butterfield, Butterfield" to the notes when a call came. Later, in battle, or in some trying circumstances or an advance of difficulties, they sometimes sang, "Damn, Damn, Damn, Butterfield, Butterfield."[13]

Dan,   Dan,   Dan,   But-ter-field, But-ter-field

The call of Taps did not seem to be as smooth, melodious, and musical as it should be, and I called in someone who could write music, and practiced a change in the call of Taps until I had it suit my ear, and then, as Norton writes, got it to my taste without being able to write music or knowing the technical name of any note, but, simply by ear, arranged it as Norton describes. I did not recall him in connection with it, but his story is substantially correct. Will you do me the favor to send Norton a copy of this letter by your typewriter? I have none." -Daniel Butterfield[14]

This account has been disputed by some military and musical historians, who maintain that Butterfield merely revised an earlier call known as the Scott Tattoo and did not compose an original work. This author believes that he did revise the earlier bugle call, but those who have power write history. An interesting fact is that Daniel Butterfield never went out of his way to claim credit for composing Taps and had it not been for Gustav Kobbe's article, the origins may never have come to light.

Butterfield continued his brigade command at the Second Battle of Bull Run and the Battle of Antietam, becoming division commander, and then Fifth Corps commander for the Battle of Fredericksburg. His corps was up against murderous fire from Marye's Heights as they began their assault throughout the city. After the debacles of Fredericksburg and the Mud March, Major General Joseph Hooker replaced General Ambrose Burnside, "The Butcher of Fredericksburg"[15] as Army of the Potomac commander and Butterfield became his chief of staff in January 1863. He was promoted to the rank of major general in March 1863.

Generals Hooker and Butterfield developed a close personal, and political, relationship during their tenure together. To the disgust of many army generals, their headquarters were frequented by women and liquor, being described as a combination of a "bar and brothel."[16] One would think if camp were running like a bar and brothel, Generals Hooker and Butterfield would be the most popular officers on the campus; however, Butterfield was not. In fact, he was widely despised by his fellow officers. This led to political infighting in the high command throughout much of the Civil War. However, by the spring of 1863, the two leaders were able to significantly enhance food, shelter, and medicine, as well as turn around the army's low morale. Butterfield instituted a long-standing tradition that is still followed by soldiers in the Army today: wearing hats or shoulder badges or patches that are unique to the unit they are a part of, in this instance, the corps. He was influenced by Major General Philip Kearny's previous division patches, which he expanded to include the entire army designing the majority of the patches himself, utilizing several corps badge shapes, which were sewn on colored cloth and into the uniforms.[17]

Just before the Battle of Gettysburg, Major General George G. Meade succeeded Hooker after the Battle of Chancellorsville. This was part of that political infighting that was previously mentioned, which occurred repeatedly throughout the Civil War. Despite not having any faith in Butterfield and his lackluster reputation, Meade kept him on as chief of staff. On July 3, 1863, at Gettysburg, Butterfield was injured by cannon fire, a discarded artillery shell fragment, which preceded Picket's charge.[18] As a result, Butterfield was sent to convalesce. A week or so later, on July 14, 1863, Meade dismissed him as chief of staff, but Butterfield continued to serve in the military and did not retire from active duty. Following the Gettysburg battle, Butterfield actively worked with another of Hooker's allies, Major General Daniel Sickles, to undermine Major General Meade. Sickles and Butterfield testified before the Joint Committee on the Conduct of the War that Meade wavered and had plans to withdraw from Gettysburg as early as July 1, damaging his reputation as a commander in the field, even though the fight was a significant win for the Union. The Pipe Creek Circular, which Meade had his staff produce before it became clear that there would be a battle at Gettysburg, served as Butterfield's primary source of support for this claim.[19]

The fall after Gettysburg, Butterfield returned to duty as chief of staff once again for Hooker, now commanding two corps in the Army of the Cumberland at Chattanooga, Tennessee. When these two depleted corps (the XI and XII Corps) were combined to form the XX Corps, Butterfield was given the 3rd Division, which he led through the first half of Sherman's March to the Sea that saw the burning of Atlanta. After being assigned to quiet duties in the western theater in Vicksburg, Mississippi, Butterfield served as the army's General Recruiting Service in New York and as colonel of the Fifth United States Infantry. However, he fell victim to fever and illness that prevented him from finishing the war in the field. In addition, he continued to be active in military music, calling on a board of officers to review the fife and drum music handbook, which the Secretary of War eventually accepted and approved.[20]

After a distinguished military career, Butterfield resigned his post in 1870 and was appointed to serve as the Assistant Treasury Secretary by President Ulysses S. Grant. Grant's brother-in-law Abel Corbin suggested that Butterfield alert traders Jay Gould and James Fisk when the government was about to sell gold, a market that Gould and Fisk hoped to corner. Gould sent Butterfield a $10,000 payment, stating that it was "to cover expenses."[21] Later on, Butterfield told Congress in testimony that the loan was for real estate and was unsecured. Fisk and Gould would sell their gold before the price fell if Butterfield gave them a tip. But after learning of the plan to manipulate gold prices, President Grant chose to sell $4,000,000 worth of government gold without informing Butterfield, which caused a panic and led to the collapse of gold prices on September 24, 1869, also known as Black Friday.[22] He would later go back to work for the American Express Company.[23]

On September 21, 1886, Daniel Butterfield married his second wife, Julia Lorillard James of New York, in a ceremony in London, England. He married his first wife, Elizabeth, in 1857 and she died in 1877. The couple retired to their Cragside estate, overlooking the

Hudson River and just across the river from the United States Military Academy at West Point. Cragside is in the town of Cold Spring, New York, where General George Washington once had a nearby encampment and used to frequently stop and drink from a spring during the Revolution.[24]

On July 17, 1901, at the age of 69, around 8:30 p.m., General Daniel Butterfield died in Cold Spring, New York. He was buried with full military honors by special order of the Secretary of War at West Point Cemetery at the United States Military Academy, although he had not attended that institution. Taps was sounded at his funeral and could be heard from his Cragside estate across the river. His cause of death was softening of the brain and apoplexy (stroke). The Davenport Daily Republican dated Thursday, July 18, 1901, reads: "General Daniel Butterfield died at Cragside tonight. He had been in poor health for a year or more and has been in a condition of semi-paralysis for some time. He leaves a widow, but no children."[25] Taps is not mentioned, nor is it mentioned on his monument at West Point. There are sixteen ornate columns on his monument recording the thirty-eight battles in which he fought or participated, and again not one mention of Taps.[26] However, for a man who could not read music or write music, and as the commander of a brigade, he knew all the bugle calls necessary to relay orders and command troops. During his time, all troops were expected to know what the calls were and how to respond. He authored the 1862 Army field manual, Camp and Outpost Duty for Infantry, laying out expectations and bugle calls to communicate orders. Butterfield was like the Mozart of his day in the fact that he could play the bugle by ear and then rearrange the melody or notes with the help of those who could read and write music.

Back at Command Sergeant Major James Bryant's funeral, the commander of the Honor Guard gives the command, "Order Arms, parade rest."

Honor Guard: Bereaved relatives, comrades, friends. You have heard the bugle. In the military world, it has a tender significance. It is the golden hour of recollection, the roll call for those who wander, and a homecoming for those like our comrade Command Sergeant Major James Bryant here today. As the notes of the bugle seem to fade away, so too have the many years since his enlistment faded away. Let us look back on the day this comrade left his home, left his loved ones, and went off to defend his country. When the call to arms was heard, James Bryant answered. Imbued with a spirit of devotion, inspired by the love of his native land, he marched off with his fellow comrades, both young and old, to preserve and defend our American heritage of freedom. The red, white, and blue of our grand old flag is brighter, and much more beautiful because of his courage, his devotion, his loyalty, and his service to our American ideas. The march for this comrade is now over, and he layeth down in a house appointed for the living where there are no more storm-tossed seas, and no more shell torn battlefields, most of all no more suffering and pain. You see, he is in the hands of our Heavenly Father, and God giveth him his beloved sleep. He is laid to rest, but let us cherish his memory, be reminded of the place he no longer fills, and be so aware of the thinning of our ranks. Let each of us be so faithful to the remaining marches, so ever true to the friendships that when the keeper of the eternal records comes to call our names for the last time, those, we leave behind may say of us as we now say of him: Here lays a mortal comrade loyal and true, a courageous defender of his country and his flag.

Mr. Bryant's service continues as two members of the honor guard approach the casket to tend to the flag. We've heard the bugle and investigated how Taps has become associated with military funerals. The earliest official reference to the mandatory use of Taps at military funeral ceremonies is found in the U.S. Army Infantry Drill Regulations for 1891, although the United States Army officially recognized it in 1874, under its former designation "Extinguish

Lights". I contend that the tradition of Taps was adopted that July day in 1862, when friend and foe first heard those notes, and it spread like wild fire throughout Civil War encampments. The tradition had to begin somewhere, so why not at its first known sounding at the funeral of a fallen soldier?

Today, in Fort Monroe, Virginia, there is a stained-glass window at the Chapel of the Centurion, formerly known as The Old Post Chapel, that honors and depicts the first-time taps were played at a military funeral.[27] Taps is steeped in tradition. On the grounds of

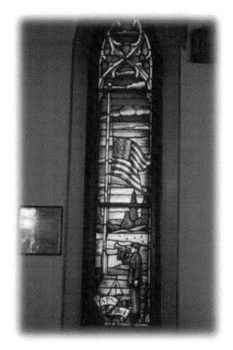

Harrison's Landing, which almost sounds like something out of Game of Thrones, at the Berkeley Plantation there is a monument commemorating the birthplace of Taps. The monument was erected by the Virginia American Legion and dedicated on July 4, 1969. The site is also rich in history, known for the Harrisons of Berkeley Plantation, including Benjamin Harrison V, a signer of the Declaration of Independence; his son William Henry Harrison, the 9th President of the United States and veteran of the United States Army, fighting in battles for the Indiana Territory and the War of 1812; and William Harrisons grandson, Benjamin Harrison, who was the 23rd President of the United States and veteran of the United States Army, obtaining the rank of General during the American Civil War.

Historian and expert on the bugle Jari Villanueva claims that the origin of the name "Taps" can be traced back to the call of Tattoo, which was used to gather soldiers for the final roll call of the day. It's possible that tattoos first appeared in the Thirty Years War (1618–1648) or in King William III's wars in the 1690s. In this context, the word "tattoo" comes from the Dutch words' "tap" (tap or faucet) and "toe" (to cut off). The provost, also known as the Officer of the Day, would beat out the signal throughout the town with the help of a drummer and sergeant when it was time to finish recreating for the evening and head back to the post. According to military protocol, it was required to take a roll call "at Taptoe time" to make sure that every soldier had returned to their billets. It's possible that Taps evolved from the word tattoo. Tattoo was also known as "Tap-toe," and like with military slang, it was abbreviated to Taps.[28]

The other, and more plausible, theory is that Taps was inspired by the beat of a drummer. The drummer of the guard would beat three distinct drum taps at four-count intervals for the military evolution Extinguish Lights, after the drum corps beat Tattoo. Extinguish Lights, as its name suggests, was the bugle call used as the last call of the day during the American Civil War, signaling the extinguishment of all lights and fires. Following the call, three single drum strokes were beat at four-count intervals. This was referred to as the "Drum Taps," or "The Taps" or "Taps" as soldiers would often say. Before the war and during the conflict, and even before the creation of the well-known bugle call, the term "Taps" is frequently mentioned. In fact, it is mentioned so much that it reminds this author of the last call for alcohol at a bar where the beer "taps" are shut down for the night. Thus, the drum beat that came after Extinguish Lights was nicknamed "Taps" by common soldiers. Similarly, the new bugle call that replaced the more formal-sounding Extinguish Lights, which Butterfield detested, also became known as "Taps" in July 1862. Therefore, the new bugle call, jokingly referred to as "Butterfield's Lullaby," serves the same function as the three drum taps commonly referred to as "Taps." The U.S. Army, nevertheless, continued to refer to it as Extinguish Lights, and it wasn't until 1891 that the name was formally changed to Taps. The mournful sound of its notes immediately inspired words that were added to the music that July night of 1862. As soon as the "Taps" were rung. "Go To Sleep, Go to Sleep"[29] is believed to be the first one considering Taps was used to extinguish lights. Numerous other versions have been created and passed on through the generations.

Although, there are no official lyrics to its lingering notes, the following are some of the more well-known passages, beginning with one by Colonel James A. Moss's found in his book Officer's Manual:

"Fades the light;
And afar
Goeth day,
Cometh night;
And a star
Leadeth all
To Their Rest."[30]

The prose of Colonel Moss may not adequately reflect the notes, but what follows are other popular versions:

Day is done, gone the sun,
From the lake, from the hill,
From the sky.
All is well, safely rest,
God is nigh.

Fades the light; And afar
Goeth day, And the stars
Shineth bright,
Fare thee well; Day has gone,
Night is on.

Thanks and praise, For our days
'Neath the sun, Neath the stars,
'Neath the sky,
As we go, This we know,
God is nigh.[31]

As with many other customs, this solemn tradition continues today. Daniel Butterfield, a Civil War general, Medal of Honor recipient, and heir to American Express, may have merely updated an earlier bugle call, but his contribution to creating the most recognized twenty-four notes on the planet earns him a place in music history, and his service to our nation is recorded in the national archives, and the annals of military history.

In Memoriam: Lt. Oliver Wilcox Norton

(December 17, 1839 – October 01, 1920)

First Sounder of the Bugle Call Taps

Chicago, Illinois — Oliver Wilcox Norton, 80, the celebrated bugler, soldier, businessman, and author, entered into rest on October 1, 1920, at his home surrounded by his loving family leaving behind a legacy that will forever resonate in the hearts of Americans with the sounding of Taps. Born on December 17, 1839, in Angelica, New York to the late Oliver William and Henrietta Norton. Young Oliver was the oldest of thirteen children. He attended Montrose Academy in Montrose, Susquehanna County, Pennsylvania in 1857. By April 21, 1861, he had joined the Union Army at the outbreak of the American Civil War.

During the **Civil War**, Norton's bugle call echoed across battlefields, a poignant melody that transcended mere notes. As a bugler in the **83rd Regiment of Pennsylvania Volunteers**, he faced the horrors of combat at **Gaines' Mill** and **Malvern Hill**. Wounded but unbroken, he joined **Gen. Daniel Butterfield's staff**, where fate intertwined their destinies.

At **Harrison's Landing**, amidst the encampment, Norton and Butterfield transformed an old French bugle call into the timeless **"Taps."** This haunting melody, played at dusk, has become a solemn eulogy for fallen comrades. Norton was the first to sound Taps, its notes carrying the weight of sacrifice across the **Army of the Potomac** and beyond.

Beyond the war, Norton's pen etched history as he wrote The Attack and Defense of Little Round Top. His writings illuminated the **Battle of Gettysburg**, particularly the fierce struggle for **Little Round Top** in July 1863. His words bridged the gap between the past and present, ensuring that valor and sacrifice would not fade into oblivion.

Norton's commitment extended beyond the war. As an officer in the **8th U.S. Colored Infantry**, he championed equality and free thought. His actions spoke louder than words, shaping a more just and compassionate world.

He was discharged from the Army in 1865, joined the organization the Grand Army of the Republic, the precursor to the American Legion, and served as commander of the Illinois Commandery of the Military Order of the Loyal Legion. He also worked for the Fourth National Bank in New York City and attended Plymouth Congressional Church in Brooklyn, New York.

Yet, for over 35 years, the authors of Taps remained anonymous. It was not until 1898 that Norton and Butterfield revealed their roles in its creation, lifting the veil of anonymity in an article and correspondence to Century Magazine. Their legacy, like the notes of Taps, now echoes through generations.

Oliver Wilcox wed Lucy Coit Fanning, the love of his life, on October 3, 1870. The famous orator and antislavery preacher, Reverend Henry Ward Beecher, who was the brother of Harriet Beecher Stowe, the author of Uncle Tom's Cabin, presided over their wedding. Together, Oliver and Lucy had five children: Ruth W. (1880–1919), Ralph Hubbard (1875–1953), Strong Vincent (1882–1959), and Gertrude H. (1875–1953). Gertrude H. passed away in infancy.

In 1872, Norton became partners in the Norton Brothers Company, which manufactured cans and sheet metal goods in Chicago, Illinois, (Note: reminding this author of Upton Sinclair's book The Jungle) and helped found the American Can Company in 1901 from several smaller companies, including Norton Brothers.

Today, we honor Lieutenant Oliver Norton not only for his poetic eloquence in his role of sounding Taps, but also for his role in shaping American business and his role as a philanthropist. Despite his name not appearing on monuments, his impact remains deeply ingrained in the hearts of those who hear Taps. As the bugle sounds its mournful refrain, we remember a bugler who composed a symphony of honor, resilience, and remembrance. His body was cremated, and his cremated human remains were scattered by his family. As part of their philanthropy, his heirs endowed several institutions that still exist today, such as Norton Hall at Chautauqua Institution in New York and the Minerva Free Library in Sherman, New York. His cause of death is unknown and may have been due to natural causes. It has been written that Oliver Norton spent his last few decades unable to see and blind.

In the quiet moments, when the sun dips below the horizon, listen closely. You may hear the echoes of Taps, carried by the wind, whispering of a life well-lived—a life that touched eternity. Rest in peace, Bugler Norton. Your notes linger, and your legacy endures.

Folding the Flag

The Flag which we honor and under which we serve is the emblem of our unity, our power, our thought, our purpose as a Nation; it has no other character than that which we give it from generation to generation. Tho silent, it speaks to us-speaks to us of the past; of the men and women who went before us, and of the records they wrote upon it.

-President Woodrow Wilson, Flag Day 1917

Chapter 7

Perfection

"Be Perfect, therefore, as your heavenly Father is perfect."
- Matthew 5:48 (NIV)

(U.S. Army photo by Elizabeth Fraser / Arlington National Cemetery)

As the crowds began to disperse around four thirty P.M. a young National Park Ranger with hopes of sitting quietly at his desk reading a book and trying to enjoy some solitude is interrupted by a bald man in a suit who dashed into the into the Custis Lee Mansion, known as Arlington House, shouting: "The president is coming! The president is coming!"[1] before racing out among the tombstones. Given the intensity of the man's shouting, one might assume that Paul Revere himself was prepared to ride through on horseback and announce the British invasion. Closing his book, rising to his feet, and shaking his head, the young National Park Service Ranger, who was at the time a college student named Paul Fuqua, exited the mansion behind the man, turned a corner, and encountered a most unexpected but already announced guest: none other than President John F. Kennedy. "Mind if we look around?,"[2] the President stated. The date was March 3, 1963, some eight months prior to his assassination and burial on the hallowed grounds where he stood, Arlington National Cemetery. It seems only fitting that Arlington National Cemetery is mentioned among the echoes of valor. Afterall, Arlington has seen its share of war, warriors, and even its own battle to a certain degree on 911. There are approximately 400,000 active-duty service members, veterans, and their family members buried on this hallowed ground spanning some 640 acres or more. According to Arlington National Cemetery's website, "This historic cemetery bears witness to American heritage and the military service and sacrifice of men and women in uniform throughout the nation's history. Families come from all over the country to bury their loved ones at Arlington National Cemetery. They come to Arlington because of the rich history of military honors that makes the service so special. The nation's veterans are laid to rest with dignity and honor by a compassionate and dedicated work force. We believe that caring for our nation's heroes and their families during their time of need is a sacred duty entrusted to us. On average, Arlington National Cemetery conducts between 27 and 30 funeral services each weekday. There are up to six committal services an hour, five times a day. Saturday services are also available for placements and services for cremated remains that do not require military honors or military chaplain support. The cemetery generally conducts between six and eight services on Saturdays."[3]

So, what does Arlington National Cemetery have to do with the folding of the United States flag? No one works harder at perfection than the Third (3d) United States Infantry Regiment known as The Old Guard. They maintain vigil at the Tomb of the Unknown twenty-four-hours a day 365-days a year in addition to funerals, maintaining horse stables, and drill and ceremony training that includes folding the flag.

The Old Guard operates out of Fort Myer formerly Fort Whipple and Fort Cass during the American Civil War. Mrs. Mary Anna Randolph Custis Lee, the wife of Confederate General Robert E. Lee, previously owned the property. She inherited it from her father, George Washington Parke Custis, who was the grandson of Martha Washington, and the step grandson of George Washington. A few short months after resigning from the United States Army, Robert E. Lee made his choice to be the commanding general of the Confederacy in defense of his beloved Virginia. Union Forces confiscated Arlington House, as it was called, due to its higher grounds overlooking Washington City, and the rest, as they say, is history.

The United States Congress passed legislation on July 16, 1862, authorizing the federal government to purchase land for the purpose of giving soldiers a proper burial. Congress placed the United States Army Quartermaster General in charge of setting up the land purchases to create national cemeteries. It was Quartermaster General Montgomery C. Megis that ordered the review of eligible sites, but the Arlington Estate was settled on as the most suitable due to it being located on a hill at a higher elevation, and being free of flooding so graves would not be unearthed, and since Robert E. Lee was now a traitor, selection of the Arlington Estate was a no brainer because it would deny the Lee family from returning home. Eventually, Lee family would be compensated for the property by the United States government. In hopes of ending the war and healing the nation President Abraham Lincoln put it this way in his second inaugural address, "With malice toward none with charity for all with firmness in the right as God gives us to see the right let us strive on to finish the work we are in to bind up the nation's wounds, to care for him who shall have borne the battle and for his widow and his orphan to do all which may achieve and cherish a just and lasting peace among ourselves and with all nations."[4] Lincoln basically wanted commerce to go back to the way it was without slavery, without armed conflict and open rebellion, and with the acquisition of Arlington as a place to honor the dead.

Again, what does this have to do with the folding of the flag and giving it ceremoniously to the primary next of kin? As previously stated, nobody works harder at perfection than The Old Guard, whose members devote an inordinate amount of time to the finest of details from the crispness of the uniform, the polishing of medals, and shining their shoes until they look like mirrors and can see their reflection, to the drill and ceremony duties they perform daily. They practice booming, thunderous artillery salutes that rattle the windows and shake the earth, crisply folding the flag until they can do it blindly and trample the Virginia hills with marching precision until their formation moves as one singular unit.

There is another unit located at the Port Mortuary on Dover Air Force Base that also has the standard of absolute perfection. This unit of Airmen receives the flag-draped coffins or transfer cases of fallen heroes of war and those serving who pass away due to accidents in training or otherwise while on active duty. Out on the flight deck, the honor guard, in a solemn manner, carries fallen soldiers in their flag-draped transfer cases to an awaiting transport vehicle, ensuring privacy and, more importantly, preserving dignity, honor, and respect for the deceased. Members of the same military branch as the fallen soldier compose the honor guard as a sign of respect for their honorable service to a grateful nation. In his book Among the Dead, John W. Harper, a twenty-one-year Air Force veteran, writes, "Officially, the dignified transfer is not considered a ceremony, as any undue pressure should never be placed onto the grieving families making them feel obligated to come to Dover. However, the military is fully committed to the care and support of the deceased families and will assist those families that desire attending the transfer."[5] In the past, presidents during their term in office have attended the transfer of fallen soldiers at Dover. In recent memory and widely publicized, Presidents George W. Bush and Barack Obama made visits to Dover during their terms in office.

"Officially, it's called the Air Force Mortuary Affairs Operation Unit. Unofficially, this is where America tries to bring some comfort to a moment that is exceedingly uncomfortable-when the bodies of those lost in overseas combat zones are brought home."[6] The silver transfer cases, draped with flags, slowly and deliberately transport the bodies of deceased soldiers down the ramp of a Lockheed C-5 Galaxy to an awaiting transport vehicle, and then to a bunkered scanning room. The carry teams, or honor guards, work with precision as a single unit, making their movements very deliberate as they solemnly move the bodies of deceased soldiers. Once in the main area of the bunker, they remove the body bags from their transfer cases one at a time, scan them for weapons, and remove them if found before entering the mortuary. According to John W. Harper, who spent several years assigned to the Port Mortuary at Dover, "This room had very thick cement walls, but there were small panes of glass that you could peer into to watch the procession. The small panes of glass were very thick, and apparently blast-proof."[7] He continues, "Occasionally I would pass through to visit that area and hear unofficial stories of ammunition or unexploded ordinances that had inadvertently slipped onto the transport planes while back in the war theatre. These stories were not routine, but also not rare, as the fallen were often rushed out of the war zone under strained conditions. It always allowed me insight into how courageous those pilots and air crews were. Priority number one for that air crew was getting the aircraft off the ground in Iraq and back to the land of the free. Those professionals at Dover, working with the initial contact of the body bags, very carefully handled whatever they encountered. They were munitions experts, well-trained in the disposal of any ordinance, and thanks to their high level of competency and professionalism, there was never an explosive incident in that building. At least not that I was ever aware of."[8]

The military is full of ordinary people from all walks of life doing extraordinary things while facing potential danger and looking death in the eyes. These ordinary people include veterans, firefighters, law enforcement officers, nurses, doctors, funeral directors, and others who respond to various situations such as fires, firefights, crime scenes, and natural disasters. Instead of running away from danger, they are trained to respond and eliminate the threat, control the situation, assist in the aftermath of a natural disaster or pandemic, and limit or contain whatever caused the emergency or crisis situation. Chaos brings out the best in those who have been trained and know how to handle it, those who do and respond appropriately do so according to their training and are the ones that become heroes and the ones for which medals are made and pinned. As difficult a task as it is to serve in any military unit, leadership is a crucial element. Leadership is best exhibited by those with passion in their hearts for doing the right thing, regardless of the circumstances. People can clearly see the care and concern, the dignity and respect, the professionalism, and the placing of their mission over their own interests in this case and our topic of discussion, military funerals, but they can also discern when someone simply doesn't want to be there, exhibits an attitude, or is disrespectful, whether intentionally or unintentionally, or flat don't care. In the military, you follow orders, and for those who don't, there are consequences. When an Honor Guard shows up to perform military rites, people see the importance of honoring their fallen comrades or loved ones. People see the diligence. They also see the call of duty, discipline, honor, and respect. In other words, people see perfection.

The mortuary building's main part receives the human remains after the body bag scan. The remains are examined and photographed, bar-coded and given an identification tag.[9] At the funeral homes where I have worked, identification tags are a must, especially if the call volume of the funeral home is high. This is just a best practice, no matter the volume of calls. It only takes one mistake in identity to bring the state funeral board or Federal Trade Commission calling, but unfortunately some people are careless and have buried the wrong person or not properly identified, labeled, and tagged cremated human remains, jewelry, etc., yet this is a discussion of another day. The point is that proper identification is important. In Mr. Bryant's case, he was out of state, so I requested the hospital nurse to send a face sheet to the trade service so when my transportation staff arrived (removal staff for you funeral directors reading this) they could properly identify him by his picture, and place a tag with his name on it and his date of birth and date of passing before he was transported back to Indiana from Ohio. Funeral directors and people who work in mortuaries must pay attention to the most minute of details. Observing the work of these professionals is akin to immersing oneself in a C.S.I. (Crime Scene Investigation) episode, minus the Hollywood drama, particularly when dealing with combat deaths or performing autopsies. Funeral directors, military personnel in the mortuary field, combat veterans, firefighters, law enforcement officers, medical examiners, coroners, and investigators have all witnessed gruesome and grotesque scenes. They can attest that the sights and smells of death are not always pleasant.

Most combat veterans that I know, whether in World War II, Korea, Vietnam, the Gulf War, Bosnia, Samalia, or Afghanistan, etc., just cannot bring themselves to talk about their combat experience because they want to spare the general public or other family members of the horrific scenes they encountered. They may even be trying to forget the things they did in the name of the United States of America. Each deceased veteran, soldier, or loved one is treated as if they are the most important person in the history of the world. We treat them with the same dignity and respect as kings, queens, the President, or other heads of state. We also train the caretakers of the deceased to uphold their dignity and respect, honoring their lives, and in our case, a life of service. We should be thanking everyone who voluntarily served in the United States Armed Forces and offering to pay for their meal, cut their grass, buy them a cup of coffee, or any other small gesture, shake their hand, or just say thank you. While we celebrate Flag Day, Memorial Day (Decoration Day), Independence Day, and Armistice Day (Veterans Day) to honor our veterans and active-duty military personnel, I believe that every veteran, regardless of whether they die in battle defending liberty or quietly at home after their call of duty, should receive honors, provided they meet the government's standards for those honors.

There is life after death. Once you are deceased the human body undergoes both physical and chemical changes. The body begins to cool to the temperature of the surrounding environment (Algor mortis). Dehydration begins followed by the gravitation of blood and bodily fluids to the dependent areas of the body (Hypostasis), then comes the reddish-purple discoloration that looks like a bruise that we embalmers call "postmortem staining" or the process of Livor mortis, where gravity begins to pull the blood to the areas closest to the ground. There is a thickening or increase in the viscosity of the blood after death caused by the loss of the liquid portion of the blood to the tissue spaces. The endogenous invasion of microorganisms in the body occurs due to the cessation of natural and metabolic activities that normally regulate the organisms during life. This results in a temporary increase in body temperature, known as postmortem caloricity, and alterations in the body's pH balance, which cause the muscles to temporarily stiffen, a condition known as rigor mortis. This is followed by postmortem staining and further decomposition. I could have given a shorter answer, which is that once you are deceased, the human body begins to decompose, starting with your blood, as it cultures bacteria and the cells begin to breakdown.[10]

Funeral directors need licenses for a variety of reasons, including enhancing public safety, combating infectious diseases, managing biohazardous waste, and utilizing potentially carcinogenic chemicals for body disinfection and preservation, which may or may not be environmentally harmful. Additionally, licensing funeral directors allows states to hold them legally accountable. Most states have licensing requirements so that funeral directors can make funeral arrangements for final disposition and carry them out legally and according to the wishes of the family. Cleaning and disinfecting the body is a must to protect public safety and prevent infectious diseases from spreading. It allows a medical examiner, coroner, and forensics professionals like, the crime scene investigator, and the pathologist to determine the necessary forensic information to help them identify the cause and manner of death. We strive for perfection, and in every case as licensed funeral professionals, we do not perform any invasive techniques, make incisions, close their eyes, and mouth, or perform embalming, shave, or cut the deceased's hair, etc. without the permission of the legal primary next of kin or the person authorized to direct disposition (PADD). When a deceased person arrives at the funeral home and is transferred to an embalming table in the prep room, and provided permission has been granted by the PADD or primary next of kin, the body is washed with soap and water, sponge bathed, hair washed, shampooed, and rinsed, styled if needed, nails trimmed, and underneath the fingernails cleaned, eyes and mouth closed with approved practices, and prepared for embalming. If you have permission to embalm, then embalm. Sounds like a good spa treatment. On a side note, funeral directors also message the arms and legs to aid arterial injection of embalming fluid and to help break rigor mortis.

If the family wants to bury their deceased veteran in their dress uniform, that's what we are going to do. If the deceased were a farmer and wore a t-shirt and blue jean overalls, then that's what we are going to do. The family will determine how the deceased is dressed, including undergarments, unless they specify the deceased went commando. For our purposes, we are discussing the military, and the deceased veteran will be wearing his or her dress uniform from their branch of service. If the deceased is active duty and killed in combat, in training, or in an accident, they receive a brand-new full military dress uniform wrinkle-free and with all rank insignias, epaulets, stripes, and oak leaf clusters; the pants are creased to a razors edge; the belt; the jacket contains all ribbons and medals measured to their precise location; a t-shirt; dress socks; and boots, all new. Some branches also use white starched gloves. The deceased veteran will be wearing this and looking razor-sharp in their casket. Perfection is the standard for everyone, but for veterans, in my experience, honoring them has to be more perfect.

Perfection is the standard for any military unit, whether it be the Old Guard of the 3rd Army Regiment, the Body Bearers of the

Marine Barracks, or the Airmen of the Air Force Mortuary Affairs Operation Unit. There are standards to get into each unit and once there, the standard is perfection. I particularly like the motto of the Marine Corps Body Bearers "The Last to Let You Down."[11] Flawless funerals are the standard to preserve lasting dignity and respect for the deceased veteran and demonstrates to the family the familial bond of love and respect that the military has for their own. In the case of President John F. Kennedy, there was tremendous pressure and stress to take the standard of perfection to a godlike level.

As the Old Guard, civilians, and the Kennedy family made preparations for his funeral, things were happening behind the scenes where the standard of perfection had to be met and pushed to an even higher standard. In his book On Hallowed Ground: The Story of Arlington National Cemetery, author Robert Poole writes, "The Old Guard not only furnished the caisson and horses for Kennedy's funeral; it also dispatched honor guard to stand watch over his casket, helped form security cordons for his funeral procession, and assigned one of its most promising young officers, 1st Lt. Samuel R. Bird, to oversee the joint services casket detail, which met their slain commander in chief at Andrews Air Force Base, stayed with him through the weekend ceremonies in fine military style. When it came to see him across the river to Arlington, they did that too."[12] Perfection is the standard, and that was just the wee hours of the morning on Saturday. President Kennedy was assassinated on Friday the afternoon before, and now he was being taken to Bethesda Naval Hospital for an autopsy, all the while the military was making preparations for a military funeral on the grandest scale and with the entire nation watching as his funeral was broadcast on television, and this with the pressure of fulfilling Mrs. Kennedy's wishes of an eternal flame that had to be completed in such a short time to honor her beloved Jack. Following the autopsy, they summoned Joseph Gawler's Sons funeral home in Washington, D.C. to carry out the embalming, dressing, casketing, and cosmetic restoration work, preparing for the president's funeral at St. Matthew Cathedral and burial at Arlington National Cemetery. He would be

only the second president buried at Arlington with William Howard Taft being the first in 1930. Both are currently the only two presidents buried at Arlington.

"On Sunday, November 24, 1963, arriving for rituals on Capitol Hill, some members of Bird's (The author is referring to 1st Lieutenant Samuel R. Bird, who oversaw the casket detail) faced the long flight of stairs to the Rotunda with a sense of foreboding. Thirty-six shallow steps led from the Capitol Plaza to the Rotunda entrance. A stand of television cameras bristled at the top of the stairs and the Kennedy family filed into place at the bottom, with Bird's casket team in between. The whole world would be watching the nine men assigned to carry a mahogany casket weighing 1,300 pounds- about the heft of a thoroughbred horse-to the top." Army specialist Douglas A. Mayfield remembers, "looking at the steep incline and thinking it looked more like a wall than steps."[13] He was one of three soldiers, two marines, two sailors, one airman, and one coastguardsman assigned to the detail to carry President Kennedy's casket.[14] With Lieutenant Bird hovering behind, the team eased Kennedy from the caisson and slowly began its ascent. As the casket detail did so, Bird sensed that the men were having trouble balancing their load. To relieve the strain, he slipped behind the squad and lifted the casket from its back corners, giving the pallbearers a boost up the stairs. With each step, the strain grew greater as they struggled to keep the casket level and struggled to make it look as if they were not struggling. Those on the lower end had to hoist the casket shoulder high, while the men in front tried to maintain their grip at waist level. With Bird close behind, watching for any signs of slippage, the casket bearers inched up the stairs, followed by Mrs. Kennedy and her two children.[15]

Down on the plaza, as the Coast Guard Band sounded the last strains of the Navy Hymn, "Eternal Father, Strong to Save," the casket detail reached the top, moved out of the bright sunlight, and disappeared into the darkened Rotunda. Under the dome, they settled Kennedy onto President Lincoln's catafalque and stepped back. Mrs.

Kennedy, dressed in black with a long veil, emerged from the shadows, clutching the hand of her daughter, Caroline. The pair strode forward through the soaring chamber and kneeled before the casket. As Mrs. Kennedy did so, she stretched out one hand to touch the box. She leaned in to kiss the flag, rose to her feet, and melted into the Rotunda again.[16]

That Sunday evening was quite lengthy for soldiers of the Old Guard. They didn't get much sleep, and the pressure from the task they were about to take on was growing. Last-minute arrangements, including polishing shoes and pressing uniforms, as well as reviewing the funeral route, procession, and ceremony itself, occupied the entire evening. Despite all of this there again was the call for perfection as Lt. Samuel Bird summoned his team from their evening routines for flag-folding practice. Each night at Retreat on military bases, soldiers practice folding the flag into a tri-cornered hat reminiscent of the hats worn by the soldiers who fought the War of the Revolution, won American independence, retired for the evening, and returned to the top of the flagpole for Reveille in the morning. Reveille is a bugle call that was not originally intended to honor the flag. In fact, in 1812 it was a drum call to signify that soldiers should rise for day duty, and sentries should leave off at night, challenging (halting people and demanding identification). As time passed, reveille came to signify the raising of the flag in the morning and honors paid to it.[17] Whereas, Retreat is the bugle call telling soldiers to retire to their quarters for the day. Retreat's original purpose was to notify sentries to start challenging until sunrise. The Continental Army used it for the first time in America during the American Revolutionary War, marking the end of the official day of duty with the lowering and folding of the flag. Command Sergeant Major Michael Hayes, Maneuver Support Center of Excellence at Fort Leonard Wood in Missouri, states, "We are honoring the nation the flag represents. We are also honoring those who have fought under the flag, and in some cases are buried under it; to protect our constitution and preserve the rights and liberty we all enjoy." He goes on to say, "Everyone needs to pay respect during these ceremonies. Although everyone does not serve under the flag, everyone enjoys the rights and liberty it stands for."[18] I agree.

The expectation of perfection continues, "The team was expected to retire the Stars and Stripes from the president's casket in traditional, slow-motion manner, transforming the familiar rectangle into a tight blue triangle. Under Bird's watchful eye, the eight men folded and unfolded the flag for hours until the crew was performing flawlessly.[19] Army Specialist Douglas Mayfield recalls, "As good as each member was individually, it was critical that we practice together over and over...since two days before we had never met and didn't know each other. If one member falters or the teams timing is off, the flag could be dropped, red and white stripes could be other than straight, and red could be showing in the triangular folded flag where only blue with white stars are supposed to be." His next statement again shows the standard of perfection. "We knew that we would be scrutinized by millions of viewers, and we wanted to give the impression that...operating in unison was second nature to us."[20]

As the clock crept toward Monday morning, Lt. Bird's team still had work to do. Filing onto a bus, and riding through an empty cemetery that would see the emergence of thousands converge on it in several hours, the team arrived at the amphitheater and saw the heavenly lights illuminating the Tomb of the Unknowns. Lieutenant Bird ordered a practice casket used by the Old Guard to train with at Arlington. Lt. Bird wanted to simulate bringing the President out of the Rotunda and down the treacherous Capitol stairs without faltering, slipping, or dropping the casket. Aiming to replicate the actual mahogany casket containing the slain president's body, the team added weights and sandbags to the casket. It would eventually hold the weight of Lt. Bird sitting on it, moving reverently at a slow pace down the stairs to the waiting caisson. Eventually Bird called a halt to the proceedings stating, "We've done all we can do tonight fellas. We're just not going to make it...Don't worry about it. We'll get it in the morning."[21]

Chapter 8

Please Accept This Flag

"Time will not dim the glory of their deeds."
-General of the Armies John J. Pershing

The folding of the flag is a precise and reverent ceremony, carried out with the utmost care and respect, but how did the presentation of the flag that we see at graveside come about? Now, everyone who read the previous chapter may have assumed that we were heading to President John F. Kennedy's funeral, and while we will eventually arrive there, I think it is important to answer the question at hand by introducing Colonel George Wilbur Cocheu (pronounced co-shoe).

You are probably wondering who this military man is, or you may have already figured out the mystery by the first line of this chapter. After long research and tracking down leads, and with the assistance of the Cadet Engagement Librarian, Laura Mosher, at the United States Military Academy at Westpoint and an article titled, Arlington's Ceremonial Horses and Funerals at the White House, I have found the origin of the folding of the flag and presenting it to the next of kin. The article mentioned by Claire A. Faulkner states, "Yet perhaps the most recognizable trapping of a military or state funeral is the flag-draped coffin. The blue of the flag is placed at the head of the coffin, over the left shoulder of the deceased. In 1918 the U.S. Army, at the suggestion of Colonel George W. Cocheu, officially began the practice of placing a flag over the coffin and presenting it to the next of kin at the conclusion of the funeral service, though the custom dates to the Napoleonic Wars of the late eighteenth and early nineteenth centuries, when a flag was used to cover the dead as they were taken from the battlefield on a caisson. Today, the flag-covered coffin is a symbol that a soldier's country assumes the solemn and sacred obligation of burying its fallen."[1]

If you recall, Colonel James A. Moss's book, Officers Manual, gives clear instructions and provides illustrations for folding the flag by two men at the sounding of the last note of Retreat in the evening. So, the folding of the flag has been done since at least 1911. Moss also wrote about what he called a "soldier's burial" in his book Memories of the Campaign Santiago published by The Mysell-Rollins Company of San Francisco in 1899. A "soldier's burial" was one that included the firing of three volleys and the sounding of Taps. If you Google folding of the flag origins you may receive this message, "The source and the date of origin of this Flag Folding Procedure is unknown. However, some sources attribute it to the Gold Star Mothers of America, while others to an Air Force chaplain stationed at the United States Air Force Academy. Some sources also indicate that the 13 folds are a nod to the original first 13 colonies." Not very informative and not very accurate.

I can tell you that the American Legion was founded on March 15, 1919, and the Gold Star Mothers was founded on June 4, 1928. I contacted the United States Air Force Academy and was told that the flag folding tradition could not have been developed by the Air Force. Why? Because the United States Air Force did not officially become an armed services branch until September 18, 1947, some scholars would argue that it was part of the Army Air Corps in 1907. My how quickly we weaponized flight, as the first flight by Orville and Wilbur Wright lasted only 12 seconds in 1903. The Air Force Academy also referred me to the United States Military Academy at Westpoint, founded on March 16, 1802, and the Naval Academy on October 10,

1845. I can also tell you that the folding the flag tradition probably started with veterans of the American Legion honoring their fallen comrades with the flag presentation to the next of kin based on Colonel Cocheu's recommendation to Army Chief of Staff, General Peyton C. March. Flags were used during the Spanish-American War in 1898 to cover the caskets of the dead. At some point, Cocheu must have noticed that the flags were not kept on the caskets during transportation home. The bodies were shipped home as cargo-on-cargo ships and left in the hands of the crews on the ship. Colonel Cocheu had witnessed these methods of caring for the dead and felt that they were not being properly honored. The thought of soldiers being left in the hands of a ship's crew and not the military bothered him enough to suggest to Army Chief of Staff, General Peyton C. March, that the caskets remain draped with the flag and the colors should be given to the next of kin as a token of the country's appreciation. He went a step further requesting a soldier of the same rank or greater to accompany the soldier home. Ultimately, General March, approved this plan in 1918 and Cocheu issued this order to the Army. What follows is from the collection of the U.S. Military Academy Library from their publication Assembly in the Fall 1966 issue. His autobiographical obituary in his own words.

GEORGE WILBUR COCHEU

No. 4144 George Wilbur Cocheu
Class of 1903
Died April 4, 1966, in Washington D.C., aged 87 in years.
Interment: Arlington National Cemetery, Arlington Virginia.

The Class of 1903 has lost one of its most able, most distinguished, and greatly beloved members. George Cocheu lived by the West Point motto (Duty, Honor, Country) and demonstrated his great affection for the Military Academy in every possible way. For the last two years, in their beautiful home on Foxhall

Road in Washington, life was not easy for the Cocheu's. George was practically blind from cataracts despite several operations, and Emma was a semi-invalid. However, they celebrated their sixtieth wedding anniversary in 1964 with their customary gracious, annual open house to, which hundreds of their myriad friends came to wish them well. The day before George's graveside service in Arlington, on April 8, 1966, Emma fell and broke her hip. She was immediately hospitalized at Walter Reed, but she followed George to rest on May 26, 1966, and lies beside him in Arlington. George filed a modest resume of his background, cadet days, and Army service with the Association of Graduates. The writer has studied it with care and sincerely believes that for anyone to attempt to edit it or to write an obituary from it would be a mistake and unfair to George Cocheu. Therefore, his resume is quoted verbatim, for it gives a warmer, more accurate picture of this highly principled, loyal son of West Point than anyone else could paint.
-M.C.T., 1903.

The following is George Cocheu's own autobiographical resume:

Family

I was born in the old Williamsburg section of Brooklyn, New York, on October 17, 1878, and graduated from Public School No. 23 and Boys High School. My mother was a direct descendant of Gerrerse Van Kowenhoven who emigrated from Holland to the New Netherlands in 1630. She was one of the eighth generation all of whom were born on Manhattan Island. She died in 1921. My father's father, Henri Cocheu, was born in Pampol, Brittany, France. He was conscripted, in 1808, into the Army of Napoleon Bonaparte and came to this country with his brother in 1820. He died in Brooklyn, in 1863. I had six brothers, four of whom are living at this time (1952). On November 12, 1904, in Johnstown, Pennsylvania, I was married to Emm a Fend Gageby, daughter of the late Major James H. Gageby, 12th U.S. Infantry, who, as a 1st Lieutenant of the 19th U.S. Infantry, in the Civil War, was a member of the famous tunnel party that escaped from Libby Prison in

Richmond, Virginia. He was a direct lineal descendant of William the Conqueror. We have no children.

How did I happen to go to West Point?

In 1889 my brother Frank, now a retired major general, entered the Military Academy, and my visits there while he was a cadet inspired me with the desire to seek an appointment. In 1897 I received an appointment as an alternate, but my principal passed the entrance examination only to be "found" the following January. In 1899 I was again an alternate, but fortunately my principal failed to report, and, after a month's preparation at the old Braden School in Highland Falls, I passed and entered with the Class of 1903 with which I graduated.

Names of Roommates

As a Plebe, I lived in camp and barracks with Ralph Glass. "Sep" Brant joined us in the fourth floor lefthand Area room of the old 8th division. The Corps consisted of only four companies, and we were assigned to "D " Company. Brant was "found" in January. I was appointed corporal in 1900 and that fall was assigned to "A " Company, where I lived in the second floor lefthand Plain room with Douglas MacArthur. When the Class of 1901 graduated in February of that year I was made acting color sergeant with Marion Howze. I was appointed sergeant and transferred to "B " Company in June 1901 which meant another move. As a Second Classman I lived with Julian Schley who o was our first sergeant. In 1902 Schley was made battalion quartermaster, and I was dropped as a sergeant but still remained in "B " Company. I lived with Paul Bunker who later, in 1904, was best man at my wedding. For the entire four years I was a member of the Cadet Choir, if it might be called a choir, and as a First Classman was its leader. Outstanding events taking place in my cadet days were our participation in the Dewey Day parade in New York; the two investigations of hazing by the Military and Congressional Committees; the famous mutiny staged by the Class of 1902; resumption of athletic relations with the Naval Academy; and, most outstanding, an occasion when Buzzard Blake was

Officer in Charge and Benny Grey, Officer of the Day, in our first-class year. Jimmie Jones, in the 12th Division, and Le w Adams, in the 1st, hauled a piece of old iron shot, swiped from Battery Knox, and a G.I. bucket, up and down the iron steps of their respective divisions at just about Tattoo. With the added noise of stones thrown by many of us from the windows of barracks against the tin roof of the old boiler house, the noise was terrific and subsided only when Jimmie and Lew got tired and the rest of us ran out of stones.

Names of Friends

Of the men in our Class, I have served most with Clifford Jones, Louie Brinton, and Douglas MacArthur, whose mother, incidentally, introduced me to the girl who later became my wife. I have counted more on a host of fine friends rather than on a few intimates and have tried to maintain friendships with officers junior to me.

War Service

I was in Yokohama, Japan, on my way home from the Philippines when war was declared in 1917. I reported immediately to the American Ambassador in Tokyo and, on his direction, proceeded to the United States. I served at the first officers' training camps at Plattsburgh Barracks and Fort Monroe. In August 1917, as a major, I was assigned as division inspector of the 78th Division at Camp Dix, New Jersey, and remained there until February 1918 when I was detailed a member of the General Staff and ordered to the Office of the Chief of Staff in Washington. I served in the office of the Executive Assistant (Deputy Chief of Staff) until January 1922 when I was ordered to the Philippines. There I served as Acting Chief of Staff and G1 of the Philippine Division and G2 of the Department. **In 1918 I conceived the idea and wrote the order, still in effect, requiring that at the funeral of any member of the military service, the flag used to cover the casket must accompany the remains wherever shipped and be presented to the next of kin after burial.**

Realizing the necessity of close contact between the War Department and the Congress, I recommended the establishment of what, in 1921, was organized as the Legislation Branch, Office of the Chief of Staff, and became its first chief under Major General J.G. Harbord, Deputy Chief of Staff. In November 1921, I was aide to the United States Senate at the funeral of the Unknown Soldier.

Recalled to active duty in May 1941, I was made Chief, Inspection Division, Office of the Quartermaster General, and served in that post until I was returned to the retired list on 31 December 1943. In 1941 I foresaw the necessity of the establishment of some system of caring for and returning to the next of kin the personal effects of officers and enlisted men killed or missing in action. In Kansas City, Missouri, I organized and personally supervised the operations of the Effects Bureau, which during its lifetime returned monies, bonds, travelers' checks, and other negotiable securities amounting to over 8 ½ million dollars and turned over $650,000 worth of other effects by mail, express, and parcel post. I am particularly proud of the fact that the operations of this Effects Bureau, which handled items from every theatre of the war, were conducted without a breath of scandal.

Other Service

On graduation, I was assigned to the Field Artillery, but, when the separation came in 1907, I was assigned to the Coast Artillery. I was the first honor graduate of the Coast Artillery School, Fort Monroe, Virginia, in 1907 and the Advanced Course in 1910. I served as an instructor and assistant professor of Chemistry, Mineralogy, and Geology at West Point in 1911 and, along with some 50 others, was relieved on 31 December 1912 under the Manchu Law. I served in the Philippines from 1915 to 1917 and again from 1922 to 1924. I graduated from the Command and General Staff School, Fort Leavenworth, in 1925 and the Army War College in 1926. I commanded the 12th Coast Artillery at Fort Monroe from 1926 to 1928, was Assistant Chief of Staff, 1st Corp Area, Boston, Massachusetts, from 1928 to 1932, and commanded the Harbor Defenses of Sandy Hook and the post of Fort Hancock, New Jersey,

1932 to 1934. I was chief of the Organization and Operations Division, Office of the Assistant Chief of Staff, G3, War Department General Staff, from 1934 until my retirement in 1938, serving a total of fourteen years and nine days as a member of the General Staff. I was on the initial General Staff list provided for in the Act of July 4, 1920.

Medals and Commendations

I was awarded the Distinguished Service Medal in January 1922, for services in World War I, with the following citation: For exceptional and meritorious and distinguished service. As a member and later as Chief of the Co-ordination Section, General Staff, a position of great responsibility, he devised many methods for improving and making more effective administrative procedure within the War Department, thereby materially facilitating the transaction of the business of the War Department and of the Army, thus rendering service of great value to the entire military establishment.

In September 1943, I was awarded the Legion of Merit for service in World War II, with the following citation: Colonel George W. Cocheu, 0-1801, Quartermaster Corps, United States Army. For exceptional and meritorious conduct in the performance of outstanding service as Chief of the Inspection Division, Quartermaster Corps since May 24, 1941. Upon his recall to active duty, Colonel Cocheu devoted all his energies towards making a constructive approach to the problems of the Quartermaster Corps. In investigating Quartermaster operations Colonel Cocheu consistently developed more effective methods for the performance of the mission of the Quartermaster Corps. He solved many organizational and operational problems of the expanding Quartermaster establishment.

In 1921 Lieutenant General William Wright, Executive Assistant to the Chief of Staff, wrote: "This officer has energy, tact, and an attractive personality. He is prompt in the discharge of his duty, an excellent staff officer, a loyal and dependable gentleman and soldier." In 1922 Major General James H. Harbord, Deputy Chief of Staff to General Pershing, wrote of me: "One of the best young general staff officers of the Army.

"In 1932 I was commended by the chief of Coast Artillery, Major General John W. Gulick, for "high efficiency in the organization and training and administration" of Fort Hancock, New Jersey.

In 1934 I received a commendation from the commanding general, 2d Corps Area, Major General Dennis E. Nolan, for the "good use made of the funds allotted to the post even in the face of trying conditions" and "commendation for the good physical condition of your post and the troops stationed there." In 1934 I was commended by the Chief of Staff, General Douglas MacArthur, for the "work in preparation for and in the conduct of the General Headquarters Command Post Exercise, September 2 to 8, 1934."

Other Information

I rose from captain to colonel in World War I. In December 1941, I wrote the letter which the President of the United States signed requesting the President in 1956 to appoint as a cadet at the United States Military Academy, Colin Kelly III, the son of Colin Kelly Jr., Class of 1927, who was killed on December 10, 1941, while attacking Japanese warships from the air off the Philippines.

In 1938 I was informed personally by the then Chief of Staff that I was four months over the age limit set by the President for promotion to higher grade. My application for retirement, after over 39 years of active service, was submitted on my 60th birthday. My wife and I purchased a home in Washington, at 3106 Foxhall Road, where we have lived in peace and quiet, except for the World War II years, enjoying contact with our friends.[2]

Folding the flag and presenting it to the primary next of kin may have taken a few years to take hold. President Theodore Roosevelt died on January 6, 1919, and was buried on a hillside overlooking the bay at Youngs Memorial Cemetery in Oyster Bay, New York on January 8, 1919.[3] What is clear is that a simple funeral was held at Christ Episcopal Church, and there was a cold, snow-covered procession. His flag-draped coffin was carried to its final resting place by his pall bearers. It is unclear whether the flag was folded and given to his wife, son, or next of kin, who may have been present. The presentation and folding of the flag was one of those small details that people just did not think to write about. On April 17, 2012, the Department of Defense standardized the verbiage for the presentation of the flag for military funeral honors. The mandated words are as follows: "On behalf of the President of the United States, (the United States Army; the United States Marine Corps; the United States Navy; the United States Air Force or the United States Coast Guard), and a grateful nation, please accept this flag as a symbol of our appreciation for your loved one's honorable and faithful service."[4]

Chapter 9

The Most Loved Man in a Generation

William Howard Taft, 27ᵗʰ President of the United States of America

For most people, you would think being elected President of the United States, where you are essentially the equivalent of royalty, would be the highlight of one's life, if not the defining moment of one's life. Yet, this was not the case for William Howard Taft, who did not desire to be president yet ran as the Republican nominee, winning the office in 1908 defeating William Jennings Bryant. Trying to continue most of President Theordore Roosevelt's policies, his next four years as president would prove exceedingly difficult for the 326-pound, extremely genial person.[1]

For Taft, the high mark in his life was in 1921, when he was appointed Chief Justice of the United States Supreme Court by President Warren G. Harding. He was extremely happy as head of the highest court in the land and still holds the distinction of being the only American in history to have served both as President of the United States and later Chief Justice of the United States Supreme Court. So, who was this ordinary man that Bishop James E. Freeman of the Washington Cathedral characterized as "The most loved man in a generation?"[2]

William Howard Taft was born in Cincinnati, Ohio, on September 15, 1857, to the late Alphonso and Louise (Torrey) Taft.[3] He had several siblings that affectionately gave him the nickname, "Big Lub."[4] He was a graduate of Woodward High School, Class of 1874; Yale University, Class of 1878; and Cincinnati Law School, Class of 1880. Admitted to the bar, he worked as a court reporter for the Cincinnati Commercial and held the position of assistant prosecuting attorney in Hamilton County from 1881 to 1883.

Taft was also assistant solicitor of Hamilton County (1885–1887). On June 19, 1886, he married "Nellie" Helen Herron, whose father was a lawyer named John Williamson Herron and classmate of future presidents Benjamin Harrison and Rutherford B. Hayes,[5] to say she guided the political career of her husband would be an understatement. Taft later became a superior court judge in Cincinnati, in 1887, solicitor general of the United States, in 1890, before being appointed to the United States Court of Appeals for the 6th Judicial Circuit (1892–1900), where he was appointed by none other than President Benjamin Harrison. He became a professor and dean of the law department at the University of Cincinnati, in 1896.[6] Hoping for an appointment to the United States Supreme Court, Taft was instead commissioned by President McKinnley as president of the Philippine Commission and became the first civil governor of the Philippine Islands (1901–1904).[7]

Surprisingly, after Associate Justice George Shiras resigned, President Theodore Roosevelt was poised to appoint Taft, and he declined the appointment to the Supreme Court only to accept the appointment as Secretary of War under Roosevelt a year later. He served from February 1, 1904 – June 30, 1908, in that role, began

American construction of the Panama Canal, and served as a conciliator in a threatened upheaval in Cuba. He posed the possibility of a probationary service for recruits before formal enlistment, directed an investigation into procurement procedures, and approved the design of a new Medal of Honor.[8] He proposed the disposal of small military posts and the concentration of the Army at brigade posts. Taft was elected President of the United States and served only a single term, from 1909 to 1913. He began his presidency as caretaker of his wife, Nellie, who "suffered a terrible stroke, which deprived her of control of her right arm and leg, and her power of speech."[9] Taft spent several hours a day and the next year looking after her and teaching her how to speak again.

Woodrow Wilson defeated Taft in his 1912 reelection bid. Following his presidency, he returned to Yale University and assumed the position of Kent Professor of Law and Legal History (1913–1921). He later became chairman of the National War Labor Board during World War I, in 1918. President Warren G. Harding finally appointed William Howard Taft to the United States Supreme Court on March 4, 1921, and he became Chief Justice following the death of Chief Justice Edward Douglas White on May 19, 1921.

Due to his own failing health, Taft retired from the bench on February 3, 1930. Two doctors issued the following bulletin: "For some years Chief Justice Taft has had very high blood pressure, associated with general arteriosclerosis and myocarditis...He has no fever and suffers no pain. His present serious condition is the result of general arteriosclerotic changes."[10] He died at his home in Washington, D.C., on Saturday, March 8, 1930, after an extended illness. Not much can be said about Taft's health without confronting his weight problem. Taft was 5 feet, 11.5 inches tall. He weighed 243 pounds when he graduated from college and, by all accounts, carried it well. By age 48, when he had been Secretary of War for two years, he weighed 320 pounds. He weighed around 335 to 340 pounds when he left the White House. He then lost weight rapidly, dropping to 270 in a year and a half. The summer before he died, he weighed 244 pounds.[11]

In his fifties, Taft developed signs of "hardening of the arteries" accompanied by a rising blood pressure. His exercise tolerance decreased, and an elevator was installed in his house. By his mid-sixties, angina and breathlessness had limited his ability to travel. Taft berated himself for the poor care he had taken of himself. By spring 1929, when he was 71, it was widely known that Taft's health was not good. Rumors occasionally arose that he might retire. Sick as he was, Taft desperately wanted to hold his place on the Supreme Court. "I am older and slower and less acute and more confused," he wrote to his brother in November 1929.[12]

Taft's last words were "Good morning,"[13] said as his physician entered his bedroom. Throughout the day, Taft just slept away. When the peaceful end came, Justice Taft was accompanied by his darling and loving wife Nellie (Helen Louise Herron Taft), a nurse, and Dr. H.G. Fuller. Death came quietly, as the former President and Chief Justice, sank imperceptibly into unconsciousness. After arriving to his residence, Doctor's Francis R. Hanger, Taft's primary care physician, and Dr. Thomas A. Clayton issued the following bulletin: "The former Chief Justice William Howard Taft died at 5:15 PM on March 8, 1930. A sudden change in his condition occurred at 4:45 PM from which he failed to rally."[14] William Howard Taft was 72 years and 174 days old. Joseph Gawler's Sons, a funeral home in Washington, D.C., received the news of William Howard Taft's death and responded to the Taft residence on Wyoming Avenue to prepare his remains for funeral ceremonies and burial. At about 6:15 PM, Walter A. Gawler and a team of at least ten assistants arrived at the Taft mansion at 2215 Wyoming Avenue in Washington, D.C.[15]

President Herbert Hoover proclaimed a thirty-day period of national mourning and directed Colonel Campbell Benjamin Hodges to oversee the arrangements for the burial at Arlington with full military honors afforded. The responsibility for arranging and conducting the funeral, however, was assigned to the Commanding General, 16th Brigade, stationed at Fort Hunt, Virginia. Despite President Hoover's appointment of Colonel Hodges, plans for the funeral the ceremonies were all scheduled for Tuesday, March 11th beginning at 0900 when Mr. Taft's body was to be escorted from his residence to the Capitol to lie in state on the Lincoln catafalque in the rotunda until noon. A procession would then form to accompany Justice Taft's body to All Souls' Unitarian Church for the funeral service. Mrs. Taft declined President Hoover's offer to use the East Room of the White House for the service and visitation, as her husband's preference was for the service to take place in the church where he was a member. Dr. Ulysses G. B. Pierce, pastor of the church and long-time friend of Mr. Taft, was to conduct both the funeral and committal services. Members of the United States Supreme Court were to be honorary pallbearers.[16]

William Howard Taft did not serve in the military as a soldier, yet he held significant roles as the Secretary of War under President Theodore Roosevelt, Commander-in-Chief as President, and served on the National War Labor Board during World War I. "As prescribed in existing regulations, all Army posts possessing the necessary equipment prepared to fire thirteen guns at reveille, one each half hour thereafter until retreat, and then a 48-gun salute to the Union on Monday, March 10, 1930. This was the salute customarily fired upon receipt of news of the death of a President or ex-President except, as in the case of Mr. Taft, when the notice was received on Sunday, March 9, 1930."[17] Additionally, in accordance with long-standing tradition and explicit orders from Army Chief of Staff General Charles P. Summerall to Secretary of War Patrick J. Hurley, Army posts were to fire twenty-one-minute guns at 1430 on Tuesday, March 11, 1930, the time set aside for the conclusion of the funeral service. For thirty days, all officers were to wear "the usual badge of military mourning around the left sleeve of the uniform coat and overcoat and on the saber," flags were to be flown at half-staff, colors and standards were to be draped in mourning. Similarly, Navy instructions prescribed that on the day of the funeral "the ensign at each naval station and on board each vessel in commission be displayed at half-mast and that a gun be fired at half-hour intervals from sunrise to sunset at each naval station and on-board flagships and all saluting ships acting singly." Officers of the Navy and Marine Corps were also to wear mourning badges for thirty days.[18]

While the size of military escorts in a former President's funeral was left to the Secretary of War, existing regulations stipulated that military honors would be rendered during the ceremonies in Washington. It was decided to have two troops, or a squadron of cavalry, escort Mr. Taft's body from his home to the Capitol. Two service bands, a battalion of infantry, a battalion of field artillery, a battalion of marines, and a company of bluejackets were to be part of the main procession from the Capitol to the church. Major General Fred W. Sladen, the commanding general of the Third Corps Area, with headquarters located in Baltimore, Maryland, was chosen by the Secretary of War to be the escort commander.

Throughout his life, Taft expressed to his wife his desire to be buried on the plot of his father, Alphonso Taft, in Cincinnati's Spring Grove Cemetery. However, at the request of the family, Mrs. Taft decided that her husband would be the first president to be buried at Arlington National Cemetery. On Monday, March 10, 1930, Gawler's funeral directors dressed and casketed President Taft. "The casket was an oversized Boyertown Solid Bronze with a full-length glass top seal with tufted satin interior and pillow."[19] The family provided the funeral directors with the Chief Justice's robe to dress him in for public viewing in the family's home. On Tuesday, March 11, 1930, "with casket in hand, a bugler called attention as the calvary men drew sabers and offered a precisely-executed "Present Arms," remaining in that order until the casket was secure on the caisson. Directly behind the flag draped casket was the funeral director, Walter Gawler, overseeing every movement of a dignified transfer"[20] as President Taft was removed from his home to lie in state under the dome of the rotunda of the United States Capitol Building. Later that morning, in a misty rain, the 2nd Squadron, 3rd Cavalry, caisson detachment, and body-bearers reached the Taft home shortly before nine o'clock in the morning. Facing the residence from the opposite side of the street, the mounted troops formed a front as the body-bearers brought the casket from the house and secured it on the caisson. Taft's remains were transferred to Washington's All Souls Unitarian Church, where he had been a longtime member.

Neither officials nor members of the family rode in the procession to the Capitol. Metro Police from the District of Columbia escorted the entire entourage, with policemen on motorcycles leading the way and the caisson following. Heavy rain fell as the procession slowly progressed toward its destination, the United States Capitol. As Taft's procession slowly made its way to Capitol Hill, it literally passed by thousands of bystanders who, despite the rain, removed their hats as the flag-draped casket came into view. When the cortege reached Lafayette Park and turned in front of the White House, President and Mrs. Hoover appeared on the east portico and stood in respectful silence, following the horse-drawn caisson down Pennsylvania Avenue, now on route to the Capitol.

As the procession reached the Capitol Plaza, there was an overwhelmingly large military presence. The Marine Corps had three squads in full dress uniform with white gloves waiting in the Rotunda. The U.S. Naval Yard's three squadrons of blue-jacketed petty officers and the Army's U.S. Calvary from Fort Myer were also present. The casket bearers met the casket on the plaza, unstrapped the oversized casket containing the body of their former commander-in-chief, and slowly ascended the marble steps. Steps on which Taft, only a year ago, stammered his words in administering the Oath of Office to President Herbert Hoover. The staff from Joseph Gawler's Sons folded back the flag and removed the head end of the casket lid after carrying the casket into the rotunda, revealing the face of the fallen leader to thousands. "An honor guard, commanded by Capt. Frank Goettge, a White House aide, was posted, as an hour and a half remained of the scheduled period of lying in state. Some 7,000 persons in two lines filed by during that time, despite interruptions each fifteen minutes when a new honor guard relief took post."[21]

The funeral directors closed the casket at high noon and moved it from the rotunda to the caisson waiting on the East Plaza, where the entire escort had assembled for the procession to the church. Water was streaming everywhere as the wind picked up, and the Army Band began leading the procession, followed by the clip clop of hooves on the pavement as the caisson and the remainder of the procession moved toward All Souls' Unitarian Church. As they did during the morning ceremony going to the Capitol, officials and family members did not ride with the procession. "As the cortege retraced its morning route as far as 16th Street, then turned north to All Souls' Unitarian Church on Harvard Street, a heavy downpour of rain with strong winds continued making it difficult for the military escort squads to maintain a precise step and formation. Despite the weather, the public lined the entire route as umbrellas were inverted inside out and hats were being toppled and held as the procession marched on at a slow pace to Chopin's (Funeral March.)"[22] History records that the procession from the Capitol to the church took almost two hours due to the weather.

Casket is Carried up the East Steps of the Capitol. (Library of Congress)

Body of President Taft lies in state in the Capitol Rotunda. (Library of Congress)

Taft requested no eulogy or sermon, a request Mrs. Taft agreed to, given his public life and the widespread knowledge of his character and values. Thousands of people stood in the cool wind and rain, demonstrating their love for him. Considerably before the arrival of the cortege and escort from the Capitol, some 900 invited guests had filled All Souls' Unitarian Church. Under the direction of Charles Lee Cooke, the ceremonial officer of the State Department, army officers acted as ushers, seating everyone in a timely and orderly fashion. Among those in attendance were President Herbert and Mrs. Hoover, Vice President Charles Curtis, cabinet members, committees of the Senate and House of Representatives, the sitting Chief Justice of the United States, and associate justices of the Supreme Court (the honorary pallbearers), state governors, military leaders, ambassadors from all major embassies in the District of Columbia, as well as other foreign and congressional delegations.

William H. Taft's funeral procession. (Library of Congress).

By 2:35 PM, the funeral procession had started its journey over to Arlington National Cemetery. Where the "US Navy Band played; the 3rd Cavalry Regiment, less one squadron; a battalion of the 13th Engineers from Fort Humphreys (later Fort Belvoir), Virginia; and a company of Marines formed a hollow square around the perimeter of the large gravesite acting as the honor guard during the committal service."[1] The family hand-picked the gravesite, which offers a view from an elevated slope overlooking the Mall of D.C., the Lincoln Memorial, and the Capitol beyond. Not far from his grave would be that of political rival William Jennings Bryant, whom he defeated for the presidency, now both lying silent at Arlington. Taft, however, would be in fine company, as a mere 75 yards or so separated him from Robert Todd Lincoln, President Abraham Lincoln's son, who was also buried at Arlington and not in Springfield, Illinois, at the Lincoln tomb. I might add that Robert Lincoln had a short military career, issued a field commission as an army captain and assigned to General Grant's staff, and a political career, serving as the Secretary of War under two United States Presidents, James Garfield (20th) and Chester Arthur (21st). Throughout his life, Robert had long expressed his intentions to be buried in the Lincoln Tomb with his family at Oak Ridge Cemetery in Springfield, Illinois. Two weeks after his death, his widow Mary

Harlan Lincoln suddenly became inspired: "...Our darling was a personage, made his own history, independently of his great father, and should have "his own place in the sun.""[2]   Lincoln's body was buried at Arlington National Cemetery in a sarcophagus designed by the sculptor James Earle Fraser.[3] He is buried together with his wife, Mary, and their son, Abraham II ("Jack"), who had died in London, England, of sepsis in 1890 at the age of 16. Weeks after Jack's death, Robert wrote to his cousin Charles Edwards, "We had a long & most anxious struggle and at times had hopes of saving our boy. It would have been done if it had depended only on his own marvelous pluck & patience now that the end has come, there is a great blank in our future lives & an affliction not to be measured."[4]

As is typical for most funerals, the flowers from his home, Capitol, and church were brought to the cemetery before the procession arrived. The gloomy pall cast over his services made the day feel more like Halloween than a spring day in March. "The rain had ushered in a sudden drop in temperature—from 51 degrees at noon to a most chilling 39 degrees at the time the funeral began at two o'clock PM.   When the ceremonies were about to conclude at Arlington, the sun would show its face for the first time blessing the day's events but leaving it still a chilly one."[5]   Clergyman recited Tennyson's "Crossing the Bar" as Taft's casket was lowered into an asphalt grave vault. The firing of three volleys commenced with seven rifles sounding off in unison for three rounds each, followed by the 3rd Cavalry's thunderous 21-gun salute, reserved only for the president and former presidents, as a final salute to the former Commander-in-Chief. The flag folded and presented to Mrs. Taft[6] as the bugler, Sergeant Frank Witchey,[7] played those now famous twenty-four notes we reverently sound as "Taps" concluding the committal service. [**Author's side note**, Sgt. Frank Witchey died in 1945 at the age of 53. He was an Army bugler that sounded Taps at the burial of the Unknown Soldier in 1921, two Presidents, Woodrow Wilson (1924) and William Howard Taft (1930), and high-ranking generals of his day.][8]

President Taft's funeral marked the first nationwide radio broadcast of a presidential funeral. With microphones concealed in flowers at the church, the NBC and CBS networks sent Taft's funeral ceremony out to millions. Over 100 stations carried the funeral. The Washington Post wrote "At the time of his retirement from the Supreme Court, he was the most beloved person in America. People described him as having an extraordinary sweetness of disposition, a heart of gold, and being void of jealousy, vindictiveness, malice, or meanness. His charity was like his frame, big and broad."[9]

Why was Taft's funeral so significant? It's the only time I have read after Colonel Cocheu's order in 1918 that a flag was folded for a president and presented to his widow. The first may have been President Theodore Roosevelt who died in 1919, but I have been unable to find a historical account documenting the occasion. Next would have been Warren G. Harding in 1923, then Woodrow Wilson, in 1924. In Wilson's instance, First Lady Edith Wilson, his widow refused a state funeral.[10] Furthermore, I haven't discovered any historical account documenting the folding of the flag at his funeral, which is why Taft's funeral and the testimony of Joseph Gawler's Sons, the funeral home of the presidents, as it is called, is so important. It is the first account that I have found where the flag has been folded and presented to the primary next of kin, and it just so happened to be the account of the first president to be laid to rest at Arlington National Cemetery, the most loved man in a generation, William Howard Taft.

In Memoriam: Technical Sergeant Frack Witchey

(September 11, 1891 – September 30, 1945)

The Maestro of the Trumpet[1]

Arlington, Virginia — Sergeant Frank Witchey, 53, The Maestro of the Trumpet, passed away on September 30, 1945. Frank was a remarkable Army bugler known for his moving renditions of Taps. Born on a farm in Iuka, Kansas, on September 11, 1891, to the late William Franklin Witchey and Delia Bridget Ryan Witchey, of which Frank was one of four children. At the age of nine, he began playing bugles and trumpets and his artistry became evident. He proudly enlisted in the United States Army in 1908. During World War I, he served in France with the Third Cavalry Regiment. Later becoming the sergeant bugler of the regiment, a position he held until his retirement in June 1938.

Frank married the love of his life, Margaret Cecilia Murphy Witchey at Fort Myer on Tuesday, July 20, 1920. They had four children.

On Armistice Day, November 11, 1921, Sgt. Witchey sounded the bugle call to "attention" three times during the **burial ceremony of the Unknown Soldier**[2] at Arlington National Cemetery. His performance was broadcast nationwide, and he followed it with a moving rendition of Taps.

Witchey's bugle was one originally issued to him by the Army. Recognizing the history of the moment, he bought it the day after his performance at the Tomb of the Unknown Soldier from the Army Quartermaster for a mere $2.50 and had it gold-plated and engraved with the names of significant events where he played Taps, becoming known, as the New York Times called it, "the most famous bugle in the United States Army."[3]

Over his nearly three decades of service, Sgt. Witchey sounded Taps at **Other Notable Funerals:** the funerals of President Woodrow Wilson (1924), Lt. Gen. Nelson Miles (1925), Col. William Jennings Bryan (1935), Maj. Gen. Leonard Wood (1927), and former President William Howard Taft (1930).[4]

Sgt. Witchey's final official act was on May 19, 1938, when he sounded Taps in uniform as a tribute to the deceased members of the Third Cavalry Regiment on its 92nd birthday.[5]

He is buried at Arlington National Cemetery in Section 18 among his comrades of World War I. Frank Witchey died at Walter Reed Hospital after a brief heart related illness.[6] His widow, Margaret, is also buried there having died on July 5, 1973.

Sgt. Frank Witchey's bugle may be silent, but its haunting melody continues to resonate, honoring those who served and reminding us of duty and sacrifice, as the legacy of his legend continues.

Chapter 10

A Chord of Three Strands

**"The cords of death entangled me; the torrents of destruction
overwhelmed me. The cords of the grave coiled around me; the
snares of death confronted me."**
- Psalm 18:4-5 (NIV)

Mark Wilson/Getty Images/AFP

The nation began preparing for the most serene funeral it had
ever seen, broadcast live on television worldwide. A diesel
engine powered backhoe made its way down the hill from the
Lee Mansion to the original gravesite of President John F. Kennedy.

A Chord of Three Strands

Now as a funeral director, I am acquainted with a gentleman, Bud Bolin, who hand-dug, with a shovel, graves where Command Sergeant Major Bryant is buried at Williams Cemetery in Winslow, Indiana, and did so for at least 40 years. Imagine, if you will, how much earth this man has moved by hand, moving it from a location just out of sight to a dirt pile with a wheelbarrow. Multiply this amount exponentially, and you will understand how much earth James Parks moved in his lifetime at Arlington National Cemetery. James Parks is the only person buried at Arlington who was also born there. He was born a slave on March 19, 1843, and died on August 21, 1929. He ended his life as a freed man, spending much of his life on the Arlington estate, witnessing the Civil War, building forts on the property, and began work as a grave digger on May 13, 1864, when he helped dig the grave of Private William Christman of Pennsylvania, who had died of rubella, becoming the first military man buried at Arlington.

Now, almost a hundred years later, Clifton Pollard would use his backhoe and dig the grave of the slain president, with Superintendent John Metzler observing. Pollard, operating his machine with surgical precision, resumed digging making a tidy job of it.[1] Digging a grave by hand would require a full day, or at least most of one, but the use of machinery allowed for the excavation of several graves in a single day. While the gravedigger continued his duties, Mrs. Kennedy was busy studying President Lincoln's funeral and planning for this unfortunate historic event. She and Bobby Kennedy went to Arlington on Saturday to look at possible burial locations for her husband, and ultimately decided on a most prominent location, situated just downhill from the Lee Mansion overlooking the Lincoln Memorial and all of Washington-the very view Kennedy had enjoyed with Paul Fuqua on his impromptu visit some eight months earlier.[2]

In Memoriam: Private William Christman
(October 1, 1844 – May 11, 1864)

First Beneath the Oaks at Arlington National Cemetery

Washington, D.C. — William Henry Christman, 19, of Lehigh County Pennsylvania, entered into rest on Wednesday, May 11, 1864. Willaim was born on October 1, 1844, in the Lower Macungie are of Lehigh County, Pennsylvania,[1] to the late Jonas and Mary Christman. He was one of four maybe five children.

William hailed from the rolling hills of Pocono Lake, Pennsylvania where his father, a blacksmith, had instilled in him a sense of honor and duty. When the Civil War erupted in 1861, William's heart swelled with patriotism, and he was eager to join. However, he did not join right away because his older brother, Barnabus, enlisted in the Union Army in June 1861 leaving a teenage William behind to care for the farm and his siblings.[2]

He left behind the anvil and hammer, donning the Union blue, and joined the 67th Pennsylvania Volunteer Infantry Regiment on March 25, 1864. His days became a blur of marching, drilling, and camaraderie. The smell of gunpowder clung to his uniform, and the distant rumble of cannons echoed in his dreams. Hoping to fight in the Battle of the Wilderness, where the earth drank the blood of thousands. However, William was spared chaos, as the war took its toll. Measles swept through the ranks, and William fell ill.

In the sterile confines of Lincoln General Hospital, William lay on a narrow cot. His fever burned, and the faces of fallen comrades haunted him. As news arrived the official order establishing Arlington National Cemetery had not yet been signed, but the need for a burial ground was urgent. The wounded and deceased piled up, their souls yearning for rest.

On May 11, 1864, William Christman breathed his last. His eyes closed, and he slipped away, leaving behind a legacy of sacrifice. The hospital chaplain whispered prayers, and the nurses wept silently. They knew they were witnessing history—the first soldier to find eternal peace in the newly consecrated soil of Arlington.

The sun dipped low as they carried William's body to the chosen spot. The Lee-Custis Mansion loomed nearby, its grandeur a stark contrast to the solemnity of the moment. The earth yielded reluctantly, as if aware of its weighty responsibility. The first shovelful of dirt fell, covering William's form. Others followed, their hands calloused from battle and grief.

The oaks stood witness, their gnarled branches reaching toward heaven. A simple wooden marker at the time bore his name: "Private William Christman, 67th Pennsylvania." The wind whispered secrets to the fallen leaves, promising to remember.

And so, Arlington began—a sanctuary for heroes, a place where valor and sacrifice intertwined. William's spirit lingered, watching over the rows that would soon fill with others like him. His sacrifice paved the way for countless more, each name etched into the collective memory of a grateful nation.

Today, Arlington National Cemetery stretches across rolling hills, its white headstones stretching toward infinity. But it all began with William Christman—a blacksmith's son, a soldier, and the first to rest beneath those ancient oaks. Visitors come, their footsteps hushed, and they pause at his marker. They read his name, trace the letters with reverence, and whisper their gratitude.

And so, Private William Christman lives on—a sentinel of honor, a guardian of memory, forever cradled by the land he helped consecrate.

With the burial site selected, the grave digger, military personnel, and grounds crew sprang into action. As Clifton Pollard was digging the grave, and the grounds crew was raking away leaves, John Metzler received an unexpected request from Mrs. Kennedy. She wanted an eternal flame installed at her husband's grave. In studying for and making preparations for her husband's funeral, Mrs. Kennedy remembered visiting the Tombe du Soldat inconnu, the French Tomb of the Unknown Soldier, and the eternal flame located there under the Arc de Triomphe, when she and President Kennedy made a visit to Paris, France, in 1961.

On the steps of the United States Capitol, huge crowds gathered, and the Secret Service and other law enforcement officials nervously watched the crowd fearing another assassination attempt at the president's funeral. In his memoir, "As I Saw It," then-Secretary of State Dean Rusk wrote about the chaos of not only arranging a funeral but making sure everything went according to plan even as they feared this was just the beginning of more troubles. Some leaders were viewed as more at-risk than others: "We were especially concerned about French President Charles de Gaulle's personal security during the Kennedy funeral," he wrote. "Political tensions were high in France, resulting in threats to his personal safety."[1]

George Ball was the Under Secretary of State at the time, and in his memoir, "The Past Has Another Pattern," echoed Rusk's fears. In addition to fears of a larger plot, there was also the reaction to consider: Would extremist groups take matters into their own hands? Ball also mentioned concerns that de Gaulle would be a target, along with leaders from the Soviet Union. Concern was so great that Ball didn't attend the funeral at all: He wrote that he was instead tasked with standing by as the first line of defense if there was another assassination attempt or other political emergency. He was actually fine with it: "I have a distaste for the pomp and panoply of state funerals," he wrote. "We were treating the dead President as a king, rather than as a warm, human, lively, glittering young American elected by the popular vote of a great nation."[2]

Bettmann/Getty Images

The death watch of Lt. Samuel Brid and his men came to a close. As the president's casket descends the Capitol steps, the Navy Band starts to assemble, playing Hail to the Chief. The Kennedy family stands on the left of the steps, gazing into the Rotunda, while the Joint Chiefs of Staff stands on the right. A very somber, quiet crowd watches as they wait patiently on this cold Monday, November 25, 1963, morning to pay their last respects to their fallen leader. A leader who a few short years earlier won the presidency by a narrow victory over Richard Nixon. A leader who two weeks ago, on November 11, 1963, made his first, and what would be his only formal visit to Arlington National Cemetery placing a wreath at the Tomb of the Unknowns, and a cemetery where he would now be laid to rest. It was also a day that saw two other funerals, including one for his alleged murderer.

As President Kennedy's casket was being taken from the White House to the Capitol, United Press International recorded the mood when news broke of the assassination of gunman Lee Harvey Oswald: "Word of this new act of violence spread rapidly, adding a note of incredulous shock to the mood of mourning."[1] For countless people watching coverage of the funeral and the developing story of the assassination at home, the word didn't need to spread — they saw it happen. When Jack Ruby shot and killed Oswald on live television, it became the first real, televised homicide — and millions of people were watching. The ratings for daytime television were through the roof over these two murders and their successive course of events and funerals of President Kennedy and Officer Tippit. As it should be, and only as a footnote, the alleged assassin Lee Harvey Oswald was buried in a private ceremony, with reporters in attendance acting as pallbearers. Oswald was interred at Rose Hill Memorial Park in Ft. Worth, Texas, with his grave marked by a flat stone that simply reads Oswald. These three men, Kennedy, Oswald, and Tippit, will forever be intertwined as a chord of three strands ensnared by the coils of the grave, and the date of their burial.

Bettmann/Getty Images

Also buried on that brisk Monday was a man just doing his job, Dallas Police Officer J.D. Tippit, who was working his normal beat in a South Oak Cliff neighborhood in Dallas, when President John F. Kennedy was shot. Within minutes, word went out to all police officers, with a vague description of Oswald as the president's possible shooter. About forty-five minutes after the president's assassination, Officer Tippit had spotted Oswald walking hurriedly then suspiciously changing directions. Fearing apprehension, Oswald pulled a .38 revolver from under his jacket and fired at least four shots at nearly point-blank range, striking Officer Tippit in the chest and right temple area. He then fled into the movie theater, the Texas Theater, where the police arrested him without causing any further casualties. Two eyewitnesses to the shooting later identified Oswald as Tippit's killer, and seven others saw Oswald running from the scene, carrying a pistol. The police arrested Oswald at the Texas Theater after he failed to purchase a theater ticket, prompting the ticket seller to report a suspicious-looking man. When he was arrested, Oswald still had the .38 caliber revolver on him that he used to kill Officer Tippit, ballistics tests later identified that revolver as the gun that killed Tippit. A couple of thousand people attended his funeral that afternoon, and it's safe to say that while Jackie Kennedy was burying her husband on the east coast, Tippit was in her thoughts. Mrs. Kennedy later sent Tippit's widow a framed photo of the Kennedy family, writing, "There is another bond we share. We must remind our children all the time what brave men their fathers were."[2]

It should also be noted that Officer Tippit's funeral was also televised in Dallas, Texas, on that Monday, November 25, 1963. The funeral was held at Berkley Hills Baptist Church. One block away from the church, at Laurel Land Cemetery, a fifteen-man motorcycle escort leads the way to his burial. Officer Tippit had an honor guard of policemen instead of military personnel at his funeral. Although he was entitled to a military service, J.D. Tippit was a World War II United States Army veteran, enlisting on July 21, 1944. He volunteered to be a paratrooper in the 513th Parachute Infantry Regiment, part of the 17th Airborne Division. He saw combat in Operation Varsity, the airborne crossing of the Rhine River in March 1945, earning a Bronze Star,[3] and remained on active duty until June 20, 1946. His fellow Dallas police officers performed a walk of honor as the funeral began, and six of his Dallas police comrades acted as his pallbearers. It is unclear as to whether there is any evidence that there was a military honor guard, draping of the flag, firing of three volleys, the sounding of Taps, or presentation and the folding of the flag at his funeral. What I can say based on the video evidence of his funeral is that the Blue was just as deep for him as the military was for President Kennedy.

Photo by Ben Saunders July 8, 2014, at Laurel Land Cemetery, Dallas, TX.

In Memoriam: J.D. Tippit
(September 18, 1924 – November 22, 1963)

Dallas Police Officer

Annona, Texas — J.D. Tippit, 39, working his normal beat in the south Oak Cliff section of Dallas, Texas, when President John F. Kennedy was shot, was gunned down in the streets of Dallas, Texas, by Kennedy's alleged, Lee Harvey Oswald, on November 22, 1963, less than two hours after President John F. Kennedy was assassinated. His murder led to the eventual capture of the alleged assassin at the Texas Theater. He will forever be connected to the American tragedy of that fateful fall day.

Born on September 18, 1944, in Annona, Texas, to the late Edgar Lee and Lizzie Mae Rush Tippit. J.D. was the eldest of six children. He grew up on a rural cotton farm, where he developed a love for hunting, fishing, and horseback riding. His father gave him the initials J.D. as a first name; they have no meaning other than to honor a character, "J.D. of the Mountains,"[1] his father read about in a high school novel. He attended Fulbright High School through the tenth grade but dropped out to help on the family farm.

When World War II broke out, J.D.'s father left to work in a war plant in Hooks, Texas, leaving the 15-year-old J.D. to operate the family farm. In 1944, the family moved to Birmingham, Texas, to be close to his father's war factory work. His commitment to service led him to enlist in the United States Army, where he volunteered for the paratroopers following basic training at Camp Wolters, Texas. After completing airborne training at Fort Benning, Georgia, in late 1944, J.D. was shipped to England and assigned to the 17th Airborne Division as an infantryman. In January 1945, he was assigned to the 513th Battalion (Parachute Infantry Regiment), 17th Airborne Division, and baptized into combat in France. On March 24, 1945, he parachuted with the 17th Division across the Rhine River near Eiersfordt, Germany, making his one and only combat jump, earning a Bronze Star Medal for his bravery. When the war ended in September 1945, Tippit was sent home and honorably discharged, returning to his family farm in Red River County, Texas.

On December 26, 1946, J.D. married his high school sweetheart, Marie Frances Gasway, in Clarksville, Texas, and together they raised their three children: Allan, Brenda, and Curtis. He found work at Sears Roebuck in Dallas, Texas, but shortly afterward, he decided to return to farming in Red River County. After several years of farming, he decided to return to Dallas in 1952, where he found a job with the city police. Assigned badge no. 848, J.D. took to police work naturally and soon developed a flair for spotting troublemakers. Fellow police officers would remark about his instinctive ability to spot suspicious people who were about to make trouble. In 1956, J.D. received a commendation for using this ability to kill a gunman in a bar before the man could kill the police officers.

Officer J.D. Tippit was laid to rest at Laurel Land Cemetery, one block from where his funeral was held at Berkley Hills Baptist Church, on Monday, November 25, 1963, the same day that President Kennedy was interred at Arlington National Cemetery. Over 1,500 mourners attended the funeral, and it was also broadcast on television. J.D. Tippit was later given a "posthumous Meritorious Citation and Medal for Valor from the Dallas Police Department."[2]

Today, we honor "a lovable guy" Officer J.D. Tippit as his legacy lives on as a symbol of courage, selflessness, and the sacrifices made by law enforcement officers in service to their communities. May he rest in peace.

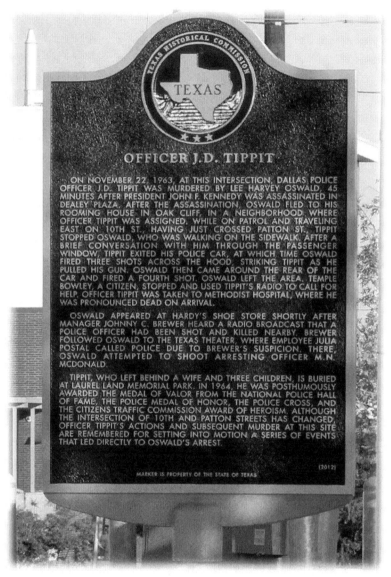

Photo by Texas Historical Commission[3]

All those watching in total silence shared a single feeling as this day of mourning in Washington reached its climax: shock. The feelings of sadness and sorrow for the president and his family, and the silent glares and blank stares of those lining the streets of Washington, DC. For those who witnessed the events of President Kennedy's funeral, there was an eerie silence. As an entire nation mourned the loss felt by every American, few truly knew the details of what was going on behind the scenes. I'm not sure I can even grasp all the moving parts from President Kennedy's assassination to what was going on behind the scenes in planning his funeral. Scholars and eyewitnesses have penned several books and articles that chronicle the events from beginning to end. The three days after his murder shows just how quickly his funeral came and went.

National Archives/Getty Images

One of life's more terrifying tendencies is one where things change completely, terribly, and permanently, all in the blink of an eye. On November 22, 1963, the assassination of the American President took place on a global scale. As Yoda might say in Star Wars, unexpected it was, unbelievable it was, and unfortunate. For those who remember the day, it was similar to the attack and shock of September 11, 2001, as people watched it on live television in horror.

A Chord of Three Strands

In a generation where news is literally streamed to our fingertips through our "magic" phones, smart phones, and the internet, we get news shared lightning fast, instantly. However, that was not the case in 1963 when these events occurred. Television was the technology and the emerging competition of the news networks, as families usually gathered around the television to see the news and experience the happenings of the day. For many Americans watching, it was their first opportunity to witness the pursuit of justice, the live broadcast of the alleged assassin's murder, and the ensuing funerals. Today, very few streaming services or television networks would suspend their programming, or even commercials, to cover such an event. Then again it might be like the 1998 movie The Truman Show, where Jim Carrey played a man named Truman Burbank, whose entire life was filmed twenty-four hours a day and broadcast live on television. The assassination of John F. Kennedy and the thirst for information about the who, what, where, when, why, and how was like watching a tragic reality show. The news back then was broadcast on the day Kennedy was shot with no commercials and no interruptions. This was a significant event that witnessed the mourning of a nation and its impact around the world. Remember, this was a time when, despite who the president was and his political affiliations, he was still the president and the leader of American ideals. You didn't have all the divisiveness that you have today. According to people growing up during that time, everyone was glued to their televisions around the clock, much like watching the 24-hour news cycle of today. And yes, the nation mourned, but none more than the illusion of Camelot, which had the Kennedy family at center stage, was now shattered by an assassin's bullet(s).

Grief is a deeply personal thing, and no two people grieve in quite the same way. No one can tell another person how to grieve, when to grieve, or how long the grief process will take. I tell people when I speak to dismiss the committal service at the cemetery that "mourning endures for a night, but joy is coming in the morning." I don't know which morning, or when, but it will happen. Could you imagine being Jackie Kennedy as she found her grief and mourning thrust upon the global stage? She had just lost her son, Patrick, on August 7, 1963, and now her husband whom she loved. The world was watching, and she handled everything with such elegance and grace. Mrs. Kennedy later told Life Magazine, "Most people think having the world share in your grief lessens your burden. It magnifies it."[1]

Still, it was her very public farewell that was credited with guiding a nation that didn't quite know how to deal with televised tragedy, the assassination of a young, charismatic president, and the unknown that came next. The president's death was widely publicized. Could you imagine the amount of misinformation or "fake news" that would be spread if his murder would have happened today, and not just the conspiracy theories, those would be exponential? And the amount of internet sleuths that would come out of the woodwork to make a name for themselves to solve the crime of the century.

The president's funeral literally began the day he died, or at least preparations did. As public as his state funeral was, the cameras did not capture every detail in its preparation. Some of those details include, being put in his first casket, a bronze casket secured from O'Neal Funeral Home in Dallas, Texas, being flown back to Bethesda Naval Hospital, where an autopsy took place, the clandestine employment of the funeral home Jospeh Gawler's and Sons, who performed embalming, dressing, re-casketing in a new mahogany casket, and completed the restoration work of the president's head. The reading of books is where people find the details that the cameras didn't always catch, but in the 21st century with the advancement of technology could you imagine the amount of cell phones that would have secretly recorded things like the initial assessment and treatment at Parkland Hospital, or the autopsy? You would not be able to stop what could become infinite leaks of information in such a high-profile case.

Bettmann/Getty Images

Two weeks after his formal visit to Arlington National Cemetery on November 11, 1963, to lay a wreath at the Tomb of the Unknown Soldiers, John F. Kennedy embarked on a mission to win the south by visiting Texas to deliver a few speeches and layout his plans for the future in a bid to "help heal a rift in his party, and to hold the state for the Democrats in 1964,"[2] and get re-elected. Suddenly, on November 22, 1963, during a visit to Dallas, Texas, with what sounded like several firecrackers popping, around 12:30 p.m., the president was shot. Many living during this time may remember Walter Cronkite, the CBS News anchor, coming on television to deliver the following news, "From Dallas, Texas, the flash apparently official. President Kennedy died at 1 p.m. central standard time, 2 o'clock eastern standard time some thirty-eight minutes ago."[3] Despite the chaos at Parkland Hospital due to Texas State law mandating Coroner Earl Rose to perform a postmortem examination (autopsy) prior to the body being released to the family or transporting it out of state, President Kennedy's body was wrapped in sheets placed inside a casket, secured from Dallas based Oneal Funeral Home located at 3206 Oak Lawn Ave. in Dallas, Texas, and transported by the Secret Service to Love Field, and flown back to Washington, D.C. aboard Air Force One.

During a program at the LBJ Presidential Library on November 12, 2013, Sid Davis, a long-time journalist and witness to the swearing-in of President Lyndon Johnson aboard Air Force One, gave this account in his own words. Mr. Davis was working for the Westinghouse Broadcasting Company in Washington, D.C., when these events occurred:

"I was on the air broadcasting the president's death when the White House travel office person grabbed me by my suit collar from behind and said I had to go with him. And I said I'm on the air, I'm not leaving, I'm not leaving damn it, I'm on the air. He said, "Well, we need a pool." I said, "Well, get Pierpoint; it's his turn." I mean we're arguing over the biggest story of the century and I'm not wanting to go to cover it. It's crazy. Yeah, I couldn't believe it when I look back it's like what was I fighting over but I did go, and we picked up Merriman Smith and Chuck Roberts of Newsweek and went down through the hospital and they had an unmarked police car waiting for us. They said we're going out to Air Force One. We took off, and we were doing 60 to 70 miles per hour through Dallas over curbs, driveways, and lawns, no matter how this police officer could get there through backyards trying to get to Air Force One before it took off back to Washington.

When we arrived at the airport, Mrs. Kennedy had just arrived with the casket, and they were in the process of loading it onto the aircraft. They had to carry it up the incline of the rear stairs. This was a 707—a big airplane, a majestic airplane—because Mrs. Kennedy and Jack Kennedy had helped design the colors. The colors you see on Air Force One today and the lettering were designed by Mrs. Kennedy and Jack Kennedy. It was a brand-new airplane that came to his administration, so they had a piece of it in history as well. They had to knock four handles off the casket because they were sticking out and they couldn't get it into the airplane. So, the Secret Service got an axe somewhere, and they knocked off the handles, and were able to manage to get the thing in there.

I went around the side of the airplane with Merriman Smith and Chuck Roberts, climbed in from another side of the aircraft, came from the front end of the plane, and went back to the midship. I saw Mrs. Johnson and President Johnson in there with a group of people. President Johnson was talking to Marie Fehmer, his secretary. I talked to Marie for a little bit, and she said they were trying to assemble and get a judge from downtown to come out and do the swearing-in. Mrs. Kennedy was in the rear with the casket. Marie told me when the president arrived on the aircraft which was maybe fifteen minutes before that of Mrs. Kennedy's arrival. The first thing he did was he asked for a hot cup of vegetable soup, and he said to Marie, "I've lived a year since this morning" and then he told her, and I overheard him tell her, that I would like for you to go and ask Mrs. Kennedy if she will stand with us at the swearing-in. And Marie went back and talked to Mrs. Kennedy or sent a message back and the message came back "Yes, I will come but I want a few minutes to compose myself." So, we waited, and by this time, the room was stifling hot, probably 120 degrees, because it was sitting under a hot sun and only one engine had been running to keep the electronics going.

It was probably a few minutes before Mrs. Kennedy appeared in the doorway and that's when the sobbing, the quiet sobbing by the young Kennedy staff. You have to understand these were young people in their 20s and 30s who had made the long march to the campaign and made him president, then they'd gone through the Bay of Pigs and the Cuban Missile Crisis and he was their hero, and now he was gone. And the sadness of this scene was evident on the faces of these young women with their mascara streaking their cheeks as they were waiting for Mrs. Kennedy. Once she came into the room, the crying became almost unbearable among everyone. The sobbing was just, uh, unbelievable. Despite everyone's sobs and crying, Mrs. Kennedy did not. She had composed herself and was standing in the doorway to the back of the plane, and we could see her.

President Johnson left his place in the middle of the room, walked over to her, took her by both hands, and he walked backward. Sort of backward, he took her and placed her to his left in the center of the room, and he pulled Mrs. Johnson over to his right. He asked for a glass of ice water, and Marie brought him some ice water. Then he looked at federal judge Sarah T. Hughes, who was appointed to the bench by President Kennedy in October 1961. Johnson said, "proceed."

Now as a pool reporter, it's my responsibility to write everything I saw. I'm just a rinky-dink reporter who covered the police station in Ohio, and now I'm covering one of the biggest stories in the world. And I have to tell you that I was worried that I wouldn't get everything I had to get because it was such an important story, but I examined her (Mrs. Kennedy) pretty carefully. I saw blood on her legs. It had congealed on both legs. On her skirt and blouse, I saw blood and speckles of brain matter. I noticed that she was unblinking. She was in grief, but she had her wits about her. She knew exactly what was going on, and she understood everything that was going on. I don't think she would have come forward had she not known what was going on. I think in the annals of history this was one of the most courageous things I've ever seen between a President and another first lady.

Where she, I believe having to suffer from probably the worst thing that could happen to a married couple losing your husband in a murderous situation—leaving the casket to come up front to attend the ceremony took a lot of courage. And I think Mrs. Kennedy felt it was important for her to be in that room. At the same time, I thought that the gesture by President Johnson asking her to come forward if she would like to stand with us because he knew the circumstances. I think that the opportunities for greatness were there in that setting for this so brief of time. The compassion shown by President Johnson, I've never seen it since. He invited all the members of the Kennedy staff on the airplane who wanted to come into the compartment. They jammed the compartment as close as they could and he asked people to get closer together so that more of the Kennedy people could attend the thing. His behavior—I never saw anybody who was more resolved than what he had to do. He had his wits totally about him.

He went over as soon as the oath of office was finished and kissed Mrs. Johnson, then he kissed Mrs. Kennedy on the cheek, then he went over to President Kennedy's secretary Evelyn Lincoln and shook her hand and held her tightly and said he was sorry this had happened. Then he fended off almost any effort on the part of anyone to come up and congratulate him, which was another sign of, I think, his greatness, as he did not want this to turn into a celebration. The somber mood that existed from the beginning was there at the end. My friend Chuck Roberts, one of the others in the press pool, was standing near me and went over to President Johnson and shook his hand. Chuck looked up at the president, who stood six feet four inches tall, and said, "Godspeed, Mr. President," and I thought I wish I could have said something like that it was so appropriate for him to have said that and then President Johnson's first order was let's get airborne because they knew they had to move that airplane out of Dallas to get back to Washington."[4]

Although the government and most funeral homes have an outline for state funerals, Jackie Kennedy insisted on several additions that were modeled after the funeral of Abraham Lincoln, including her decision to hold vigil in the East Room of the White House, laying in state at the Capitol Rotunda, walking behind the caisson to Saint Matthew's Catholic Cathedral for requiem mass, to having the Irish Guard perform their silent drill at the graveside known as the Queen Anne Drill (the first and only time that a foreign army has been invited and delivered those honors at the graveside of a United States President, but more importantly she wanted an eternal flame to forever burn at Jack's grave at Arlington National Cemetery. Before that, though, JFK's body was rushed back to Washington, D.C. — and Jackie refused to change out of her bloodstained pink suit until the morning after the assassination, when she and the president's casket returned to the White House's East Room. (That outfit has since been donated to the National Archives but will not be displayed until at least 2103.)[5]

Without a doubt, it was a military operation. Lt. Bird and his honor guard of men representing each branch of the armed forces were now escorting the coffin out of the Capitol as the 21-hour death watch ended. The nation watched as the president's flag-draped casket was carried down the Capitol steps and placed on the waiting caisson, strapped down, and transported to Saint Matthew's Roman Catholic Cathedral while Mrs. Kennedy, Ted, and Bobby Kennedy walked the nearly three and a half miles behind the caisson. The Marine Corps. Band led the procession,[6] which included ten bagpipers from the Scottish Black Watch (Royal Highland Regiment)[7] (on a side note it sounds like something out of Game of Thrones like the Knight's watch.) Then there were the cadets of the Irish Defense Force and military units, dignitaries from the United States Congress, and heads of other nations Around 800,000 people witnessed the funeral procession in person, while millions around the world watched it on television or listened by radio. Six white horses pulled the caisson that carried the body of President Kennedy as he lay in his casket, traveling to the requiem funeral mass at St. Matthews. Most catholic services that I have attended last about an hour or so, but President Kennedy's funeral rites lasted exactly one hour and 16 minutes. The majority of the service, conducted by Cardinal Richard Cushing, was performed in Latin. Afterwards, the funeral procession for one of the nation's most endearing presidents was being escorted, approximately four miles, to Arlington National Cemetery.

Bettmann/Getty Images

One interesting note, as with most funerals, there is silence during the service, but on this fall Monday, it was more like a golf event where everyone was quiet. People by their very nature are pretty loud, but when the estimated quarter of a million mourners converged on Washington, D.C., to pay their final respects to President Kennedy, one of the things witnesses reported and recorded was the silence. In their book "Four Days: The Historical Record of the Death of President Kennedy," United Press International and American Heritage Magazine documented how quiet the crowds were, lines of people that stretched for miles remained silent listening to the sounds of drums, bagpipers, and music played by the Marine Corps. Band: "As they turned to look at the flag-covered coffin, [mourners] seldom showed tears, and most had a kind of blankness."[8]

The crowd's silence was compared to that that had settled over the city during another presidential funeral. An 1865 newspaper report documenting Abraham Lincoln's funeral was reportedly one that could have been written about Kennedy's: "The ... procession, with a slow and measured tread, moved from the home of mourning on its mission with the remains of the illustrious dead. Despite the enormous crowd, the silence was profound. To a certain extent, the entire nation joined in on the silence. Nielsen reported (via Reuters) that 81% of homes with a television were watching the funeral. When surveys were conducted later, the majority of people who watched the funeral reported having a physical reaction to it, and perhaps an even better measure of how the nation mourned along with the Kennedy family was when the televisions were turned off. A massive drop in viewers was noted at the same time that JFK's funeral mass started: America, it seemed, had gone to their own religious sanctuaries, and prayed."[9]

As God Bless America played, President Kennedy's casket was placed back on the caisson for the final time. The requiem mass ended and the journey to his final resting place began. Members of the armed forces surround the caisson, accompanied by the presidential flag.

Bettmann/Getty Images

One of the most iconic sights of John F. Kennedy's funeral dates back to that of George Washington. The caparisoned horse or riderless horse, boots turned backward in the stirrups, is reminiscent of a period in history when horses were sacrificed to accompany their riders into the afterlife.[10] On this day, for President Kennedy, that horse was an

Army Quartermaster-issued gelding named Black Jack, who was anything but submissive throughout the funeral procession.

Black Jack and his handler, Private First-Class Arthur Carlson, escorted the president's caisson and casket throughout the funeral parade, and not only did the crowds and the sound of a grate being dragged along the pavement completely spook him, but he also danced, pranced, and pawed for miles. Carlson was unable to do anything; as protocol dictated, he basically had to stay silent and keep walking, with 1,200 pounds of pent-up panic beside him. Carlson's discipline was impressive, and even more so when it's taken into account that along the way, Black Jack actually stomped on his foot outside St. Matthews. He recalled to WSFA News 12, "I was actively afraid that the horse would get away from me."[11] When Black Jack retired from military service in 1973, Mrs. Kennedy, demonstrating that she too had not forgotten his service, bought him. His longtime human companion, Nancy Schado, described his uncharacteristically difficult behavior on the day of the funeral as something deep: "He wasn't used to assassinations. He was showing his objection to what happened. Animals sense things."[12] Black Jack passed away in 1976 and was interred at Fort Meyer, close to Arlington National Cemetery, after being cremated.

Just prior to their departure from Saint Matthews, President Kennedy's daughter Caroline was holding her mother's hand, with her uncle, Ted Kennedy, standing behind. Robert Kennedy, the United States Attorney General, stood next to Mrs. Kennedy, and little John, Jr., who turned three the day his father was buried, stood with others as the caisson was about to depart. Mrs. Kennedy leaned down to say something to little John. What happened next was iconic.

Apic/Getty Images

On the final leg, a caisson carried the casket to Arlington National Cemetery for burial. Moments after the casket was carried down the front steps of the cathedral, Jacqueline Kennedy whispered to her son, after which he saluted his father's coffin; the image, taken by photographer Stan Stearns, became an iconic representation of the 1960s. (The children were deemed to be too young to attend the final burial service, so this was the point where the children said goodbye to their father.)[13] Dan Farrell, a photographer for the New York Daily News, also captured this iconic photo. One of the sights that was not seen by the television cameras was the press box, which was packed with journalists and photographers looking to get any vantage point they could of the funeral procession. Stan Stearns said this about John Junior's salute. "As the caisson was rolling out to Arlington Cemetery, I asked every photographer I could if they had the salute. Duh! Nobody saw it. Everyone I talked to had been concentrating on Jackie and the caisson." Stearns, however, had seen Jackie pause to say something to her young son, and with the forethought that makes a really, really good photographer, he kept his camera on the little boy. "One exposure on a roll of 36 exposures," he reflected later.[14]

(Photo Credit: © Wally McNamee/CORBIS/Corbis via Getty Images)

As the caisson carrying President Kennedy's flag draped coffin moves towards Arlington National Cemetery, the Marine Band plays "Onward Christian Soldiers." The flag at Arlington is at half-staff as a crowd awaits the arrival of the funeral cortege. The route runs from St. Matthews Cathedral down M Street Northwest, through the campus of George Washington University on 23rd Street Northwest, down to Parkway Drive, passing the Lincoln Memorial, crossing the Potomac River on Memorial Drive into Virginia, and hanging a left on Eisenhower Drive before turning right on McClellan Drive and entering through McClellan Gate into Arlington National Cemetery. Several hours after the funeral cortege disbanded. It took several hours for the lengthy and extremely slow-moving procession to go just a few miles.

Echoes of Valor: The Timeless Tradition of Military Funerals in America

As Mrs. Kennedy and Robert Kennedy exited their limousine and took their positions, the United States Air Force bagpipers played Mist Over the Mountain as they slowly moved toward the gravesite. Robert and Jackie Kennedy stood nearby, observing as the flag-draped casket was being removed from the caisson. The military honor guard moved step-by-step, precisely as they had practiced the night before. Cardinal Cushing led the pall bearers carrying the flag-draped casket of the president to the grave. The Irish Defense Forces stood in salute, while members of the armed services stood at attention. Military jets streaked over the assembled throng as the honor guard placed the casket on the lowering device over the grave. Attorney General Robert F. Kennedy and Mrs. Jacqueline Kennedy were positioned near the grave, and as pallbearers removed the flag from the casket and held it over the grave with such discipline, Air Force One made a flyby, dipping its wings in salute. The Irish Guard then conducts their silent drill, known as the Queen Anne Drill, at the graveside before following orders to march away. French President Charles de Gaulle, other heads of state, and other dignitaries gathered to salute the fallen leader as Cardinal Cushing began the committal service by sprinkling holy water and blessing the grave of the martyred president.

After Cardinal Cushing's final words, the twenty-one-gun salute commenced as thunderous booms of artillery fire erupted rattling the windows of the Custis Lee Mansion. Cardinal Cushing offers a prayer, then blesses the casket again and offers the Lord's Prayer. Jackie, Teddy (Edward), and Bobby Kennedy approach the coffin. The firing party, deployed above the president's grave, stiffened at Sergeant Malcom's command, raised their M-1 rifles to port arms in one fluid motion, and swung them into position firing, executing a perfect three-round volley[15] in salute to this Navy veteran who happened to be President. Once the firing of the three volleys concluded, Sergeant Keith Clarke stood and sounded a most interesting rendering of Taps cracking the sixth note as if the bugle and bugler were crying or in mourning at this somber moment with the nation watching and with ordinary citizens in the crowd expressing their grief.

As the Navy hymn "Eternal Father, Strong to Save was played, the flag was folded by the eight servicemen acting as pall bearers. Without a wrinkle, the flag crisply passed down the line of eight men, resolved into a perfect blue triangle in the white-gloved hands of Specialist Mayfield. Clutching the ensign to his heart, Mayfield stepped smartly across the turf to Arlington Nation Cemetery Superintendent, John Metzler, who took the flag and held it while Cardinal Cushing blessed the eternal flame, still inert in its evergreen bed. When Cushing was done, Mrs. Kennedy stepped forward to accept the flag from Metzler, who offered it with these words: "Mrs. Kennedy, this flag is presented to you in the name of a most mournful nation." He felt a catch in his throat. "Please accept it." She took the ensign, her eyes filling with tears behind the black veil. "She did not speak," Metzler said. "I do not believe that she could at that moment."[16]

An Irish cadet honor guard, with arms outstretched, stand in formation as the U.S. flag is lifted from the coffin of President John F. Kennedy during his funeral services at Arlington National Cemetery in Arlington, Virginia, on November 25, 1963. The cadets, 18- and 19-year-old soldiers, had been whisked from their remote barracks in County Kildare the day before and were flown to the U.S. to perform a special ceremonial drill at the funeral of the slain president. He had been captivated by the drill when he saw it performed in Dublin months earlier. (Library of Congress)

The eternal flame. There is nothing else like it in history. The idea for an eternal flame came from President and Mrs. Kennedy's trip to Paris, France, and the French Tomb of the Unknown. An ever-burning reminder and one of the most powerful symbols of John F. Kennedy's legacy. The moment was somber and just as powerful as its imagery, but behind the scenes, it had been a wild scramble to get the temporary flame installed. The Army Corps of Engineers was under a tremendous amount of pressure to get this done in less than twenty-four hours. Superintendent John Metzler found out about Mrs. Kennedy's request around 3 o'clock p.m. on Sunday, November 24, 1963. This is the afternoon before President Kennedy's funeral. According to Lt. General Walter K. Wilson Jr.'s book, "Engineer Memoirs," (via the U.S. Army Corps of Engineers), the hurried work was done from scratch even as the lying-in-state had begun. The flame was cobbled together — there wasn't even time for plans to be drawn up — and was based around a propane tank and a tiki torch. Thirty hours and one test-lighting later, Jackie lit the eternal flame.[17]

Robert Poole said in his book On Hallowed Ground: The Story of Arlington National Cemetery, "While workers at Arlington dug a trench for the gas line, army engineers welded the basket and torch into a single unit. The device was delivered to the cemetery by nine p.m. Sundy and set in place at the head of Kennedy's grave. The gas tank, hidden in a thicket of bamboo near the Lee mansion, would be operated by an army sergeant, ready to open the valve on a signal from graveside.[18] Fresh-cut pine boughs were heaped around the burner to hide the unsightly contrivance. With all elements in place, the patchwork creation was ready for a test run. A burst of light flared on the dark hillside. The eternal flame was up and running by midnight."[19] At the conclusion of the president's funeral, Cardinal Cushing commits the president's body. Mrs. Kennedy then steps forward, takes the torch, and lights the eternal flame. She passes the torch to Robert Kennedy, who symbolically does the same, and he then passes it to his other brother Edward (Teddy) who does the same. Fleeing to their awaiting cars to receive dignitaries after the service, Mrs. Kennedy remained stoic. Cardinal Cushing walked over to President Kennedy's mother, Rose Kennedy, to offer her some comfort. Only one thing remained and that was the lowering of the casket into the ground and sealing in the vault, which was done shortly after three-thirty p.m.

Wally McNamee/Getty Images

Only the second president to be buried at Arlington National Cemetery, but a ceremony that will not be forgotten by those attending that day—a day that changed how we honor our dead forever. As Mrs. Kennedy and her entourage headed back across the Potomac, Superintendent John Metzler made some observations, "Practically all of the dignitaries were either filing by or just standing looking at the casket as though in a trance, Ever so slowly they moved off as though they were reluctant to leave...The first sergeant of the Special Forces...stood quietly by the head of the grave, removed his hat, and placed it on the frame of the eternal flame. He saluted and departed." Others spontaneously followed suit, leaving hats and medals by the grave.[20] Thus began the swarm of thousands who flooded the gates of Arlington to pay their respects to the late president and the other soldiers buried there, a most hallowed ground, and a sacred place. It is fair to say that every soldier buried at Arlington is receiving the same type of honors. What I mean is that, throughout this book, I have endeavored to demonstrate or present the origins of the four components of a military service.

Colonel Cocheu ordered in 1918 that deceased soldiers are to arrive with their flag-draped coffin, and later, it's folded and presented to the next of kin. The firing party presents arms and fires three volleys over the grave; while the bugler sounds Taps. Today, the U.S. military fires a 21-gun salute in honor of a national flag, the sovereign or chief of state of a foreign nation, a member of a reigning royal family, and the president, ex-presidents, and president-elect of the United States.[21]

President Kennedy's death marked the end of one era and the beginning of another, the Vietnam War. President Johnson would send thousands of troops to Vietnam including some of the best officers from the Old Guard at Fort Myer who served during the funeral of President Kennedy. "Among those who so eagerly joined the fight was fresh-faced, patriotic 1st Lt. Sam Bird, who had so ably headed the casket team for Kennedy's funeral. Promoted to captain, Bird led a combat company in fierce fighting until 1967, when his helicopter came under heavy enemy fire. Several rounds hit Bird, including one that blew away a quarter of his skull. By some miracle, Bird survived the brain injury, living another seventeen years. He was greatly diminished but still proud of the way his men had performed for President Kennedy in November 1963.[22]

In Memoriam: Major Samuel Richard Bird
(January 27, 1940 – October 18, 1984)

Honor Guard Commander at Funeral of President John F. Kennedy

---

Wichita, Kansas — Samuel Richard Bird, 44, of Wichita, Kansas, entered into rest on Thursday, October 18, 1984, surrounded by his loving family. Sam was born on January 27, 1940, in Wichita, Kansas, to the late Richard Ely Bird and Pauline Frances Houston Bird. He was their only child.

Sam was a graduate of the Missouri Military Academy in 1957, where he received the Legion of Honor for industry, integrity, and abiding loyalty, and was a company commander his senior year. In 1961, he graduated with honors from the prestigious military academy, the Citadel, and received a commission as a second lieutenant in the United States Army.

He attended infantry school, then Ranger School. He was the officer-in-charge of the casket detail, or honor guard, of the Old Guard, assigned to guard and President John F. Kennedy's casket.

After graduating from Airborne School and becoming an Airborne Ranger, Sam Bird received a promotion to captain in 1965. He had a distinguished military career, earning numerous medals and meritorious service awards including 2-Bronze Stars, National Defense Service Medal, the Air Medal, Vietnam Service Medal, Army Good Conduct Medal, and the Army Presidential Unit Citation, just to name a few. (Note: From this author's point of view, he should have been awarded the Purple Heart.) Despite the number of officer's deaths in Vietnam, he was a "soldier's soldier," always putting the welfare of his men first and, unlike so many other officers in the military, he never had them do anything that he himself was unwilling to do.

Sam was an overcomer. Sam's 27th birthday coincided with his assignment to Bravo Company on his final day in Vietnam, January 27, 1967. His men had secretly planned a birthday party and even arranged to have a cake flown in. They were going to "pay back the old man." However, orders were issued for Bravo to lead an airmobile assault on a North Vietnamese regimental headquarters. Sam's helicopter was about to touch down at the attack point when it was ripped by enemy fire. His left ankle and right leg were shattered by slugs. Another struck the left side of his head, removing nearly a quarter of his skull. He spent several months recovering at the VA Hospital in Memphis, TN, which left him blind in his left eye and partially in his right, confined to a wheel for the rest of his life. Despite the pain, he persevered and battled to regain control of his right arm, neck, and back, enabling him to sit upright, and his speech function also improved over time.

Few men knew it, but he had been in charge of a special honors unit of the Old Guard, which serves at the Tomb of the Unknown Soldier in Arlington National Cemetery, and participates in the Army's most solemn ceremonies. He was the kind of guy whose eyes would mist during the singing of the National Anthem. Sam figured patriotism was just a natural part of being an American. But he knew that morale was a function not so much of inspiration as of good boots, dry socks, extra ammo, and hot meals. Sam's philosophy was to put his troops first. On that foundation, he built respect, one brick at a time. His men ate first; he ate last. Instead of merely learning their names, he made it a point to get to know the men. A lot of the soldiers were high school dropouts and would-be tough guys, just a few years younger than himself. Some were scared, and a few were still in partial shock at being in a shooting war.

Sam patiently worked on their pride and self-confidence. Yet there was never any doubt as to who was in charge. An officer once said of him, "Sam can dress a man down till his ears burn, and the next minute that same guy is eager to follow him into Hell."[1] He praised his men in public and criticized them in private.

In Memoriam

He had the support of his loving and wonderful family. In 1972, he married his high school sweetheart, Annette Okarche Blazie. They built a house like Sam had dreamed of — red brick with a flagpole out front. He had developed the habit of addressing God as "Sir" and spoke to him often. He never asked to be healed. While saying grace at the table, he thanked God for sending him Annette, and for "making it possible for me to live at home in a free country."

In 1976, he and Annette traveled to The Citadel for his 15th class reunion. World War II hero General Mark Clark, the school's president emeritus, asked about his wounds and said, "On behalf of your country, I want to thank you for all you did." With pride, Sam answered "Sir, it was the least I could do." Later, Annette chided him gently for understating the case. After all, he had sacrificed his health and career in Vietnam. Sam gave her an incredulous look. "I had friends who didn't come back," he said. "I'm enjoying the freedoms they died for."[2]

Historian William Manchester described him as "a lean, sinewy Kansan, the kind of American youth whom Congressmen dutifully praise each Fourth of July and whose existence many, grown jaded by years on the Hill, secretly doubt." There can be no doubt about Sam—about who he was, how he lived, and how he led. Major Samuel R. Bird was buried on a fall afternoon, as they say, "with honors," including the folding and presentation of the flag to his wife, Annette, at Maple Grove Cemetery in Wichita, Kansas. As his honor guard walked from his final resting place, they knew they were the honored ones. Thank you, Major Bird, for your devoted service.

Chapter 11

In Honored Glory

On fame's eternal camping ground
Their silent tents to spread,
And glory guards, with solemn round
The bivouac of the dead.[1]
-from the poem Bivouac of the Dead by Colonel Theodore O'Hara, 1847

(U.S. Army photo by Elizabeth Fraser / Arlington National Cemetery / released)

Just before the crowd at his funeral dispersed, two men of the Honor Guard of the American Legion and Veterans of Foreign Wars approached the casket of Command Sergeant Major James Bryant. One of the men, a former Marine, handed the funeral director his cane as the pair lifted the flag straight above the casket then shifted a few short steps to the side as they began slowly and crisply folding the flag. The two veterans create thirteen folds, forming a triangle that some say resembles a cocked hat, a tribute to the soldiers under General George Washington and the sailors and Marines under Commodore John Paul Jones. In some circles, the thirteen folds each have a meaning and tender significance, representing the thirteen original colonies that started the United States of America. Although there are scripts expressing the symbolism of each fold, I have found nothing official in the U.S. Flag Code or anywhere else in law that currently says the meaning of each fold is to be recited at a funeral as the flag is folded. However, according to William F. Tuerk, the Under Secretary for Memorial Affairs of the U.S. Department of Veteran's Affairs says, "Honoring the burial wishes of veterans is one of the highest commitments for the men and women of Veterans Affairs. A family may request the recitation of words to accompany the meaningful presentation of the American flag as we honor the dedication and sacrifice of their loved ones."[2] One such script is as follows:

The **first** fold of our flag is a symbol of life.

The **second** fold signifies our belief in eternal life.

The **third** fold is made in honor and tribute of the veteran departing our ranks, who gave a portion of his or her life for the defense of our country to attain peace.

The **fourth** fold exemplifies our weaker nature as citizens trusting in God; it is to Him we turn for His divine guidance.

The **fifth** fold is an acknowledgment to our country, for in the words of Stephen Decatur, "Our country, in dealing with other countries, may she always be right, but it is still our country, right or wrong."

The **sixth** fold is for where our hearts lie. It is with our heart that we pledge allegiance to the flag of the United States of America, and to the republic for which it stands, one nation under God, indivisible, with liberty and justice for all.

The **seventh** fold is a tribute to our armed forces, for it is through the armed forces that we protect our country and our flag against all enemies.

The **eighth** fold is a tribute to the one who entered into the valley of the shadow of death, that we might see the light of day, and to honor our mother, for whom it flies on Mother's Day.

The **ninth** fold is an honor to womanhood, for it has been through their faith, love, loyalty, and devotion that the character of men and women who have made this country great have been molded.

The **tenth** fold is a tribute to the father, for he, too, has given his sons and daughters for the defense of our country since he or she was first-born.

The **eleventh** fold, in the eyes of Hebrew citizens, represents the lower portion of the seal of King David and King Solomon and glorifies, in their eyes, the God of Abraham, Isaac, and Jacob.

The **twelfth** fold, in the eyes of a Christian citizen, represents an emblem of eternity and glorifies, in their eyes, God the Father, the Son, and Holy Ghost.

The **last** fold, when the flag is completely folded, the stars are uppermost, reminding us of our national motto, "In God We Trust."[3]

Although the script of the meaning of the folds was not recited at the funeral of CSGTM James Bryant, his funeral was more traditional, where the military honors included his flag-draped coffin, the firing of three volleys, the sounding of Taps, and now the silent folding and presentation of the flag.

Officer presenting the flag: This flag, our beloved star-spangled banner is close to the hearts of all loyal Americans. It was first placed on Command Sergeant Major James Bryant's casket by the authority of the government of our United States, and as it was close to his heart as a loyal American, so was it first in his heart as a true soldier. The gentle breeze caresses the folds of no other flag more beautiful than our own Old Glory. You see, there is no such red in a budding rose, in a falling leaf, or a sparkling wine; there is no such white in an April blossom, in a crescent moon, or a mountain snow; and there is no such blue in a woman's eye, ocean's depths, or in Heaven's dome. On behalf of the President of the United States of America, through the American Legion and Veterans of Foreign Wars, I am honored to present you with this flag of our country under which your husband so honorably and faithfully served. May it be a comfort to you in the years to come in everything for which it stands. Keep it always as a lasting reminder of your husband, a soldier loyal and true. Please accept it with the deep appreciation of a grateful nation.

These three shell casings represent the three volleys you heard fired here today, in keeping with the highest traditions of the United States Army.

The officer presenting the flag would have added the following if CSGTM James Bryant had been a Marine: The Marine Corps is rich in tradition. One of those traditions is that at the conclusion of church services on Marine Corps bases throughout the world, the final hymn is sung prior to the congregation being dismissed. It is the Marine Corps verse of the Navy Hymn.

Eternal Father, grant we pray,
To all Marines, both night and day.
The courage, honor, strength, and skill
Their land to serve, thy law fulfill.
Be thou the shield forevermore.
From every peril to the Corps.
-J.E. Sein, 1966

Semper Fi, Marine

In his first inaugural address, President Ronald Reagan outlined for us the American way of life and why we are the greatest country in the world. Through research for this book, I found a YouTube video by Nate Wylie Studios titled "We Are Americans" [4] that rearranges Reagan's inaugural address to make the point that we need to remember those who paid the ultimate price, made the ultimate sacrifice by giving their lives in the defense of the freedoms we as Americans enjoy. Here is what President Regan said in that nicely put-together video, and the entire inaugural address will be at the end of the book in the appendix. These words ring true today, and we have our armed forces to thank.

"If we look to answer as to why for so many years we achieved so much, prospered as no other people on Earth, it was because here in this land we unleashed the energy and individual genius of man to a greater extent than has ever been done before. Freedom and the dignity of the individual have been more available and assured here than in any other place on Earth. The price for this freedom at times has been high, but we have never been unwilling to pay that price.

Those who say that we're in a time when there are not heroes, they just don't know where to look. The sloping hills of Arlington National Cemetery, with its row upon row of simple white markers bearing crosses or Stars of David. They add up to only a tiny fraction of the price that has been paid for our freedom.

Each one of those markers is a monument to the kind of hero I spoke of earlier. Their lives ended in places called Belleau Wood, The Argonne, Omaha Beach, Salerno, and halfway around the world on Guadalcanal, Tarawa, Pork Chop Hill, the Chosin Reservoir, and in a hundred rice paddies and jungles of a place called Vietnam.

Under one such marker lies a young man, Martin Treptow, who left his job in a small-town barbershop in 1917 to go to France with the famed "Rainbow Division." There, on the western front, he was killed trying to carry a message between battalions under heavy artillery fire.

We're told that on his body was found a diary. On the flyleaf under the heading, 'My Pledge,' he had written these words: 'America must win this war. Therefore, I will work, I will save, I will sacrifice, I will endure, I will fight cheerfully and do my utmost, as if the issue of the whole struggle depended on me alone.'

We must realize that no arsenal or no weapon in the arsenals of the world is so formidable as the will and moral courage of free men and women. It is a weapon our adversaries in today's world do not have. It is a weapon that we, as Americans, do have. Let that be understood by those who practice terrorism and prey upon their neighbors.

As for the enemies of freedom, those who are potential adversaries, they will be reminded that peace is the highest aspiration of the American people. We will negotiate for it, sacrifice for it; we will not surrender for it, now or ever. We are Americans." -Ronald Reagan, 1981.[5]

It has long been debated and mostly resolved as to how we honor our veterans and their bravery. President Regan mentioned the burial grounds, but there are monuments that have been erected and organizations formed to honor our veterans. The Civil War had Arlington National Cemetery and the organization Grand Army of the Republic, which celebrated and commemorated the soldiers of that war. For the soldiers of the American Expeditionary Force (AEF) returning from the Great War (the war to end all wars), it was important for soldiers to maintain connections to their military comrades once their time of service was up and they were back stateside. However, those who did not return once the war ended brought about reform on how to best commemorate and honor Americans who had fought to save the world. It is human nature to shape the memory of death after it occurs. We have all seen movies where the army jeep pulls up and two soldiers get out and give that knock on the door. We see the widow with tears streaming down their face, and their inconsolable grief as the officer-in-charge reports the death of their spouse or loved one. The way in which a nation remembers an event can shape the history of the event itself. Were America's soldiers' heroes who saved the world or governmental pawns caught up in an event that really didn't concern America? Nonetheless, they formed other organizations like the American Legion and Veterans of Foreign Wars to stay connected with their comrades. Over time, these organizations would expand their membership by adding auxiliaries to include wives, sons, and daughters.

In August of 1918, the American War Mother's was founded to convince the nation that huge efforts must be made to preserve and conserve food so that neither the fighting men nor the nation went hungry. Their purpose "To keep alive and develop the spirit that prompted world service; to maintain the ties of fellowship born of that service and to assist and further any patriotic work; to inculcate a sense of individual obligation to the community, State and Nation; to assist in any way in our power the men and women who served and were wounded or incapacitated in the World War; to foster and promote friendship and understanding between America and its Allies of the World War."[6] Others were formed as well and even still exist today like America's Gold Star Mothers. The Gold Star Mothers was founded by Grace Darling Whitaker Seibold on June 4, 1928. The circumstances that led to the creation of the American Gold Star Mothers was similar to those that occurred in tens of thousands of American homes during the Civil War, and World War I (the Great War). A child was called to serve, then gone to war. There was worry and fear for his or her safety and the not knowing period of if and when they were coming back; then that dreaded knock at the door and the message that their soldier had paid the ultimate sacrifice. For those left behind, there is a lifetime of loss and grief, and a sadness felt by the many reminders of a life lived and one of sacrifice and service. To some, it is like an open wound that never heals or one that is always there but calloused over.

With kind permission of the Dean and Chapter of Westminster

There were many questions raised: where should the fallen rest? How should they be honored? Will we ever get them home? Many of these questions have been answered with statues, monuments, national cemeteries, and how we honor those who have served in honored glory by draping the flag on the casket, firing three volleys, sounding Taps, and folding and presenting the flag. As a result, "the United States of America followed the example set forth by Britain and France when it laid the body of an unidentified soldier to rest at Arlington National Cemetery and designated it the "Unknown Soldier."[7] Britain was the first to bury its Unknown Warrior on Armistice Day (Veteran's Day) November 11, 1920, amongst the kings in Westminster Abbey, followed by France in January of 1921 and Belgium in November 1922. After the War to End All Wars (World War I 1914-1918), most of America's fallen soldiers came home.

Author's side note: For those who do not know Congress declared November 11, 1921, a legal holiday to honor all those who participated in World War I and an elaborate ceremony in Washington, D.C. would pay tribute to the symbolic unknown soldier of World War I.

These veterans were honored in cemeteries where the families could place flowers on their graves, coins on their headstones, and beer or sippin whiskey at the grave. While others remained nameless and seemingly lost yet identified as to their country of origin. During World War I, the armed forces used aluminum identification discs, the precursor to "dog tags" to aid in the process of identifying remains of soldiers killed in the line of duty on the battlefield. As a result of the War to End all Wars (World War I), the War Department created the Graves Registration Service as part of the Quartermaster Corps. In fact, there was great debate among the powers that be in the government and lobbyist groups, but more importantly the call from parents to repatriate their deceased soldier. This time period in history did not have all the luxuries or technological advances that help us identify a human body as we do today. When entering military service, a person goes through rigorous tests and medical evaluations to determine if you are fit enough to be a soldier or member of the armed forces. Once sworn in and boot camp arrives your service record starts, but your medical history begins at the Military Entrance Processing Station (MEPS). Outside of clothing or personal items there may or may not have been aluminum identification discs or dog tags to help in identifying a body. Bodies on the battlefield were buried on the battlefield and graves marked with a cross and country of origin as best they could. Today, in the twenty-first century, we have DNA, saliva, blood, fingerprints, hair follicles, skin swatches from inside the mouth, dental records, etc. in helping identify soldiers, as well as scanning equipment and X-rays.

Burial of the Unknown Soldier at Arlington represented the primary official means by which the United States collectively memorialized the war. There were local parades and wreath-laying ceremonies at the base of new monuments throughout the country.[8] Not since the assassination of President Lincoln had Washington prepared for a state event on the grandest scale, the only difference is that this time the state funeral is to celebrate the life and return of one of our own, the American Unknown. On March 4, 1921, Congress approved a resolution providing for the burial of an unidentified

American soldier of the World War in Arlington National Cemetery Memorial Amphitheater on Armistice Day 1921. The American Graves Registration Service in Europe was charged with the selection of the remains of four soldiers from among America's unknown dead who had died in combat areas; one of those four would be selected as the nation's Unknown Soldier: "No one will ever know whether the unknown American soldier buried at Arlington National Cemetery came from Maine or California, whether he died on the Somme, in Belleau Wood, in the Argonne or at St. Mihiel. His body was chosen from the graves of all the unknown American dead in France so that these questions can never be answered."[9] After each of the four selected was exhumed from their place in France, each body was examined to determine that each had been a member of the American Expeditionary Forces, had died of wounds received in combat, and that there were no identifying clues whatsoever. The Quartermaster General's office handled the preparation of each soldier's remains and each body was placed in a separate transfer case draped with the American flag. Then each one was placed on a truck bound for Châlons-sur-Marne for the selection ceremony.

Once all four caskets arrived safely to their destination October 23, 1921, French troops carried the transfer cases into city hall for the selection ceremony. Major Robert P. Harbold of the Quartermaster Corp. was the officer in charge of the ceremonies. The outside of the city hall was decorated with French and American flags, while the inside, the aisles and corridors were ornamented with palms, potted trees, and flags, and a catafalque had been constructed and set up in the main hall. Another room was decorated for the reception of the four unknown soldiers and a third was prepared for the ceremony in which the chosen unknown soldier was to be transferred to a different casket. An honor guard of French soldiers stood vigil until American troops arrived from Coblenz, Germany to take their place. A combined effort between the two forces maintained a constant watch. On October 24, 1921, the caskets of the four soldiers were shuffled like a deck of cards. "Originally, instructions called for a commissioned officer to make the selection. At the last minute, however, Major General Harry L. Rogers, the Army Quartermaster General, learned that the French had delegated this honor to an enlisted man when they chose their Unknown Soldier in 1920. Rogers consequently authorized this duty to be given to one of the enlisted men participating in the ceremony. Major Robert P. Harbold, the officer in charge, chose Sergeant Edward F. Younger. Inside the Hôtel de Ville (City Hall), the four American unknowns lay in identical caskets. Younger's task was to choose one to be buried at Arlington."[10]

In his own words Sergeant Younger remembers feeling "overwhelmed." He states, "I took the flowers and advanced to the little temporary shrine through a line of French troops. I entered the door … and stood alone with the dead…. For a moment I hesitated, and said a prayer, inaudible, inarticulate, yet real. Then I looked around. That scene will remain with me forever. Each casket was draped with a beautiful American flag…. I began a slow march around the caskets. Which should it be? Thoughts poured like torrents through my mind. Maybe these buddies had once been my pals. Perhaps one of them had fought with me, had befriended me, had possibly shielded me from a bullet that might have put me in his place. Who would even know?"[11]

On Memorial Day 1930, Younger placed roses on the Tomb, reenacting his selection of the Unknown Soldier nine years earlier in France. (Library of Congress)

Younger went on to recount, "I was numb. I couldn't choose…. Three times I walked around the caskets; then something drew me to the coffin second to my right on entering…. I couldn't walk another step. It seemed as if God raised my hand and guided me as I placed the roses on the casket. This, then, was to be America's Unknown Soldier, and by that simple act I had started him on his road to destiny. I tarried a moment, then remembered my task was done. I saluted the casket and reported that the order had been fulfilled."[12] Thus, began his journey home to the United States to his Tomb at Arlington National Cemetery.

On October 25, 1921, a special funeral train departed Paris at midday and arrived at Le Havre at around one o'clock p.m., following the final respects paid by French officials and members of patriotic societies, who left tributes, medals, wreaths, and flowers for the Unknown Soldier. An American Army honor guard, a large contingent of French Army troops, a French Army band, a detachment of French sailors, representatives of various French societies and associations, and mounted gendarmes all waited at the docks, creating a military scene at the docks. After taking out the flower pieces from the train, thirty French soldiers formed the column for the dockside parade. The American military personnel assigned as body bearers removed the casket from the funeral car and placed on an awaiting caisson while "Aux Champs" was being played by the band and flowers were being dropped by French schoolchildren on the caisson. The procession then headed toward the Pier d'Escale, where the naval cruiser, USS Olympia, the former flagship of Admiral Dewey, was waiting to transport the Unknown Soldier back to his American homeland. While traveling along the Boulevard Strassbourg, the procession made a brief stop at the municipal hall, where the city council presented the Unknown Soldier a wreath.[13]

Ceremony At The Pier, Le Havre, France (Library of Congress)

At the pier, after speeches by American and French officials Minister Andre Maginot, Minister of Pensions as it was called back then, recognized as the Minister of Veterans Affairs today, (sounds like something out of a Harry Potter book) presented the Croix de Chevalier de la Legion d'Honneur (the highest French order of merit established by Napoleon Bonaparte in 1802 as the Legion of Honor) to the Unknown Soldier.

Minister of Pensions André Maginot presents the French Legion of Honor to the
Unknown Soldier in Le Havre, France, October 25, 1921.
(Bibliothèque nationale de France)

The casket of the "Unknown Soldier" was lifted onto the
Olympia by the Army's Body Bearers. Six sailors and two marines
relieved the Army body bearers and brought the casket onboard ship
while the cruiser's band played Chopin's "Funeral March" and a group
of American Marines on the wharf presented arms. The coffin was
carried to the stern, where it was decorated, and Rear Adm. Lloyd H.
Chandler, commanding the Olympia, members of his staff, and French
and American authorities marched behind it. Flowers were used as
tributes, some of which were brought on board by French
schoolchildren. As the Olympia set sail around 3:20 p.m., accompanied
by eight French naval boats and the US destroyer Rueben James (DD-
245), which would eventually become the first American warship to be
sunk in World War II. The thunderous booming of artillery erupted as
a 17-gun salvo was given as the Olympia cleared the harbor and another
eruption of thunderous volleys began shortly after they left French
territory.

American ceremony preparation fell to Brigadier General Harry H. Bandholtz, who oversaw the Military District of Washington. He made public his plans for the following events: the October 19, 1921, reception of the Unknown Soldier's body from the Navy at the Washington Navy Yard; the November 9, 1921, movement of the body in procession to the Capitol; the November 10, 1921, lying in state in the rotunda; and the November 11, 1921, grand finale, Armistice Day, and the procession to Arlington National Cemetery, with funeral service in the Memorial Amphitheater, and burial to follow at the newly built tomb.

It was a drizzly, rainy day on November 9th when Olympia made her way up the Potomac River, stopping at military posts along the way to accept and return salutes, before docking at the Washington Navy Yard at around 4 o'clock p.m. The 3d Cavalry and its mounted band from Fort Myer, Virginia, General Bandholtz, the escort commander, and various military and civilian officials, such as the Army Chief of Staff, General of the Armies John J. Pershing, Chief of Naval Operations, Admiral Robert E. Coontz, Commandant of the Marine Corps, Maj. Gen. John A. Lejeune, Secretary of War, John Weeks, and Secretary of the Navy, Edwin Denby, were present to receive the body of the Unknown Soldier. A military presence was felt as two squadrons of the 3d Cavalry were already lined up on the far side of the dock area, facing the cruiser when the Olympia docked. The mounted band was to the left of these squadrons, at a right angle to their formation. The band and the ship's complement of marines marched off and formed a line at the near edge of the pier facing the cavalry squadrons after members of the crew installed the gangplank. Next, completing the box formation, the military and civilian dignitaries positioned themselves to the right of the cavalrymen and across from the mounted band.

A body bearer detail consisting of sailors and marines from the ship's company carried the casket to the gangplank after the Navy buglers on board the Olympia sounded the alarm. The cruiser started firing minute guns at the same time that the ship's band started playing Chopin's "Funeral March."[14] In the manner befitting a full admiral, the boatswain piped the Unknown Soldier ashore as the coffin was brought through the rails. The coffin was followed by Admiral Chandler and his fully attired staff, who were bareheaded and had their hats pressed against their chests. As the army saluted, the civil dignitaries on the dock took off their hats. The boatswain blew his pipe to announce that the party had left the ship as the Navy parade came to a stop when it passed the foot of the gangplank. After that, the ship's band stopped playing the funeral march, the national anthem was played by the band, and a marine bugler sounded four flourishes.

Music was paramount as the Olympia's band resumed the funeral march, and music took center stage. The welcoming of the Unknown Soldier was a jubilant event rather than a somber funeral procession. Proceeding through the box formation, the procession reached a draped caisson situated between the two cavalry squadrons on the distant end. The dockside greeting concluded with the casket being removed from the ship's detail and placed on the caisson by eight Army body bearers from the Third Cavalry abruptly bringing the reception ceremony to its end. The calvary band's performance of "Onward Christian Soldiers" led the march to the Capitol. The nation's unknown soldier's flag-draped coffin was led to the Capitol Rotunda. As has happened for numerous presidents and dignitaries following their respective deaths, the body of the unknown was now to lie in state under a guard of honor consisting of a few men from the Army, Navy, and Marine Corps. The Army body bearers lifted the casket from the horse-drawn caisson, brought it through the honor cordon and into the rotunda, and set it down on the Lincoln catafalque, with the foot of the casket facing west. In most burials at cemeteries the feet are to the east, but this was how the unknown would rest on this day as thousands of people filed by to pay their respects. Shortly after the flag-draped coffin was brought into the Capitol, President Warren G. Harding and Mrs.

Harding made their way up the east stairs, passed through the honor cordon, and entered the Rotunda. Mrs. Harding covered the coffin with a large white ribbon that she had handmade. Then President Harding advanced, laying a large wreath of crimson roses on the coffin, and pinned a silver National Shield with forty-eight gold stars on the ribbon. Then, in that order, Vice President Calvin Coolidge, Speaker of the House Frederick H. Gillette, Chief Justice William Howard Taft, Secretary Weeks, and Secretary Denby advanced and laid wreaths for the Army, Navy, Congress, and Supreme Court, respectively. "The assembled dignitaries then filed out of the rotunda leaving the guard of honor to maintain a vigil through the night."[15]

The public was allowed entry on Thursday, November 10, 1921, the following day. Throngs of people filed by the flag draped casket. Among the groups of individuals walking four abreast past the bier were representatives of several patriotic and fraternal organizations. After obtaining authorization to carry out short ceremonies, a few groups gathered on the Senate wing's steps, went through the north entrance to the rotunda, laid wreaths, and carried out their ceremonies before filing out alongside the general public by the west door. Numerous international envoys stopped over to offer their condolences, leaving behind flowers, medals, and other gifts. "More than 90,000 individuals filed past the casket, that day, including the highest officials of the government, members of the diplomatic corps, gold star mothers, and private citizens, to pay homage to the Unknown Soldier who symbolized all the nation's unknowns."[16] The funeral procession exited the Capitol much as it came in, with the Unknown Soldier placed on an awaiting caisson. Eight body bearers had been selected to handle the casket, five were Army noncommissioned officers, two were Navy petty officers, and one was a Marine Corps noncommissioned officer. Nine general officers and three flag officers, all of whom had served in World War I, had been appointed as honorary pallbearers. At eight o'clock a.m. the body bearers, followed by the honorary pallbearers, carried the casket of the Unknown Soldier from the rotunda and down the east steps to the awaiting caisson.

Casket Is Carried Down East Steps Of The Capitol, 1921.
(Library of Congress)

Again, the Army Band sounded the funeral dirge as the military escorts stood at present arms. Positioned on the Capitol Mall near the Washington Monument, a field artillery battery brought in from Camp Meade, Maryland, began firing minute guns simultaneously as the funeral procession made its way to Arlington National Cemetery. Except for a scheduled pause at noon to observe a two-minute period of silence during the funeral service, the battery continued to fire a round each minute until the end of all ceremonies. You will find music is a large part of just about any funeral, but this was more of a national celebration than a national period of mourning. More music but this time from the Army Drum Corps to help maintain the quick-time cadence at which the procession was to move. Recipients of the Medal of Honor marched behind the drum corps. All those who had received this highest military decoration were invited, but only those who had done so during World War I received government-funded invitations.

"The medal of honor winners marched eight abreast, ranging from front to rear according to the dates of their medals, those holding the oldest medals leading. It was behind this honored group that the carriage bearing former President Woodrow Wilson, who would pass away a few years later, February 3, 1924, joined the procession."[17] The Army band played throughout the entire parade. Again, this was more of a celebration than a period of mourning. The National Anthem was played, a bugler sounded attention three times to commemorate the two-minutes of silence, afterword, "America" was sung, then President Harding delivered his address, paid tribute to the Unknown Soldier and made a plea for an end to all wars. When President Harding finished his address a quartet from the Metropolitan Opera Company sang, he "placed upon the casket of the Unknown Soldier the Medal of Honor and the Distinguished Service Cross."[18] Following President Harding's presentation, other high-ranking dignitaries, and heads of state from other nations also presented decorations, gifts, and honors of high order, some of which had never before been given to a foreigner, then hymns and scriptural readings followed. The service concluded as the audience sang "Nearer My God to Thee."

President Harding's Address At Memorial Amphitheater Service, 1921.
(Library of Congress)

In preparation for the committal service, the Marine Corps Band left the amphitheater and took up a spot close to the tomb playing "Our Honored Dead" as the casket, preceded by the clergy, was moved in procession from the apse and placed in the tomb. During this transfer, the Army body bearers again were flanked by the honorary pallbearers. President and Mrs. Harding; Vice President and Mrs. Coolidge; the head of the American National War Mothers, Mrs. R. Emmett Digney, who had lost a son in the conflict, and Mrs. Julia McCudden, who represented the British War Mothers and had lost three boys, were arranged behind the coffin. The heads of foreign delegations followed in line, followed by the Secretaries of State, War, and Navy as well as American and foreign military officials. While the rest of the audience made their way from the amphitheater to the area surrounding the tomb, the band began playing "Lead Kindly Light."

Burial of WWI Unknown Soldier In Arlington National Cemetery.
(Library of Congress)

Bishop Charles H. Brent conferred the rites at the committal service. Congressman Hamilton Fish III, who was the only World War I veteran in Congress at the time, had introduced legislation leading to the approval and construction of the Tomb of the Unknown, came forward and laid a wreath at the tomb.[19] I think it is also important to note that what happened with the celebration and commemoration of the Unknown Soldier impacted every American. Rendering tribute on behalf of all Native American Indian tribes was Chief Plenty Coups, Chief of the Crow Nation. Chief Plenty Coup paid tribute to the Unknown Soldier laying "his war bonnet and coup stick at the tomb."[20] With three salvos of artillery, the sounding of Taps, played by Sergeant Frank Witchey, and the national salute, the ceremonies ended for "an unknown American soldier who gave his life in the Great War"[21] as his flag draped casket covered with wreaths of roses was lowered into the crypt, the bottom of which had been covered with a layer of soil from France.

Chief Plenty Coups at the WWI Unknown Soldier's funeral.
(Library of Congress)

So why even mention the Tomb of the Unknowns? To this author the answer is clear. First of all, I wanted to see if we could pinpoint the origins of the folding of the flag, but as we now know was ordered by Colonel George W. Cocheu in 1918, well at least the presentation of it. The actual first time a flag was folded at a military funeral is relatively unknown. I had read an article by author Marc Leepson titled "The First Union Civil War Martyr: Elmer Ellsworth, Alexandria, and the American Flag." After reading the article, I looked into other sources on the Ellsworth incident that resulted in his death or the "Marshall House Incident."[22] Somewhere in my research I read that the blood-stained Confederate flag that Colonel Elmer Ellsworth took down from the Marshall House because of its defiance to the Union had been folded and presented to Mrs. Lincoln. The flag was presumably tucked in a drawer, but that did not keep young Tad Lincoln from running up and down the hall of the White House playing with it. Colonel Ellsworth was shot and killed by the owner of the Marshall House, James Jackson. Colonel Ellsworth was the first war casualty of the Civil War, well officer, who was a friend of President Lincoln, and Lincoln was reported to have burst to tears at hearing about Ellsworth's death.[23] So, I didn't want the first reporting of the folding of the flag to be one of rebellion. Then again, the writer may have taken liberty and wrote the flag was folded when it could have just been rolled up. Folding the flag back then was probably done like you fold a towel, just folded and not into a triangle.

The second reason to mention the Unknown Soldier is to see if there is any video footage, photographs, or reports or writings that allude to the flag being presented to President Harding. I found no evidence to support that claim. If anything, I found that after Chief Plenty Coups presented his coup stick to the Unknown Soldier and the casket had been lowered into the vault and in the picture you can see the wreath and flag covered casket lowered in the tomb. The Library of Congress also has three clips of rare Army video from Armistice Day, November 11, 1921, of the burial of the Unknown Soldier. The video shows the casket still draped with the flag and wreaths of flowers on top of the flag and lowered into the tomb. A screen shot of that video is shown on the next page. It is definitely against the civics lessons we learned in school about not letting the flag touch the ground or those views written in books by Colonel James A. Moss.

Unknown Soldier of WWI being lowered into the Tomb. (Library of Congress)

Chief Plenty Coups presented his coup stick to the Unknown Soldier.
(Library of Congress)

Finally, The Tomb of the Unknown Soldiers at Arlington National Cemetery is a tribute to all veterans living, and to those who gave their life in service to their country, and to those veterans that came home and are buried in countless private and national cemeteries around the country and around the world. Sergeant Younger's personal reflection of the selection process, a selection process which was repeated for three more unknown soldiers (World War II, Korea, and Vietnam) and entombed in their respective vaults at the Arlington National Cemetery Memorial Amphitheater, paints the picture of what it means to be an Unknown Soldier.

Author's side note: Only the Vietnam unknown has been disinterred and returned to his family after a mitochondrial DNA test identified him as Air Force Pilot Lt. Michael Joseph Blassie. Lt. Blassie was reinterred with full military honors at Jefferson Barracks National Cemetery in St. Louis, Missouri on July 11, 1998, just over 24 years after laying with unknowns at Arlington.

Sgt. Younger gave meaning that resonated with those that had lost their loved ones in war. Those who experienced the Tomb went there and some even traveled overseas to the burial places of known and unknown soldiers on the battlefields of Europe and military cemeteries there to express their personal grief. The Tomb of the Unknowns is a place that all can go to express their collective loss, again their personal grief. Younger likened the Unknown to one of his "buddies" implying that this unknown soldier could have been the son of any mother who did not have a gravesite to visit. Back in 1932 American Legion Commander Louis Johnson spoke of the mother of the Unknown Soldier saying, "We know not whether he was our friend lost in battle, nor the manner of his going. All we know is that he was born of a mother and that he had love before he had breath. We know he loved and was loved in his mother's arms, and, as a boy enjoyed life, stepping forth to meet manhood, the fruition of a mother's dreams. We know he lived for peace, died for peace, and dying found that peace that passeth understanding."[24]

Command Sergeant Major James Bryant was not unknown, but he received a funeral service that expressed Duty, Honor, and Respect in keeping in line with the highest traditions of the United States military. He received a service of gratitude, but more importantly, thank you for your faithful service and a grateful nation.

Those words from my perspective go out to all the families that I have served as a funeral director, will serve, and who have loved ones that gave up a part of themselves to serve this great nation and those serving in the United States military now, thank you for your service.

We conclude this chapter as we began with another part of the poem written by Theodore O'Hara "The Bivouac of the Dead:"[25]

Rest on, embalmed and sainted dead!
Dear as the blood ye gave;
No impious footstep here shall tread
The herbage of your grave;
Nor shall your glory be forgot
While Fame her record keeps,
Or Honor points the hallowed spot
Where Valor proudly sleeps.

As the Honor Guard Chaplain prays: (concluding Command Sergeant Major James Bryant's military honors.) Bow with me in prayer please. Almighty and merciful Father, we come to thee in this moment of thanksgiving for the life of our comrade and for his service to our beloved country. We beseech thee to look with mercy upon each of us assembled here today and with thine own tenderness console and comfort those bereaved by the hand of death. Heavenly Father, hear our prayer on behalf of our comrade allow him to enter thy house eternal to rest in peace. Bless our country with freedom, peace, and righteousness giving you praise for it all. In Jesus precious name. Amen.

Soldier, may you Rest in Peace.

Appendix

Inaugural Address 1981

-Ronald Wilson Regan[1]

Senator Hatfield, Mr. Chief Justice, Mr. President, Vice President Bush, Vice President Mondale, Senator Baker, Speaker O'Neill, Reverend Moomaw, and my fellow citizens:

To a few of us here today this is a solemn and most momentous occasion, and yet in the history of our nation it is a commonplace occurrence. The orderly transfer of authority as called for in the Constitution routinely takes place, as it has for almost two centuries, and few of us stop to think how unique we really are. In the eyes of many in the world, this every-4-year ceremony we accept as normal is nothing less than a miracle.

Mr. President, I want our fellow citizens to know how much you did to carry on this tradition. By your gracious cooperation in the transition process, you have shown a watching world that we are a united people pledged to maintaining a political system which guarantees individual liberty to a greater degree than any other, and I thank you and your people for all your help in maintaining the continuity which is the bulwark of our Republic.

The business of our nation goes forward. These United States are confronted with an economic affliction of great proportions. We suffer from the longest and one of the worst sustained inflations in our national history. It distorts our economic decisions, penalizes thrift, and crushes the struggling young and the fixed-income elderly alike. It threatens to shatter the lives of millions of our people.

Idle industries have cast workers into unemployment, human misery, and personal indignity. Those who do work are denied a fair return for their labor by a tax system which penalizes successful achievement and keeps us from maintaining full productivity.

But great as our tax burden is, it has not kept pace with public spending. For decades we have piled deficit upon deficit, mortgaging our future and our children's future for the temporary convenience of the present. To continue this long trend is to guarantee tremendous social, cultural, political, and economic upheavals.

You and I, as individuals, can, by borrowing, live beyond our means, but for only a limited period of time. Why, then, should we think that collectively, as a nation, we're not bound by that same limitation? We must act today in order to preserve tomorrow. And let there be no misunderstanding: We are going to begin to act, beginning today.

The economic ills we suffer have come upon us over several decades. They will not go away in days, weeks, or months, but they will go away. They will go away because we as Americans have the capacity now, as we've had in the past, to do whatever needs to be done to preserve this last and greatest bastion of freedom.

In this present crisis, government is not the solution to our problem; government is the problem. From time to time, we've been tempted to believe that society has become too complex to be managed by self-rule, that government by an elite group is superior to government for, by, and of the people. Well, if no one among us is capable of governing himself, then who among us has the capacity to govern someone else? All of us together, in and out of government, must bear the burden. The solutions we seek must be equitable, with no one group singled out to pay a higher price.

We hear much of special interest groups. Well, our concern must be for a special interest group that has been too long neglected. It knows no sectional boundaries or ethnic and racial divisions, and it crosses political party lines. It is made up of men and women who raise our food, patrol our streets, man our mines and factories, teach our children, keep our homes, and heal us when we're sick -- professionals, industrialists, shopkeepers, clerks, cabbies, and truckdrivers. They are, in short, "We the people," this breed called Americans.

Well, this administration's objective will be a healthy, vigorous, growing economy that provides equal opportunities for all Americans with no barriers born of bigotry or discrimination. Putting America back to work means putting all Americans back to work. Ending inflation means freeing all Americans from the terror of runaway living costs. All must share in the productive work of this "new beginning," and all must share in the bounty of a revived economy. With the idealism and fair play which are the core of our system and our strength, we can have a strong and prosperous America, at peace with itself and the world.

So, as we begin, let us take inventory. We are a nation that has a government -- not the other way around. And this makes us special among the nations of the Earth. Our government has no power except that granted it by the people. It is time to check and reverse the growth of government, which shows signs of having grown beyond the consent of the governed.

It is my intention to curb the size and influence of the Federal establishment and to demand recognition of the distinction between the powers granted to the Federal Government and those reserved to the States or to the people. All of us need to be reminded that the Federal Government did not create the States; the States created the Federal Government.

Now, so there will be no misunderstanding, it's not my intention to do away with the government. It is rather to make it work -- work with us, not over us; to stand by our side, not ride on our back. Government can and must provide opportunity, not smother it; foster productivity, not stifle it.

If we look to the answer as to why for so many years we achieved so much, prospered as no other people on Earth, it was because here in this land we unleashed the energy and individual genius of man to a greater extent than has ever been done before. Freedom and the dignity of the individual have been more available and assured here than in any other place on Earth. The price for this freedom at times has been high, but we have never been unwilling to pay that price.

It is no coincidence that our present troubles parallel and are proportionate to the intervention and intrusion in our lives that result from unnecessary and excessive growth of government. It is time for us to realize that we're too great a nation to limit ourselves to small dreams. We're not, as some would have us believe, doomed to an inevitable decline. I do not believe in a fate that will fall on us no matter what we do. I do believe in a fate that will fall on us if we do nothing. So, with all the creative energy at our command, let us begin an era of national renewal. Let us renew our determination, our courage, and our strength. And let us renew our faith and our hope.

We have every right to dream heroic dreams. Those who say that we're in a time when there are not heroes, they just don't know where to look. You can see heroes every day going in and out of factory gates. Others, a handful in number, produce enough food to feed all of us and then the world beyond. You meet heroes across a counter, and they're on both sides of that counter. There are entrepreneurs with faith in themselves and faith in an idea who create new jobs, new wealth, and opportunity. They're individuals and families whose taxes support the government and whose voluntary gifts support church, charity, culture, art, and education. Their patriotism is quiet, but deep. Their values sustain our national life.

Now, I have used the words "they" and "their" in speaking of these heroes. I could say "you" and "your," because I'm addressing the heroes of whom I speak -- you, the citizens of this blessed land. Your dreams, your hopes, your goals are going to be the dreams, the hopes, and the goals of this administration, so help me God.

We shall reflect the compassion that is so much a part of your makeup. How can we love our country and not love our countrymen; and loving them, reach out a hand when they fall, heal them when they're sick, and provide opportunity to make them self-sufficient so they will be equal in fact and not just in theory?

Can we solve the problems confronting us? Well, the answer is an unequivocal and emphatic "yes." To paraphrase Winston Churchill, I did not take the oath I've just taken with the intention of presiding over the dissolution of the world's strongest economy.

In the days ahead I will propose removing the roadblocks that have slowed our economy and reduced productivity. Steps will be taken aimed at restoring the balance between the various levels of government. Progress may be slow, measured in inches and feet, not miles, but we will progress. It is time to reawaken this industrial giant, to get government back within its means, and to lighten our punitive tax burden. And these will be our first priorities, and on these principles there will be no compromise.

On the eve of our struggle for independence a man who might have been one of the greatest among the Founding Fathers, Dr. Joseph Warren, president of the Massachusetts Congress, said to his fellow Americans, "Our country is in danger, but not to be despaired of . . .. On you depends the fortunes of America. You are to decide the important questions upon which rests the happiness and the liberty of millions yet unborn. Act worthy of yourselves."

Well, I believe we, the Americans of today, are ready to act worthy of ourselves, ready to do what must be done to ensure happiness and liberty for ourselves, our children, and our children's children. And as we renew ourselves here in our own land, we will be seen as having greater strength throughout the world. We will again be the exemplar of freedom and a beacon of hope for those who do not now have freedom.

To those neighbors and allies who share our freedom, we will strengthen our historic ties and assure them of our support and firm commitment. We will match loyalty with loyalty. We will strive for mutually beneficial relations. We will not use our friendship to impose on their sovereignty, for our own sovereignty is not for sale.

As for the enemies of freedom, those who are potential adversaries, they will be reminded that peace is the highest aspiration of the

American people. We will negotiate for it, sacrifice for it; we will not surrender for it, now or ever.

Our forbearance should never be misunderstood. Our reluctance for conflict should not be misjudged as a failure of will. When action is required to preserve our national security, we will act. We will maintain sufficient strength to prevail if need be, knowing that if we do so we have the best chance of never having to use that strength.

Above all, we must realize that no arsenal or no weapon in the arsenals of the world is so formidable as the will and moral courage of free men and women. It is a weapon our adversaries in today's world do not have. It is a weapon that we as Americans do have. Let that be understood by those who practice terrorism and prey upon their neighbors.

I'm told that tens of thousands of prayer meetings are being held on this day, and for that I'm deeply grateful. We are a nation under God, and I believe God intended for us to be free. It would be fitting and good, I think, if on each Inaugural Day in future years it should be declared a day of prayer.

This is the first time in our history that this ceremony has been held, as you've been told, on this West Front of the Capitol. Standing here, one faces a magnificent vista, opening up on this city's special beauty and history. At the end of this open mall are those shrines to the giants on whose shoulders we stand.

Directly in front of me, the monument to a monumental man, George Washington, father of our country. A man of humility who came to greatness reluctantly. He led America out of revolutionary victory into infant nationhood. Off to one side, the stately memorial to Thomas Jefferson. The Declaration of Independence flames with his eloquence. And then, beyond the Reflecting Pool, the dignified columns of the Lincoln Memorial. Whoever would understand in his heart the meaning of America will find it in the life of Abraham Lincoln.

Beyond those monuments to heroism is the Potomac River, and on the far shore the sloping hills of Arlington National Cemetery, with its row upon row of simple white markers bearing crosses or Stars of David. They add up to only a tiny fraction of the price that has been paid for our freedom.

Each one of those markers is a monument to the kind of hero I spoke of earlier. Their lives ended in places called Belleau Wood, The Argonne, Omaha Beach, Salerno, and halfway around the world on Guadalcanal, Tarawa, Pork Chop Hill, the Chosin Reservoir, and in a hundred rice paddies and jungles of a place called Vietnam.

Under one such marker lies a young man, Martin Treptow, who left his job in a small-town barbershop in 1917 to go to France with the famed Rainbow Division. There, on the western front, he was killed trying to carry a message between battalions under heavy artillery fire.

We're told that on his body was found a diary. On the flyleaf under the heading, "My Pledge," he had written these words: "America must win this war. Therefore, I will work, I will save, I will sacrifice, I will endure, I will fight cheerfully and do my utmost, as if the issue of the whole struggle depended on me alone."

The crisis we are facing today does not require of us the kind of sacrifice that Martin Treptow and so many thousands of others were called upon to make. It does require, however, our best effort and our willingness to believe in ourselves and to believe in our capacity to perform great deeds, to believe that together with God's help we can and will resolve the problems which now confront us.

And after all, why shouldn't we believe that? We are Americans.

God bless you and thank you.

Note: The President spoke at 12 noon from a platform erected at the West Front of the Capitol. Immediately before the address, the oath of office was administered by Chief Justice Warren E. Burger.

In his opening remarks, the President referred to Rev. Donn D. Moomaw, senior pastor, Bel Air Presbyterian Church, Los Angeles, Calif.

The address was broadcast live on radio and television.
Date: 01/20/1981

Correct Method of Folding the United States Flag[1]

Per VA FORM 27-2008, MAY 2024

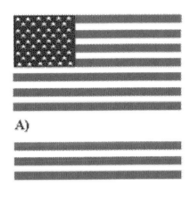

(A) Straighten out the flag to full length and fold lengthwise once, folding the lower striped section of the flag over the blue field.

(B) Fold it lengthwise a second time to meet the open edge, making sure that the union of stars on the blue field remains outward in full view.

(C) A triangular fold is then started by bringing the striped corner of the folded edge to the open edge.

(D) The outer point is then turned inward, parallel with the open edge, to form a second triangle.

(E) The diagonal or triangular folding is continued toward the blue union until the end is reached, with only the blue showing and the form being that of a cocked (three-corner)

Bivouac of the Dead[1]

By Colonel Theodore O'Hara, 1847

The muffled drum's sad roll has beat
The soldier's last tattoo;
No more on life's parade shall meet
That brave and fallen few.
On Fame's eternal camping-ground
Their silent tents are spread,
And Glory guards, with solemn round,
The bivouac of the dead.

No rumor of the foe's advance
Now swells upon the wind;
Nor troubled thought at midnight haunts
Of loved ones left behind;
No vision of the morrow's strife
The warrior's dream alarms;
No braying horn nor screaming fife
At dawn shall call to arms.

Their shriveled swords are red with rust,
Their plumed heads are bowed,
Their haughty banner, trailed in dust,
Is now their martial shroud.
And plenteous funeral tears have washed
The red stains from each brow,
And the proud forms, by battle gashed
Are free from anguish now.

The neighing troop, the flashing blade,
The bugle's stirring blast,
The charge, the dreadful cannonade,
The din and shout, are past;

Nor war's wild note nor glory's peal
Shall thrill with fierce delight

Those breasts that nevermore may feel
The rapture of the fight.

Like the fierce northern hurricane
That sweeps the great plateau,
Flushed with the triumph yet to gain,
Came down the serried foe,
Who heard the thunder of the fray
Break o'er the field beneath,
Knew well the watchword of that day
Was "Victory or death!"

Long had the doubtful conflict raged
O'er all that stricken plain,
For never fiercer fight had waged
The vengeful blood of Spain;
And still the storm of battle blew,
Still swelled the gory tide;
Not long, our stout old chieftain knew,
Such odds his strength could bide.

Twas in that hour his stern command
Called to a martyr's grave
The flower of his beloved land,
The nation's flag to save.
By rivers of their father's gore
His first-born laurels grew,
And well he deemed the sons would pour
Their lives for glory too.

For many a mother's breath has swept
O'er Angostura's plain --
And long the pitying sky has wept
Above its moldered slain.
The raven's scream, or eagle's flight,
Or shepherd's pensive lay,
Alone awakes each sullen height
That frowned o'er that dread fray.
Sons of the Dark and Bloody Ground
Ye must not slumber there,
Where stranger steps and tongues resound

Along the heedless air.
Your own proud land's heroic soil
Shall be your fitter grave;
She claims from war his richest spoil --
The ashes of her brave.

Thus 'neath their parent turf they rest,
Far from the gory field,
Borne to a Spartan mother's breast
On many a bloody shield;
The sunshine of their native sky
Smiles sadly on them here,
And kindred eyes and hearts watch by
The heroes sepulcher.

Rest on embalmed and sainted dead!
Dear as the blood ye gave;
No impious footstep shall here tread
The herbage of your grave;
Nor shall your glory be forgot
While fame her records keeps,
Or Honor points the hallowed spot
Where Valor proudly sleeps.

Yon marble minstrel's voiceless stone
In deathless song shall tell,
When many a vanquished ago has flown,
The story how ye fell;
Nor wreck, nor change, nor winter's blight,
Nor Time's remorseless doom,
Shall dim one ray of glory's light
That gilds your deathless tomb.

In Memoriam: Colonel Theodore O'Hara

(February 11, 1820 – June 6, 1867)

Poet and Officer for the US Army in the Mexican-American War

Colonel Theodore O'Hara was born on February 11, 1820, in Danville, Kentucky, to the late Kean and Helen Sue Hardy O'Hara.[1] He also had a sister, Susanna (O'Hara) Hardie, who married Henry Hardie on June 13, 1825. Theodore left an indelible mark on American history through his poetry and military service. As a poet, he penned verses that continue to resonate across generations. His most famous work, "Bivouac of the Dead,"[2] graces countless cemetery memorials, honoring fallen soldiers, including his own memorial at Frankfort Cemetery in Frankfort, Kentucky and inscribed on McClellan's Gate at Arlington National Cemetery. Originally written to honor his fellow Kentuckians who perished in the Mexican War, but later honored veterans on both sides of the American Civil War.

O'Hara's journey was multifaceted. He studied law under the tutelage of future Vice President and Confederate Secretary of War, John C. Breckinridge, and was admitted to the bar in 1842. However, his passion lay in journalism, and he pursued a career in newspapers working for the "Frankfort Yeoman" and later the "Louisville Daily Times."

During the Mexican–American War (1846 – 1848), O'Hara served as a captain and quartermaster with the Kentucky volunteers under General Gideon J. Pillow. His conduct in battles earned him commendations and respect. He also participated in a filibustering expedition to Cuba in 1850, driven by his belief in American expansion. He suffered a severe leg injury during the Battle of Cárdenas while commanding a regiment during the expedition.

Despite being Honorably discharged on October 15, 1848, at the conclusion of the Mexican-American War, O'Hara found himself practicing law and working in journalism until the Army came calling again in 1855, serving for a year with the 2nd US Cavalry.

In 1856 having been brought up on charges of drunkenness by then Lt. Colonel Robert E. Lee and under threat of court martial, O'Hara resigned and moved to Mobile, Alabama, where he became editor of the Mobile Register until the outbreak of the Civil War. As the Civil War unfolded, O'Hara joined the Confederate cause holding the rank of colonel and contributed to the war effort. He raised the "Mobile Light Dragoons"[3] in the city and was elected company captain, before joining the 12th Alabama Volunteer Infantry where he rose to the rank of lieutenant colonel. He later served on the staff of General Albert Sidney Johnston and General John Breckenridge. After the war, O'Hara became a merchant in the cotton business until wiped out by a devastating fire. He retired to a friend's plantation in Alabama where he died from a bilious fever as a result of malaria and exacerbated by heavy consumption of alcohol.

Yet, it is his poetic legacy that endures. "Bivouac of the Dead" eloquently captures the sacrifice of those who gave their lives for their country.

Colonel Theodore O'Hara passed away on June 6, 1867, and was initially buried in Columbus, Georgia. In 1873, the legislature of the Commonwealth of Kentucky decided their native son needed to come home. With the funding of the Commonwealth's legislature, O'Hara's remains were disinterred and returned to his birth state of Kentucky. He was reinterred at Frankfort Cemetery on September 15, 1874. He leaves behind a legacy of honor, courage, and literary brilliance. His words continue to echo through time, reminding us of the price paid by those who rest in the bivouac of eternity.

May his memory be forever cherished.

Index

Endnotes

PROLOGUE

1 Layden, Tim. (2024). *Indianapolis 500 is a reflection of what Memorial Day means most* | Motorsports on NBC. (May 26, 2024). [Video]. YouTube.
2 108ᵗʰ Runing of Indianapolis 500. *Pre-race Ceremony*. May 26, 2024. https://www.nbcsports.com/
3 Ibid.

CHAPTER 1. MILITARY FUNERALS

1 Sheeler, Jim. (2008). *Final Salute: A story of Unfinished Lives*. New York: Penguin Press. P. 77.
2 Bush, G. W. (2001, September 14). *President George W. Bush Speaks From Ground Zero 2001*. Retrieved from Youtube.com: https://www.youtube.com/watch?v=f9NEwe1JvrI September 14, 2001
3 Soldiers Creed. https://www.army.mil/values/soldiers.html
4 Indiana Funeral Directors Association. Book of Facts 2021-2022. Indianapolis, Indiana. 2021. P. 100. https://www.infda.org
5 Army Techniques Publication (ATP 1-05.02) *Religious Support to Funerals and Memorial Events*. Headquarters Department of the Army. Washington D.C., 27 November 2018. ARN14071_ATP 1-05x02 FINAL WEB 1.pdf (army.mil)
6 Ibid.
7 Ibid.
8 Ibid.
9 Ibid.
10 Ibid.
11 Ibid.
12 Ibid.
13 *Burial at Sea* . (2024, May 03). Retrieved from EPA United States Environmental Protection Agency: https://www.epa.gov/ocean-dumping/burial-sea

CHAPTER 2. LOOKING DEATH IN THE EYES

1 Yancey, Rick. (2013) New York: Penguin Random House. P. 60.
2 1964: Stefan Westmann: How it felt to kill a man | The Great War Interviews | BBC Archive (youtube.com) Originally recorded in 1963. [Video]. YouTube.
3 Indiana Code § 23-14-54-1. IGA | 2024 Indiana Code. https://iga.in.gov/laws/2024/ic/titles/001

4 https://www.vba.va.gov/pubs/forms/VBA-27-2008-ARE.pdf

CHAPTER 3. FLAG AN AMERICAN SYMBOL

1 Leepson, Marc. (2007) *Flag An American Biography*. New York: Thomas Dunne Books. P. 21.
2 Williams, Robin. *The Flag*. March 21, 1982.
   https://www.youtube.com/watch?v=Q_L1vLv84vs&t=4s
3 Washington, G. (1776, January 1). General Orders, 1 January 1776. *Founders Online*. National Historical Publications and Records Commission. Retrieved from https://founders.archives.gov/documents/Washington/03-03-02-0001#GEWN-03-03-02-0001-fn-0003

4 McCullough, David. (2005) *1776*. New York: Simon and Schuster. P. 69.

CHAPTER 4. MASONS AND THE MILITIA

1 Leepson, Marc. (2014) *What So Proudly We Hailed: Francis Scott Key, A Life*. New York: Thomas Dunne Books. P. 202.

IN MEMORIAM: JOHN PAUL JONES

1 Jones, John Paul. https://www.usna.edu/PAO/faq_pages/JPJones.php
2 Greyfield, Donald. *Find a Grave*, database, and images (https://www.findagrave.com/memorial/554/john_paul-jones: accessed July 7, 2024), memorial page for John Paul Jones (6 Jul 1747–18 Jul 1792), Find a Grave Memorial ID 554, citing United States Naval Academy Chapel, Annapolis, Anne Arundel County, Maryland, USA; Maintained by Find a Grave.

CHAPTER 3. FLAG AN AMERICAN SYMBOL

1 Canby, George; Balderston, Lloyd. *The Evolution of the American Flag. Philadelphia: Ferris & Leach*, 1917. *p. 48.*
2 McGrath, Jane, and Kathryn Whitbourne. "*Did Betsy Ross Really Make the First American Flag?*" Updated June 30, 2022. https://history.howstuffworks.com/history-vs-myth/betsy-ross-flag.htm
3 Canby, William. (March 1870) "*The History of the Flag of the United States*" https://*www.ushistory.org/betsy/more/canby.htm.*
4 Canby, George; Balderston, Lloyd. *The Evolution of the American Flag. Philadelphia: Ferris & Leach*, 1917.

IN MEMORIAM: ELIZABETH GRISCOM CLAYPOOLE

[1] *Find a Grave*, database, and images
(https://www.findagrave.com/memorial/904/betsy-ross: accessed July 22, 2024),
memorial page for Betsy Ross (1 Jan 1752–30 Jan 1836), Find a Grave Memorial
ID 904, citing Betsy Ross House Grounds, Philadelphia, Philadelphia County,
Pennsylvania, USA; Maintained by Find a Grave.

CHAPTER 3. FLAG AN AMERICAN SYMBOL

[1] Zall, Paul M. (1976). *Comical Spirit of Seventy-Six: The Humor of Francis Hopkinson.*
San Marino, California: Huntington Library. p. 10
[2] Furlong, William Rea; McCandless, Byron (1981). *So Proudly We Hail.* Washington,
D.C.: Smithsonian Institution Press. p. *100.*
[3] Patterson, Richard S. and Richardson Dougall, The Eagle and the Shield: A
History of the Great Seal of the United States, Washington: U.S. Government
Printing Office, 1976 (released 1978). P. 42.
[4] Joint Committee on Printing, U.S. Congress (2007). *Our Flag* (Rev. ed.109th
Congress, 2nd Session ed.). Washington, D.C.: U.S. Government Printing Office.
[5] Williams, Earl P. Jr. (October-December 2012). "Did Francis Hopkinson Design
Two Flags? NAVA News. P. 7.
[6] Ibid. P. 7-9.
[7] Patterson, Richard S. and Richardson Dougall. P. 35-38.
[8] Ibid. P. 43.
[9] Williams, Jr., Earl P., "The 'Fancy Work' of Francis Hopkinson: Did He Design
the Stars and Stripes?," Prologue (quarterly of the National Archives), Vol. 20,
No. 1 (Spring 1988), pp. 42–52.
[10] Patterson, Richard S. and Richardson Dougall. P. 43.
[11] Furlong, William Rea; McCandless, Byron (1981). *So Proudly We Hail.* Washington,
D.C.: Smithsonian Institution Press. p. *101.*

IN MEMORIAM: FRANCIS HOPKINSON

[1] Williams, Earl P. Jr. (October-December 2012). "Did Francis Hopkinson Design
Two Flags? NAVA News. P. 7-9.
[2] Ibid.

DRAPING THE CASKET WITH OLD GLORY

[1] Klicker, PhD., Ralph L. and Joan J. Klicker, MSN. (2018). *A Walk-Through Time:
A History of Funeral Service.* New York: Thanos Institute. P. 198.

[1] Department of Veterans Affairs. (2024, May). Retrieved from Application For United States Flag For Burial Purposes: https://www.vba.va.gov/pubs/forms/VBA-27-2008-ARE.pdf

[2] American Legion (2024). How is the flag to be displayed on a fully open or half open casket? https://www.legion.org/flag/questions-answers/91522/how-flag-be-displayed-fully-open-or-half-open-casket#:~:text=When%20a%20casket%20is%20fully%20open%20%28full%20couch%29%2C,to%20cover%20the%20closed%20half%20of%20the%20casket.

[3] Hartvigsen, John M., *Draping a Casket with the Flag*, January 7, 2019. *https://flag-post.com/draping-a-casket-with-the-u-s-flag/*

[4] Blitz, Matt, The Hoe Cake was George Washington's Favorite Food, Published June 22, 2017. The Hoe Cake Was George Washington's Favorite Food (foodandwine.com)

[5] Lear, Tobias. "I, 15 December 1799," *Founders Online,* National Archives, https://founders.archives.gov/documents/Washington/06-04-02-0406-0001. [Original source: *The Papers of George Washington*, Retirement Series, vol. 4, *20 April 1799–13 December 1799*, ed. W. W. Abbot. Charlottesville: University Press of Virginia, 1999, pp. 542–546.]

[6] Lear, Tobias. "II, 14 December 1799," *Founders Online,* National Archives, https://founders.archives.gov/documents/Washington/06-04-02-0406-0002. [Original source: *The Papers of George Washington*, Retirement Series, vol. 4, *20 April 1799–13 December 1799*, ed. W. W. Abbot. Charlottesville: University Press of Virginia, 1999, pp. 547–555.]

[7] Ibid.

[8] Ibid.

[9] Knox, J. H. Mason, Jr. "The Medical History of George Washington, His Physicians, Friends and Advisers," *Bulletin of the Institute of the History of Medicine,* 1 (1933), 174-91.

[10] The Death of George Washington | George Washington's Mount Vernon.

[11] Lear, Tobias. "II, 14 December 1799," *Founders Online,* National Archives.

[12] Ibid.

[13] Ibid.

[14] Ibid.

[15] A Brief History of Alexandria-Washington Lodge No 22, A. F. & A. M.; Of its first Worshipful Master, General George Washington; Of its priceless heirlooms contained in its Museum, and a guide thereto. https://aw22.org/wp-content/uploads/2020/11/brochure-1.pdf

[16] Van Beck, Todd. (2020, February). *Rest In Peace Mr. President – George Washington.* Funeral and Cemetery News, NOMIS Publications, Inc.

[17] Lear, Tobias. "To John Adams from Tobias Lear, 15 December 1799," *Founders Online,* National Archives, https://founders.archives.gov/documents/Adams/99-02-02-4081.

[18] Klingenmaier, Richard. (Spring 2012). *The Burial of General George Washington: The Lesser-Known Participants.* The Alexandria Chronicle. P. 5.

[19] Ibid. P. 3.

[20] Ibid. P. 1.

[21] Ibid. P. 3.

[22] Ibid. P. 3.

[23] Ibid. P. 1.

[24] Van Beck, Todd. (2020, February).

[25] Klingenmaier, Richard. (Spring 2012. P. 1-2.

[26] Van Beck, Todd. (2020, February).

[27] *Columbian Sentinel* and *Massachusetts Federalist,* 28 December 1799.

[28] Ronald E. Heaton and James R. Case, Comp. *The Lodge at* Fredericksburgh*: A Digest of the Early Records.* Norristown, PA: Ronald E. Heaton (printed in USA) 1975, and J. Travis Walker, *A History of Fredericksburg Lodge No. 4, A.F. & A.M.,* (1752-2002) (Fredericksburg VA: Sheridan Books Inc., 2002).

[29] Callahan, Bro. Charles H. *Alexandria Washington Lodge No. 22.* April 30, 2022. Alexandria, Virginia. https://templarhistory.com/alexandria-washington-lodge-no-22/

[30] Ibid.

[31] Tobias Lear, "The last illness and Death of General Washington, Journal Account," Dec. 15, 1799, *National Archives, Founders Online,* [Original source: *The Papers of George Washington, Digital Edition*]. https://www.mountvernon.org/library/digitalhistory/digital-encyclopedia/article/christopher-sheels-1776#6

[32] Neil, Edward D. (1868) The *Fairfaxes of England and America in the Seventeenth and Eighteenth Centuries* New York: Joel Munsell, 1868. P. 182. ttps://www.mountvernon.org/library/digitalhistory/digital-encyclopedia/article/fairfax-family#note3

[33] "George Washington to George William Fairfax, 27 February 1785," *The Papers of George Washington: Confederation Series,* Vol. 2, eds. W.W. Abbot and Dorothy Twohig (Charlottesville: University Press of Virginia, 1992), 388.https://www.mountvernon.org/library/digitalhistory/digital-encyclopedia/article/fairfax-family#note1

[34] Faulkner, Claire. *Arlington's Ceremonial Horses and Funerals at the White House.* https://www.whitehousehistory.org/arlingtons-ceremonial-horses-and-funerals-at-the-white-house-1

[35] Henriques, Peter. (2000). *The Death of George Washington: He Died as He Lived.* Mount Vernon: The Mount Vernon Ladies Association. P. 56.

[36] Funeral Ministers | George Washington's Mount Vernon.

[37] Bier Carriers | George Washington's Mount Vernon.

[38] Mary G. Powell, The History of Old Alexandria, Virginia, From July 13, 1749, to May 24, 1861(Richmond, Virginia: The William Byrd Press, Inc., 1928), 208.

[39] Pallbearers | George Washington's Mount Vernon.

[40] Callahan, Bro. Charles H. Alexandria Washington Lodge No. 22 - Templar History. Apr. 30, 2022,

[41] Ibid.

[42] Ibid.

[43] Ibid.

[44] Hartvigsen, John M., *Draping a Casket with the Flag,* January 7, 2019.

[45] Brieg, James. March 2, 2013. Wrapped in a flag - Gettysburg Flag Works Blog Gettysburg Flag Works Blog

[46] Earle, Alice Morse. (1893). *Customs and Fashions in Old New England.* New York: Charles Scribner's Sons. P. 368.

CHAPTER 5. HONOR OUR FALLEN COMRADE

[1] Headquarters, Military District of Washington, *FACT SHEET: GUN SALUTES,* May 1969. https://history.army.mil/faq/salute.html

[2] Twenty-One Gun Salute (navy.mil)

[3] Comerford, Tim (Mass Communication Specialist),. Salutations with a Bang! The Military Gun Salute (dodlive.mil) Published March 19, 2014.

[4] Earle, Alice Morse. (1893). P. 372.

[5] ARN32297-TC_3-21.5-000-WEB-1.pdf (army.mil) P. 14-1.

[6] Moss, James A. Officer's *Manual.*(1911). Mensashe Wisc.: George Banta Publishing Co. P. 315-316.

CHAPTER 6. YOU'VE HEARD THE BUGLE

[1] Hoggan, Melanie. *93-year-old WWII Vet Carries on Tradition of Playing 'Taps'.* May 27, 2009. Montana: Shelby Promoter. www.cutbankpress.com.

[2] Knapp, Jason. Army Veteran. Interviewed by author. September 10, 2023.

[3] Grant, Ulysses S. (1879). Ulysses S. Grant Quote on the Mexican-American War - Shot Glass of History

[4] Polk, James K. May 11, 1846: War Message to Congress. May 11, 1846: War Message to Congress | Miller Center

[5] Moss, James A. Officer's *Manual.*(1911). P. 316.

[6] Villanueva, Jari (2001). "Twenty-Four Notes That Tap Deep Emotions: The Story of America's Most Famous Bugle Call. Baltimore: JV Music. P. 4. (https://www.tapsbugler.com/store-2 store-2/#!/24-Notes-That-Tap-Deep-Emotions-Download/p/19534157/category=4218342

[7] Today in Masonic History - Daniel Adams Butterfield is Born (masonrytoday.com) written by Brother Eric C. Steele.

[8] Butterfield, Daniel · Union Notables · Exhibitions at Schaffer Library (schafferlibrarycollections.org)

[9] Daniel Adams Butterfield | U.S. Civil War | U.S. Army | Medal of Honor Recipient (cmohs.org)

[10] Villanueva, Jari (2001). P. 5.

[11] Ibid. P. 5-6.

[12] Kobbe, Gustav. "The Trumpet in Camp and Battle." *The Century Magazine* LVI, no. 4 (August 1898); P. 537-543.

[13] Villanueva, Jari (2001). P. 6.

[14] Villanueva, Jari (2001). P. 7.

[15] Hopkins, William Palmer. (1903). *The Seventh Regiment Rhode Island Volunteers in the Civil War 1862–1865.* Providence, RI: The Providence Press. p. 56.

[16] Hyde, Bill. (2003). *The Union Generals Speak: The Meade Hearings on the Battle of Gettysburg.* Baton Rouge: Louisiana State University Press, P. 30. "Says bar room and brothel."

[17] Villanueva, Jari (2001). P. 11-12.

[18] Ibid P. 239.

[19] Ibid. P. 239- 275.

[20] Ibid. P. 275.

[21] Smith, Jean Edward. (2001). *Grant.* New York: Simon & Schuster. P. 483.

[22] Black Friday, September 24, 1869, | American Experience | PBS

[23] Easton Free Press, *Butterfield is Dead,* July 18, 1901.

[24] Villanueva, Jari (2001). P. 13.

[25] Davenport Daily Republican. *Passing of Noted Veteran.* Davenport, Iowa, Thursday, July 18, 1901.

[26] *Daniel Adams Butterfield (1831-1901) - Find a Grave Memorial*

[27] Villanueva, Jari (2001). P. 16.

[28] Ibid. P. 28.

[29] Villanueva, Jari (2001). P. 40.

[30] Moss, James A. Officer's *Manual.* (1911) P. 316.

[31] Villanueva, Jari (2001). P. 40.

CHAPTER 7. PERFECTION

[1] Poole, Robert M. (2009). *On Hallowed Ground: The Story of Arlington National Cemetery.* New York: Bloomsbury Publishing. P. 209

[2] Ibid. P. 209.

[3] https:// www.arlingtoncemetery.mil/Funerals/Funeral-Information

4 Goodwin, Doris Kearns. *Team of Rivals: The Political Genius of Abraham Lincoln.* New York: Simon Schuster, 2005. p. 699.

5 Harper, John W. (2016). *Among the Dead: My Years in the Port Mortuary.* South Carolina: CreateSpace Independent Publishing Platform. P. 78.

6 Dover Air Force base: Behind the scenes at America's military mortuary (northjersey.com), October 2, 2019.

7 Harper, John W. (2016). P. 79.

8 Ibid. P. 79.

9 Ibid. P. 81.

10 Mayer, R. G. (2012). Embalming: History, Theory, and Practice. FifthEdition. New York: McGraw Hill. P. 111. New York: McGraw Hill.

11 *8th And I "The Old Post of the Corps".* (2023). Retrieved from Marine Barracks, Washington, D.C.: https://www.barracks.marines.mil/Units/Company-B/Body-Bearers/

12 Poole, Robert M. (2009). P. 217.

13 Ibid. P. 217.

14 Ibid. P. 218.

15 Ibid. P. 218.

16 Ibid. P. 218.

17 FM_3-21.5_Drill_and_Ceremonies.pdf (army.mil)

18 Retreat and Reveille: Pay your respects to the flag | Article | The United States Army September 11, 2017.

19 Poole, Robert M. (2009). P. 220.

20 Ibid. P. 220.

21 Bird, Annette, and Tim Prouty. (1993). *So Proudly He Served: The Sam Bird Story.* Witchita: Okarche Books. P. 87.

CHAPTER 8. PLEASE ACCEPT THIS FLAG

1 Faulkner, Claire. *Arlington's Ceremonial Horses and Funerals at the White House.*

2 Cocheu, George Wilbur. *No. 4144 George Wilbur Cocheu Class of 1903.* Assembly Fall 1966. New York: Unites States Military Academy Library. P. 82.

3 Morris, Edmund (2010). *Colonel Roosevelt.* Vol. 3. New York: Random House. P. 554.

4 Department of Defense. (2021, October 13). *Military One Source.* Retrieved from What to Expect During Military Funeral: https://al.ng.mil/Portals/52/What%20to%20Expect%20During%20Military%20Funeral%20Honors.pdf

CHAPTER 9. THE MOST LOVED MAN IN A GENERATION

[1] Van Beck, Todd. (2022, March). *Rest In Peace Mr. President – William Howard Taft.* Funeral and Cemetery News, NOMIS Publications, Inc.

[2] Patterson, Michael Robert. William Howard Taft – President of the United States Chief Justice of the United States Supreme Court March 2, 2024. https://www.arlingtoncemetery.net/whtaft.htm

[3] Yenne, Bill. (2015). *The Complete Book of US Presidents.* Birmingham, Alabama: Sweet Water Press. P. 130.

[4] *Rosen, Jeffrey (2018). William Howard Taft: The American Presidents Series. New York: Time Books, Henry Holt & Co.P. 12.*

[5] Schneider, Dorothy; Schneider, Carl J. (2010). *First Ladies: A Biographical Dictionary* (3rd ed.). Facts on File. pp. 172–181.

[6] Taft, William Howard. February 1980. Collection: William Howard Taft papers | Archives at Yale. https://web.library.yale.edu/mssa

[7] Blassingame, Wyatt. (1968). *The Look-It-Up-Book of Presidents.* New York: Random House.

[8] William Howard Taft (army.mil). March 2, 2001. https://www.history.army.mil/books/Sw-SA/TaftWH.htm

[9] *Rosen, Jeffrey (2018). P. 61-62.*

[10] Van Beck, Todd. (2022, March).

[11] Ibid.

[12] Ibid.

[13] Ibid.

[14] Patterson, Michael Robert. *William Howard Taft – President of the United States, Chief Justice of the United States Supreme Court.* March 2, 2024. htps://www.arlingtoncemetery.net/whtaft.htm

[15] Hills, Duane E., and Adams, Alice A. (2022) *One Block West of the White House: Joseph Gawler's Sons, Undertaker of the* Presidents. Silver Spring, Maryland: Historic Hills Publishing. P. 354-357.

[16] Mossman, B.C.; Stark, M.W. (1991). "77-606843". *The Last Salute: Civil and Military Funerals 1921-1969.* Washington, D.C.: Department of the Army. CMH Pub 90-1. P. 19.

[17] Ibid. P. 19.

[18] Ibid. P. 20.

[19] Van Beck, Todd. (2022, March).

[20] Hills, Duane E., and Adams, Alice A. (2022) P. 358.

[21] Mossman, B.C.; Stark, M.W. (1991). P. 22.

[22] Ibid. P. 22.

CHAPTER 9. THE MOST LOVED MAN IN A GENERATION

[1] Ibid. P. 22.

[2] Swick, Gerald D.; McCreary, Donna (Summer 1998). "His Own Place In The Sun" (PDF). *Lincoln Lore*. 1853: 3–6. Retrieved December 23, 2022. *[Undated letter from Mary Harlan Lincoln to Katherine Helm, either held in the "Mary G. Townsend Collection"(Giant in the Shadows: The Life of Robert T. Lincoln by Jason Emerson), or in an unnamed private collection (Swick & McCreary).*

[3] "Burial Detail: Lincoln, Robert Todd (section 32, grave S-13)". *Army Cemeteries Explorer – Arlington National Cemetery*. Retrieved May 17, 2024.

[4] Schwartz, Thomas F. (Autumn 2007). "A Death in the Family : Abraham Lincoln II "Jack" (1873–1890)" (PDF). *For the People*. Vol. 9, no. 3. Abraham Lincoln Association. pp. 1, 4. Archived from the original (PDF) on October 17, 2013. Retrieved February 11, 2019.

[5] Hills, Duane E., and Adams, Alice A. (2022). P.365.

[6] Hills, Duane E., and Adams, Alice A. (2022). P.366.

[7] Villanueva, Jari. (2021). *Frank Witchey Tomb Bugler*. https://www.tapsbugler.com/frank-witchey-tomb-bugler/

[8] Frank, Tim, ANC Historian. *Frank Witchey: The Maestro of the Trumpet*, November 5, 2021.

[9] Ibid. P. 366.

[10] Hills, Duane E., and Adams, Alice A. (2022). P. 313-338.

IN MEMORIAM: TECHNICAL SERGEANT FRACK WITCHEY

[1] ANC Blog (arlingtoncemetery.mil) Frank Witchey: The Maestro of the Trumpet. November 5, 2021

[2] Ibid.

[3] Ibid.

[4] Ibid.

[5] Witchey, Who Sounded Taps For the Unknown Soldier, Retires." *Washington Post*, June 5, 1938.

[6] Frank Witchey - Technical Sergeant, United States Army (arlingtoncemetery.net)

CHAPTER 10. A CHORD OF THREE STRANDS

[1] Breslin, Jimmy. *Digging JFK Grave Was His Honor*. The New York Herald Tribune, November 26, 1963.

[2] Poole, Robert M. (2009). P. 212.

IN MEMORIAM: PRIVATE WILLIAM CHRISTMAN

[1] WilliamChristmanHistory.pdf (tobyhannatwphistory.org)

[2] William Henry Christman (1844-1864) - Find a Grave Memorial

[1] Rusk, Dean. (1990), *As I Saw It.* New York: W.W. Norton and Company. P. 321.
[2] Ball, George. (1982). *The Past Has Another Pattern.* New York: W.W. Norton and Company P. 331.

[1] United Press International. (1964). *Four Days: The Historical Record of the Death of President Kennedy.* New York: American Heritage Publishing Co. P. 90.
[2] Nation: The Others | TIME November 27, 1964.
[3] Bugliosi, Vincent (2007). *Reclaiming History: The Assassination of President John F. Kennedy.* W. W. Norton. p. 66.

IN MEMORIAM: J.D. TIPPIT

[1] J.D. Tippit / 1924-1943 Biography (jdtippit.com).Videotaped interview of Wayne, Don and Edward Tippit, November 13, 1999, Dale K. Myers Collection. Copyright 2018 Oak Cliff Press, Inc. All Rights Reserved.
[2] J. D. Tippit (1924-1963) - Find a Grave Memorial. *Find a Grave*, database and images (https://www.findagrave.com/memorial/3433/j_d-tippit: accessed July 29, 2024), memorial page for J. D. Tippit (18 Sep 1924–22 Nov 1963), Find a Grave Memorial ID 3433, citing Laurel Land Memorial Park, Dallas, Dallas County, Texas, USA; Maintained by Find a Grave.
[3] Dooley-Awbrey, Betty (2013). *Why Stop? A Guide to Texas Roadside Historical Markers.* Rowman & Littlefield. p. 93.

[1] O'Rourke, Meghan. JFK assassination: Jacqueline Kennedy mourned in public with grace, purpose, and blood on her suit. (slate.com). November 21, 2013.
[2] Kelly, DB. *What JFK's Funeral Was Really Like.* What JFK's Funeral Was Really Like (grunge.com)/ August 9, 2023.
[3] Cronkite, Walter. (November 22, 1963). *Announcement of the Death of JFK.* CBS News. https://www.cbsnews.com/news/cronkite-remembers-jfk/
[4] The LBJ Presidential Library. *November 22, 1963, Personal Perspective.* (October 30, 2013). [Video]. YouTube. https://www.youtube.com/watch?v=uHR23oDHf90
[5] McDowell, E. (2023, May 19). Jackie Kennedy's pink suit is locked in a vault and will be hidden from public view until 2103. Here are surprising facts about the famous outfit. Retrieved from Business Insider:

https://www.businessinsider.com/jackie-kennedy-pink-suit-facts-location-storage-2023-5

6   Mossman, B.C.; Stark, M.W. (1991). P. 198.

7   NBC News (1966). *There was a President*. New York: Random House. P. 139.

8   United Press International. (1964). P. 94.

9   Kelly, DB. *What JFK's Funeral Was Really Like*. August 9, 2023.

10   The Story of the Horse - Riding into the Afterlife - Archaeology Magazine - July/August 2015

11   McFarland, Matt. *'Black Jack' Famous Kennedy Funeral Horse Dies*. February 8, 2006. https://www.wsfa.com/story/4473361/black-jack-famous-kennedy-funeral-horse-dies/

12   Kelly, DB. *What JFK's Funeral Was Really Like*. August 9, 2023.

13   PeriscopeFilm. *Funeral Procession and Burial of President John F. Kennedy. November 25, 1963. XD13194*. https://archive.org/details/xd-13194-john-f-kennedy-funeral-vwr

14   Kelly, DB. *What JFK's Funeral Was Really Like*. August 9, 2023.

15   Poole, Robert M. (2009). P. 224.

16   Poole, Robert M. (2009). P. 225.

17   Wilson, J. W. (1978). *Engineer Memoirs*. Mobile: US Army Corps of Engineers. P. 194-197.

18   Poole, Robert M. (2009). P. 220.

19   Manchester, William. (1967). The *Death of a President*. New York: Harper & Row. P. 552.

20   Poole, Robert M. (2009). P. 225.

21   21 Gun Salute (arlingtoncemetery.mil)

22   Collins, B.T. *The Courage of Sam Bird*. Reader's Digest, May 1989, 49-54.

In Memoriam: Major Samuel Richard Bird

1   Collins, B.T. *The Courage of Sam Bird*. Reader's Digest, May 1989, 49-54.

2   Ibid.

CHAPTER 11. IN HONORED GLORY

1   O'Hara, Theodore. (1847) *The Bivouac of the Dead*. South Carolina: Ye Palmetto Press.

2   American Legion. (2024) American Flag-Folding Procedures. *VA Clarifies Policy on Flag-Folding Recitations "13-Fold" Ceremony, Other Scripts Approved*. https://www.legion.org/flag/folding.

3   National Flag Foundation. (2022) Education and News: *The Meaning Behind the 13 Folds of the United States Flag*. https://nationalflagfoundation.org/the-meaning-behind-the-13-folds-of-the-united-states-flag/

4 Wylie, Nate. (November 16, 2020). *"We Are Americans" Patriotic Speech by Ronald Regan*. [Video]. YouTube. https://www.youtube.com/watch?v=9h7xD4mIcdw

5 Regan, Ronald Wilson. (January 20, 1981). Inaugural Address 1981. Ronald Regan Presidential Library and Museum. [Video]. https://www.reaganlibrary.gov/archives/speech/inaugural-address-1981

6 Fenelon, Holly S. (2012). *That Knock at the Door: The History of Gold Star Mothers in America*. iUniverse Books: Bloomington, Indiana. P. 44.

7 Ibid. P. 100.

8 I bid P. 102.

9 McNutt, William Slaven. (November 11, 1921). The Solder Comes Home. The American Legion Weekly. P. 6.

10 Frank, Tim, ANC Historian. *A Humble Sergeant: Edward F. Younger and the Unknown Soldier, October 20, 2021.*

11 Ibid.

12 Younger, Edward F. "I Chose the Unknown Soldier," *This Week,* November 8, 1936.

13 Mossman, B.C.; Stark, M.W. (1991). P. 8-9.

14 Mossman, B.C.; Stark, M.W. (1991). P. 10. https://history.army.mil/books/Last_Salute/Index.htm

15 Ibid. P. 12.

16 Fenelon, Holly S. (2012). P. 54.

17 Mossman, B.C.; Stark, M.W. (1991). P. 14.

18 Ibid. P. 17.

19 Troncone, Anthony C. (1993). *Hamilton Fish Sr. and the Politics of American Nationalism, 1912–1945.* New Brunswick, N.J.: Rutgers The State Univ. of New Jersey.

20 Mossman, B.C.; Stark, M.W. (1991). P. 18.

21 Worthington, R.C. Homecoming. *The American Legion Magazine,* November 1938, p. 3.

22 Leepson, Marc. *The First Union Civil War Martyr: Elmer Ellsworth, Alexandria, and the American Flag.* The Alexandria Chronicle. Fall 2011. P. 4.

23 Bayne, Julia Taft. *Tad Lincoln's Father* (Lincoln, NE: Bison Books, 2001), P. 39-40.

24 Gardner, Alexander. *Known But To God.* American Legion Monthly. January 1933, p. 188.

25 O'Hara, Theodore. (1847) *The Bivouac of the Dead.*

APPENDIX

1 Regan, Ronald Wilson. (January 20, 1981). Inaugural Address 1981.

1 About VA Form 27-2008 | Veterans Affairs (May 2024). https://www.vba.va.gov/pubs/forms/VBA-27-2008-ARE.pdf

[1] Sanders, "Theodore O'Hara," *ExploreKYHistory*, accessed August 4, 2024, https://explorekyhistory.ky.gov/items/show/105.

[2] Ibid. O'Hara, Theodore. (1847) Bivouac of the Dead poem. - National Cemetery Administration (va.gov). https://www.cem.va.gov/history/BODpoem.asp

[3] Poore, R. (2013, May 23). Civil War-era editor largely remembered for poem. Retrieved from Newspapering: https://newspapering.blogspot.com/2013/05/civil-war-era-editor-largely-remembered.html.

References

Dept. of the Navy. (1976). Naval Documents of the American Revolution 7 . (Washington, D.C: Naval History Division. Retrieved from https://archive.org/details/navaldocumentsof07unit

"*Burial Detail: Lincoln, Robert Todd (section 32, grave S-13)*". *Army Cemeteries Explorer*. (2024, May 17). Retrieved from Find a Grave: https://www.findagrave.com/memorial/628/robert_todd-lincoln

"*II, 14 December 1799,*" *Founders Online, National Archives, [The Papers of George Washington, Retirement Series, vol. 4, 20 April 1799–13 December 1799, ed. W. W. Abbott. Charlottesville: University Press of Virginia. 1999. p. 547-555.* (1799, December 14). Retrieved from Founders Online: https://founders.archives.gov/documents/Washington/06-04-02-0406-0002

108th Runing of Indianapolis 500. Pre-race Ceremony. (2024, May 26). Indianapolis, IN: NBC.

1964: Stefan Westmann: How it felt to kill a man | The Great War Interviews | BBC Archive (youtube.com) Originally recorded in 1963. [Video]. YouTube. (1964, November 11). Retrieved from YouTube: https://www.youtube.com/watch?v=B8log371ADA&t=248s

8th And I "The Old Post of the Corps". (2023). Retrieved from Marine Barracks, Washington, D.C.: https://www.barracks.marines.mil/Units/Company-B/Body-Bearers/

Adams, J. (1775, 28 November-December). *VIII. Rules for the Regulation of the Navy of the United Colonies, 28 November – December 1775.* Retrieved from Founders Online: VIII. Rules for the Regulation of the Navy of the United Colonies, 28 November – December 1775

Allen, G. W. (1913). A Naval History of the American Revolution, Vol. 1. Boston: Houghton Mifflin.

American Legion. (2023). Retrieved from American Flag-Folding Procedures: https://www.legion.org/flag/folding

America's First Veterans. (8, November 2019). Retrieved from American Revolution Institute: https://www.americanrevolutioninstitute.org/wp-content/uploads/2020/06/Americas-First-Veterans-catalog-revised2.pdf

ANC. (2023). James Parks (1843-1929). *Arlington National Cemetery*. Arlington, VA. Retrieved from https://www.arlingtoncemetery.mil/Explore/Notable-Graves/African American/James-Parks

Arlington National Cemetery Honor, Remember, Explore. (2024). Retrieved from Funeral Information: https:// www.arlingtoncemetery.mil/Funerals/Funeral-Information

Army, Headquarters Department of The. (2021, May 03). ARN32297-TC_3-21.5-000-WEB-1.pdf (army.mil) P. 14-1. *Drill and Ceremonies*. Washington, D.C.

Associated Press. Bugler's Note Still Plays on Him". (1988, November 22).

Bauman, R. (November 1989). "The Man Who Wrote Taps.". *The Retired Officer*, 24-26, 28-29.

Bayne, J. T. (1931). *Tad Lincoln's Father*. Lincoln, NE: Bison Books.

Bell, G. W. (2001, March 2). William Howard Taft . *Secretaries of War and Secretaries of the Army*. Washington, D.C: Center of Military History. Retrieved from https://www.history.army.mil/books/Sw-SA/TaftWH.htm

Bernstein, R. B. (2009). "Appendix: The Founding Fathers, A Partial List". In *The Founding Fathers Reconsidered* (pp. 176-180). New York: Oxford University.

Betsy Ross. (1998, April 25). Retrieved from Find A Grave: https://www.findagrave.com/memorial/904/betsy-ross

Billings, J. D. (2009, July 21). Billings, John D. Hardtack and Coffee or The Unwritten Story of Army Life. . Boston: George and Co., 1887. Reprinted by Nebraska Press, 1993.

Bird, A. a. (1993). *So Proudly He Served: The Sam Bird*. Wichita: Okarche Books.

Black Friday, September 24, 1869, . (1869, September 24). Retrieved from American Experience: https://www.pbs.org/wgbh/americanexperience/features/grant-black-friday/

Blankenship, T. (1985, July). Blankenship, Ted. "Modernization Means Playing Taps for a Noble Instrument." Army. 14-15.

Blanton, W. B. (1932). "Washington's Medical Knowledge and Its Sources," Annals of Medical History, 4.

Blassingame, W. (1968). *The Look-It-Up-Book of Presidents*. New York: Random House.

Blitz, M. (2017, June 22). *The Hoe Cake was George Washington's Favorite Food*. Retrieved from Food and Wine: https://www.foodandwine.com/

Booth, R. H. (1977, December). "Butterfield and Taps.". *Civil War Times Illustrated XVI*, pp. 34-39.

Brighton, R. (1985). *The Checkered Career of Tobias Lear.* Portsmouth, NH: Portsmouth Marine Society.

Budreau, L. M. (2010). *Bodies of War: World War I and the Politics of Commemoration in America, 1919-1933.* New York: New York University Press.

Buescher, J. (2011, August 21). *"All Wrapped up in the Flag".* Retrieved from Teachinghistory.org: https://teachinghistory.org/history-content/ask-a-historian/23852

Bush, G. W. (2001, September 14). *President George W. Bush Speaks From Ground Zero 2001.* Retrieved from Youtube.com: https://www.youtube.com/watch?v=f9NEwe1JvrI September 14, 2001

Butterfield is Dead. (1901, July 18). *Easton Free Press.*

Butterfield, D. A. (1863). *Camp and Outpost Duty For Infantry.* New York: Harper and Brothers.

Butterfield, J. L. (1904). *A Biographical Memorial of General Daniel Butterfield including many Addresses and Military Writings.* New York: The Grafton Press.

Callahan, C. (2022, April 30). *Alexandria Washington Lodge No. 22.* Retrieved from Templar History: https://templarhistory.com/alexandria-washington-lodge-no-22/

Callahan, C. H. (1913). *Washington the Man and the Mason.* Washington: National Publishing Co.

Canby, G., & and Balderston, L. (1909). *The Evolution of the American Flag.* Philadelphia: Ferris & Leach.

Carola, C. (2021, November 10). *'Driving force': Hamilton Fish III and the Tomb of the Unknown Soldier.* Retrieved from Times Union: https://www.timesunion.com/hudsonvalley/news/article/Hamilton-Fish-III-tomb-unknown-soldier-16605860.php

Chandler, M. (1960, January 1). Of Garry Owen in Glory: The History of the 7th U.S. Cavalry. The Turnpike Press.

Cocheu, G. W. (Fall 1966, Fall). No. 4144 George Wilbur Cocheu Class of 1903. *Assembly*, 82.

Cocheu, L. C. (1947). *The Cocheu Family.* Retrieved from Internet Archive: https://ia903101.us.archive.org/6/items/cocheufamily00coch/cocheufamily00coch.pdf

College, T. O. (2024). *Butterfield, Daniel · Union Notables · Exhibitions at Schaffer Library.* Retrieved from schafferlibrarycollections.org: https://exhibits.schafferlibrarycollections.org/s/union-notables/item/975

Collins, B. (1989, May). The Courage of Sam Bird. . *Reader's Digest*, pp. 49-54.

Comerford, T. (2014, March 19). *(Mass Communication Specialist),. Salutations with a Bang! The Military Gun Salute (dodlive.mil)*. Retrieved from USN History: https://usnhistory.navylive.dodlive.mil/Recent/Article-View/Article/2686256/salutations-with-a-bang-the-military-gun-salute/

Congress, U. S. (n.d.). Francis Hopkinson (id: H000783). Biographical Directory of the United States Congress. Retrieved from https://bioguide.congress.gov/search/bio/H000783

Cooper, S. (1836). *A Concise System of Instructions and Regulations for the Militia and Volunteers of the United States*. Philadelphia: Robert P. Desilver.

Coski, J. M. (2012). *The Army of The Potomac At Berkeley Plantation–The Harrison's Landing Occupation of 1862*. Richmond: Page One Inc.

Cronkite, W. (1963, November 22). *Announcement of the Death of JFK. (Cronkite Remebers JFK-November 20, 2003)*. Retrieved from CBS News: https://www.cbsnews.com/news/cronkite-remembers-jfk/

Custer, E. B. (1890). *Following The Guidon*. New York: Harper and Brothers.

Daniel Adams Butterfield (1831-1901) - Find a Grave Memorial. (2000, August 13). Retrieved from Find a Grave: https://www.findagrave.com/memorial/11734/daniel_adams-butterfield

Daniel Adams Butterfield | U.S. Civil War | U.S. Army | Medal of Honor Recipient (cmohs.org). (Chartered 1958). Retrieved from Congressional Medal of Honor Society: https://www.cmohs.org/recipients/daniel-a-butterfield

December [1799]," Founders Online, National Archives, [Original source: The Diaries of George Washington, vol. 6, 1 January 1790–13 December 1799, ed. Donald Jackson and Dorothy Twohig. Charlottesville: University Press of Virginia, 1979, p. 377-380. (2022, January 6). Retrieved from Founders Online: https://founders.archives.gov/documents/Washington/01-06-02-0008-0012

DeKraft, E. (1818). Rules, Regulations, and Instructions for the Naval Service of the United States... . Washington, D.C: E. De Kraft.

Department of Defense. (2021, October 13). *Military One Source*. Retrieved from What to Expect During Military Funeral: https://al.ng.mil/Portals/52/What%20to%20Expect%20During%20Military%20Funeral%20Honors.pdf

Department of Defense. (2024). *Military One Source*. Retrieved from Flag Presentation Protocol:

https://download.militaryonesource.mil/12038/MOS/Brochures/MFH-FlagPresentationProtocol-Brochure.pdf

Department of the Army. (1991, September 6). U.S. Army FM 12 – 50, U.S. Army Bands, U.S. Army Element, School of Music, Department of the Army. Washington D.C: Government Printing Office.

Department of the Army Headquarters. (2013, November 12). *Religious Support to Funerals and Memorial*. Retrieved from ATP 1-05.02: https://movfw.org/uploads/Documents/chaplain/Religious-Support-at-Funerals-ATP-1-05.02.pdf

Department of the Unted States Army. (2024). *Honor the Fallen: A Chaplain's Guide* . Retrieved from The Coalition of Spirit-Filled Churches: https://www.spirit-filled.org/documents/funeral_book_final.pdf

Department of Veterans Affairs. (2024, May). Retrieved from Application For United States Flag For Burial Purposes: https://www.vba.va.gov/pubs/forms/VBA-27-2008-ARE.pdf

Ditzel, P. (1974, August). The Story of Taps. *The American Legion Magazine*, pp. 10-13.

Downey, F. (1971). *Fyfe, Drum and Bugle*. Ft. Collins: The Old Army Press.

Earle, A. M. (1893). *Customs and Fashions in Old New England*. New York: Charles Scribner's Sons.

Editors, H. (2009, November 24). This Day in History: Congress adopts the Stars and Stripes. A&E Television Networks. Retrieved from History: https://www.history.com/this-day-in-history/congress-adopts-the-stars-and-stripes

Faulkner, C. (2023). *Arlington's Ceremonial Horses and Funerals at the White House*. Retrieved from The White House Historical Association: https://www.whitehousehistory.org/arlingtons-ceremonial-horses-and-funerals-at-the-white-house-1

Faust, D. G. (2008). *This Republic of Suffering Death and The American Civil War*. New York: Vintage Books.

Fenelon, H. S. (2012). *That Knock at the Door: The History of Gold Star Mothers in America*. Bloomington, Indiana: iUniverse Books.

Foundation, N. F. (2022). The Meaning Behind the 13 Folds of the United States Flag. *Education and News*. Retrieved from https://nationalflagfoundation.org/the-meaning-behind-the-13-folds-of-the-united-states-flag/

Francis Hopkinson biography at the Library of Congress Performing Arts Digital Library. (2015, September 30). Retrieved from Library of Congress: https://www.loc.gov/item/ihas.200035713

Frank, T. A. (2021, October 20). *A Humble Sergeant: Edward F. Younger and the Unknown Soldier*. Retrieved from Arlington National Cemetery Honor, Remember, Explore: https://www.arlingtoncemetery.mil/Blog/Post/11465/A-Humble-Sergeant-Edward-F-Younger-and-the-Unknown-Soldier

Furlong, W. R. (1981). *So Proudly We Hail*. Washington, D.C: Smithsonian Institution Press.

Gardner, A. (1933, January). Known But To God. *American Legion Monthly*, p. 188.

George Wise Wilson Gunn, "Let George Do It! He Was a Pallbearer of George Washington: A Portrait of George Wise of Virginia, 1799," unpublished paper. (1999).

Goodwin, D. K. (2005). Team of Rivals: The Political Genius of Abraham Lincoln . New York: Simon Schuster.

Greyfield, D. (1998, April 25). *Find a Grave, John Paul Jones*. Retrieved from Find A Grave: https://www.findagrave.com/memorial/554/john_paul-jones

GUIDON Staff, F. L. (2017, September 11). Retreat and Reveille: Pay your respects to the flag. U.S. Army. Retrieved from https://www.army.mil/article/108998/retreat_and_reveille_pay_your_respects_to _the_flag

Hamill, J. (1986). *The Craft: History of English Freemasonry*. UK: Aquarian Press.

Harper, J. W. (2016). *Among the Dead: My Years in the Port Mortuary*. South Carolina: CreateSpace Independent Publishing Platform.

Hartvigsen, J. M. (2019, January 7). *Draping a Casket with the Flag, January 7, 2019*. Retrieved from flag-post.com: Many Voices, One Flag: https://flag-post.com/draping-a-casket-with-the-u-s-flag/

Hastings, G. E. (1926). *The Life and Works of Francis Hopkinson*. Chicago: University of Chicago Press.

Heaton, R. E. (2002). *A History of Fredericksburg Lodge No. 4, A.F. & A.M., (1752-2002)* . Fredericksburg, VA: Sheridan Books Inc.

Henriques, P. (2000). *The Death of George Washington: He Died as He Lived*. Mount Vernon: The Mount Vernon Ladies Association.

Hills, D. E. (2022). *One Block West of the White House: Joseph Gawler's Sons, Undertaker of the Presidents*. Silver Spring, Maryland: Historic Hills Publishing.

Historical Society of Pennsylvania. (2023). *The Tobias Lear Journal: An Account of the Death of George Washington*. Retrieved from Historical Society of Pennsylvania: https://hsp.org/history-online/digital-history-projects/tobias-lear-journal-account-death-george-washington

Hogan, E. (1774). *The Pennsylvania State Trials: Containing the Impeachment, Trial, and Acquittal of Francis Hopkinson, and John Nicholson, Esquires. The Former Being Judge of the Court of Admiralty, and the Latter, the Comptroller-general of the Commonwealth of Pennsylvan.* Philadelphia.

Hoggan, M. (2009, May 27). *93-year-old WWII Vet Carries on Tradition of Playing 'Taps'.* Retrieved from Pioneer Press: https://www.cutbankpioneerpress.com/shelby_promoter/news/article_b71fb317-2209-5703-828c-a7e9948e321e.html

Hopkins, W. P. (1903). *The Seventh Regiment Rhode Island Volunteers in the Civil War 1862–1865.* Providence, RI: The Providence Press.

Howe, E. (1853). *Camp Duty for Drum, Fife, and Field Bugle.* New York: H.B. Dodworth and Co.

Howe, E. (1862). Howe's United States Regulation Drum and Fife Instructor, For the Use of the Army and Navy…Also the Complete Bugle Calls for the Infantry, Artillery and Cavalry. Boston: Howe.

Hyde, B. (2003). *The Union Generals Speak: The Meade Hearings on the Battle of Gettysburg.* Baton Rouge: Louisiana State University Press.

Indiana General Assembly 2024 Session. (2024). Retrieved from Indiana Code § 23-14-54-1. IGA | 2024 Indiana Code.: https://iga.in.gov/laws/2023/ic/titles/4#4-23

International., U. P. (1964). *Four Days: The Historical Record of the Death of President Kennedy.* New York: American Heritage Publishing Co., Inc. Retrieved from https://archive.org/details/fourdayshistoric0000unit

Jacob, M. C. (1991). *Living the Enlightenment: Freemasonry and Politics in Eighteenth-Century Europe.* New York: Oxford University Press.

Jacobs, E. C. (1978, July). A Prelude to the Bugle Call Taps. *Military Medicine, 143, no. 7*, pp. 486-487.

Johnson, M. M. (1924). *The Beginnings of Freemasonry in America.* New York: George H. Doran Company.

Judson, A. M. (1986). *History of the 83rd Regiment Pennsylvania Volunteers.* Erie, Pa: B.F.H. Lynn Publishers, 1865. Reprinted by Morningside Publishers, Dayton, Ohio.

Kelly, D. (2023, August 9). *What JFK's Funeral was Really Like*. Retrieved from Grunge: https://www.grunge.com/1360622/what-jkfks-funeral-really-like/

Kelly, M. (2019, October 2). *Dover Air Force base: Behind the scenes at America's military mortuary*. Retrieved from Northjersy.com: https://www.northjersy.com/story/news/columnists/mike-kelly/2019/10/02/dover-air-force-base-behind-scenes-americas-military-mortuary/2222857001/

Klicker, P. R. (2018). *A Walk-Through Time: A History of Funeral Service*. New York: Thanos Institute. P. 198.

Klingenmaier, R. (Spring 2012). The Burial of General George Washington: The Lesser-Known Participants. *The Alexandria Chronicle*.

Knapp, J. (2023, September 10). Army Veteran on Origin of Taps, Myth. (B. Saunders, Interviewer)

Knox, J. H. (1933). Bulletin of the Institute of the History of Medicine, Vol. 1, No. 5. In *"The Medical History of George Washington, His Physicians, Friends and Advisers* (pp. 174-91). Baltimore, MD: Johns Hopkins University Press.

Kobbe, G. (1898, August). The Trumpet in Camp and Battle. *The Century Magazine LVI, no. 4*, pp. 537-543.

Lacy, L. A. (1976). *The Soil Soldiers–Civilian Conservation Corps in the Great Depression*. Radnor, Pennsylvania: Chilton Book Company.

Layden, Tim. Indianapolis 500 is a reflection of what Memorial Day means most [Video]. YouTube. (2024, May 26). Indianapolis, IN: Motorsports on NBC.

Lear, T. (1799, December 15). I, Journal Account Tobias Lear, "The last illness and Death of General Washington. *Founders Online*. National Archives [Original source: The Papers of George Washington, Digital Edition]. Retrieved from https://founders.archives.gov/documents/Washington/06-04-02-0406-0001

Lear, T. (1799, December 14). *II, 14 December 1799*. Retrieved from Founders Online, National Archives: https://founders.archives.gov/documents/Washington/06-04-02-0406-0002

Lear, T. (1799, December 15). *To John Adams from Tobias Lear*. Retrieved from Founders Online, National Archives, : https://founders.archives.gov/documents/Adams/99-02-02-4081

Lear, T. (1799, December 10). Tobias Lear Diary. (1799-1801) Tobias Lear Diary, Historical Society of Pennsylvania (Am.09238). Philadelphia, Pennsylvania.

Lee, B. (1993, November). The Broken Note. *Washingtonian Magazine*, pp. 48-49.

Leepson, M. (2007). *Flag An American Biography* . New York: Thomas Dunne Books.

Leepson, M. (2014). *What So Proudly We Hailed: Francis Scott Key, A Life*. New York: Thomas Dunne Books.

Leepson, M. (Fall 2011). The First Union Civil War Martyr: Elmer Ellsworth, Alexandria, and the American Flag. *The Alexandria Chronicle.* , pp. 1-7.

Lovette, L. P. (1939). *Naval Customs–Traditions and Usage*. Annapolis, Md: United States Naval Institute.

Lowens, I. (1963, December 1). Accurate Listing of Funeral Music. List of music from President Kennedy's funeral procession. Washington D.C.: The Washington Star.

Luce, S. B. (1884). *Text-Book of Seamanship: The Equipping and Handling of Vessels Under Sail or Steam*. New York: D. Van Nostrand.

Manchester, W. (1963). *The Death of A President*. New York: Harper & Row.

Mayer, R. G. (2012). *Embalming: History, Theory, and Practice. Fifth Edition. New York: McGraw Hill. P. 111*. New York: McGraw Hill.

McCullough, D. (2005). *1776*. New York: Simon and Schuster.

McDowell, E. (2023, May 19). *Jackie Kennedy's pink suit is locked in a vault and will be hidden from public view until 2103. Here are surprising facts about the famous outfit*. Retrieved from Business Insider: https://www.businessinsider.com/jackie-kennedy-pink-suit-facts-location-storage-2023-5

McFarland, M. (2006, February 8). *'Black Jack' Famous Kennedy Funeral Horse Dies*. Retrieved from WSFA 12 News: https://www.wsfa.com/story/4473361/black-jack-famous-kennedy-funeral-horse-dies/

McGrath, J. a. (2014, July 2). *Did Betsy Ross Really Make the First American Flag?* Retrieved from History.com: https://www.history.com/news/did-betsy-ross-really-make-the-first-american-flag

McGratten, A. (1995). The Trumpet in Funeral Ceremonies in Scotland and England During the 17th Century. *Historic Brass Society Journal, 7*, 168-184.

McNutt, W. S. (1921, November 11). The Solder Comes Home. *The American Legion Weekly*, p. 6.

McPherson, J. M. (1992). *Ordeal by Fire The Civil War and Reconstruction*. New York: McGraw-Hill, Inc.

Military. (1891). Infantry Drill Regulations, United States Army with Interpretations 1891. New York: D. Appleton and Co. Retrieved from https://archive.org/details/InfantryDrillRegulationsUnitedStatesArmywithInterpr etations1891

Miller, T. M. (1991). *Artisans and Merchants of Alexandria, Virginia, 1780-1820, Vol. 1, ed.* Maryland: Heritage Books, Inc., 1991, 7; The Writings of George Washington, 33:279 & 279n, 281-282, and 282n; 34:214.

Moeller, H. W. (2002, January). Two Early American Ensigns on the Pennsylvania State Arms. *NAVA News (173)*, 41-41.

Moen, M. a. (2002). *Heroes Cry Too A WWII Ranger Tells His Story of Love and War.* Elk River, MN: Meadowlark Publishing, Inc.

Moss, J. A. (1911). *Officer's Manual.* Mensashe Wisc: George Banta Publishing Co.

Mossman, B. a. (1991). *The Last Salute: Civil and Military Funerals 1921-1969.* Washington, D.C: Department of the Army. CMH Pub 90-1.

Naval Regulations, Issued by Command of the President of the United States of America, January 25, 1802. (1970). Annapolis, Md: Naval Institute Press.

Neil, E. D. (1868). The Fairfaxes of England and America in the Seventeenth and Eighteenth Centuries . New York: Joel Munsell. Retrieved from https://www.mountvernon.org/library/digitalhistory/digital-encyclopedia/article/fairfax-family#note3

Nevins, J. H. (1997). *What Death More Glorious—A Biography of General Strong.* New York: Belle Grove Pub Co.

News, C. (2013, October 18). Irish cadets who performed at JFK funeral to offer final salute. Retrieved from https://www.cbsnews.com/news/irish-cadets-who-performed-at-jfk-funeral-to-offer-final-salute/

News, N. (1966). *There was a President.* New York: Ridge Press. Retrieved from https://archive.org/details/therewaspresiden00nbcn

News, T. D. (1993). *The day JFK died : thirty years later : the event that changed a generation.* Kansas City : Andrews and McMeel. Retrieved from https://archive.org/details/dayjfkdiedthirty0000unse

Norton, A. a. (1984). *Our Norton Family.* Sun City, Ariz: Published by the Authors.

Norton, O. W. (1903). *Army Letters, 1861-1865.* Chicago: Chicago: O.L. Deming, 1903. Reprinted with additional material by Morningside, 1990.

Norton, O. W. (1909). *Strong Vincent and His Brigade at Gettysburg, July 2, 1863*. Chicago: Chicago.

Norton, O. W. (1913). *The Attack and Defense of Little Round Top* . New York: Neale Publishing Co.

O'Hara, T. (1847). The Bivouac of the Dead. The R. Clarke Co. Retrieved from https://www.cem.va.gov/history/BODpoem.asp

Origin of the 21-Gun Salute. (1969, May). Retrieved from Headquarters, Military District of Washington, FACT SHEET: GUN SALUTES: https://history.army.mil/faq/salute.html

Origins of the Twenty-One Gun Salute. (2024, June 05). Retrieved from https://www.history.navy.mil/browse-by-topic/heritage/customs-and-traditions0/twenty-one-gun-salute.html

Passing of Noted Veteran. (1901, July 18). *Davenport Daily Republican*. Davenport, Iowa: Davenport Daily Republican.

Patterson, D. T. (22, March 2018). Patterson, Daniel T. Station Bills Etc. of the U.S. Ship North Carolina Ship's Manuscript, 1825. U.S. Naval Academy. *Naval History and Heritage Command*. Annapolis, MD. Retrieved from https://www.history.navy.mil/content/history/nhhc/research/library/research-guides/z-files/zb-files/zb-files-p/patterson-daniel-todd.html

Patterson, M. R. (2024, March 2). William Howard Taft – President of the United States Chief Justice of the United States Supreme Court.

Patterson, R. S. (1978). *The Eagle and the Shield: A History of the Great Seal of the United States.* Washington: Office of the Historian, Bureau of Public Affairs, Dept. of State : for sale by the Supt. of Docs., U.S. Govt. Print. Off.

PeriscopeFilm. (1963, November 25). Funeral Procession and Burial of President John F. Kennedy. November 25, 1963. XD13194. Retrieved from https://archive.org/details/xd-13194-john-f-kennedy-funeral-vwr

Polk, J. K. (1846, May 11). May 11, 1846: War Message to Congress. Washington: University of Virginia Miller Center. Retrieved from https://millercenter.org/the-presidency/presidential-speeches/may-11-1846-war-message-congress

Poole, R. M. (2009). *On Hallowed Ground: The Story of Arlington National Cemetery*. New York: Bloomsbury Publishing.

Poore, R. (2013, May 23). *Civil War-era editor largely remembered for poem*. Retrieved from Newspapering: https://newspapering.blogspot.com/2013/05/civil-war-era-editor-largely-remembered.html

Powell, E. A. (2015, July/August). Riding Into The Afterlife. *Archaeology Magazine*. Retrieved from https://archaeology.org/issues/july-august-2015/collection/horses-companions-in-the-afterlife/the-story-of-the-horse/

Powell, M. C. (1928). The History of Old Alexandria, Virginia P. 91, 94, 259-260; The Diaries of George Washington, Vol. 4, 123n, Vol. 5:19, 38, 41, 43, 152, 187-8, 220, 247, 414, 414n; Vol. 6, 303, 307, 313, 357. Richmond: William Byrd Press.

Press, A. (1988, November 22). Bugler's Note Still Plays on Him.

Printing, J. C. (2007). *Our Flag by U.S. Congress (2007). (Rev. ed.109th Congress, 2nd Session ed.)*. Washington, D.C.: U.S. Government Printing Office.

Rauser, F. (1892). Music on the March, 1862-65, With the Army of the Potomac. Philadelphia: William Fell and Co.

Reed, R. M. (2014). *Lincoln's Funeral Train The Epic Journey from Washington to Springfield*. Atglen, PA: Schiffer.

Regan, R. W. (1981, January 20). Inaugural Address 1981. Washington, D.C. Retrieved from https://www.reaganlibrary.gov/archives/speech/inaugural-address-1981

Reid, T. (1963, December 16). After Action Report, President Kennedy Funeral (Interment Ceremony). 3rd U.S. Infantry Records.

Rohm, F. W. (1998). *No Braver Man—The Story of Fritz Rohm, Bugler, 16th PA Cavalry*. Fredericksburg, VA: Sergeant Kirkland's Press.

Rosen, J. (2018). *William Howard Taft: The American Presidents Series*. New York: Time Books, Henry Holt & Co.

Ruiz, S. (2023, August 30). Cradle to Grave: The Only American Both Born and Buried at Arlington National Cemetery. Retrieved from https://www.military.com/history/cradle-grave-only-american-both-born-and-buried-arlington-national-cemetery.html

Russell, B. (1799, December 28). Columbian Centinel & Massachusetts Federalist (Boston, Mass.) 1799-1804. Boston, Massachusetts: Columbian centinel.

Safranek, V. (1916). *Complete Instructive Manual for Bugle, Trumpet and Drum*. New York: Carl Fisher.

Sanders. (2024, August 4). *Theodore O'Hara*. Retrieved from ExploreKYHistor: https://explorekyhistory.ky.gov/items/show/105

Schlichter, Norman C. "The Birth of Taps." Pennsylvania Guardsman 42 (May 1939); 3. (n.d.).

Schneider, D. a. (2010). First Ladies: A Biographical Dictionary (3rd ed.). Facts on File. 172–181. Infobase Publishing.

Schwartz, T. F. (Autumn 2007). A Death in the Family : Abraham Lincoln II "Jack" (1873–1890)" (PDF). For the People. Vol. 9, no. 3. Abraham Lincoln Association. pp. 1, 4. Archived from the original on October 17, 2013. Retrieved February 11, 2019.

Science, N. A. (2015). *Types of Funeral Services and Ceremonies 2nd Ed.* Oklahoma City: Funeral Service Education Resource Center.

Scott, W. (1835). *Infantry tactics ; or, Rules for the exercise and manœuvres of the United States' infantry.* New York: George Dearborn. Retrieved from https://archive.org/details/bub_gb_B_MVAAAAYAAJ

Sheeler, J. (2008). *Final Salute: A story of Unfinished Lives.* New York: Penguin Press.

Shinseki, E. K. (2003, May). Soldiers Creed. https://www.army.mil/values/soldiers.html. U.S. Army. Retrieved from https://www.army.mil/values/soldiers.html

Sledge, M. (2005). *Soldier Dead: How We Recover, Identify, Bury, and Honor Our Military Fallen.* New York: Columbia University Press.

Sousa, J. P. (1985). *A Book of Instruction for The Field Trumpet and Drum.* Washington, D.C: Published by the Author. Reprinted by Ludwig Music, Cleveland, Ohio.

Steele, E. C. (2024). *Today In Masonic History*. Retrieved from MasonryToday.com: Today in Masonic History - Daniel Adams Butterfield is Born (masonrytoday.com) written by Brother Eric C. Steele.

Stevenson, D. (1986). *The First Freemasons: Scotland's Early Lodges and their Members, 2nd edition.* Scotland, UK: Aberdeen Univ Pr; Reprint edition (January 1, 1989).

Strube, G. A. (1870). *Strube's Drum and Fife Instructor.* New York: D. Appleton & Co.

Swick, G. D. (Summer 1998). His Own Place In The Sun" (PDF). Lincoln Lore. 1853: 3–6. Retrieved December 23, 2022. 3-6. Retrieved from https://www.friendsofthelincolncollection.org/wp-content/uploads/2018/11/LL_1998-Summer.pdf

Taft, W. H. (1980, February). Collection: William Howard Taft papers | Archives at Yale. Retrieved from https://web.library.yale.edu/search/google/William%20Howard%20TAft

The George Washington Masonic National Memorial. (2024). Alexandria, VA: The George Washington Masonic National Memorial Association, Inc. Retrieved from https://gwmemorial.org/

The LBJ Presidential Library. Personal Perspective. [Video]. YouTube. (2013, October 30). *November 22, 1963*. Retrieved from https://www.lbjlibrary.org/exhibitions/permanent/november-22-1963

Torreon, B. S. (2015, April 10). *Military Funeral Honors and Military* . Retrieved from Congressional Research Service: https://sgp.fas.org/crs/misc/RS21545.pdf

Troncone, A. C. (1993). Hamilton Fish Sr. and the Politics of American Nationalism, 1912–1945. New Brunswick, NJ: Rutgers The State Univ. of New Jersey.

United States Congress. (1843). Rules and Regulations for the Navy..., 27th Cong. 3d Sess., H. Doc. 148 . Washington, D.C.

United States Environmental Protection Agency. (2024, May 03). *Burial at Sea*. Retrieved from EPA United States Environmental Protection Agency: https://www.epa.gov/ocean-dumping/burial-sea

Van Beck, T. (2020, February). Rest In Peace Mr. President – George Washington. *Funeral and Cemetery News* . NOMIS Publications, Inc.

Van Beck, T. (2022, March). Rest In Peace Mr. President – William Howard Taft. *Funeral and Cemetery News*. NOMIS Publications, Inc.

Villanueva, J. (2001). *Twenty-Four Notes That Tap Deep Emotions: The Story of America's Most Famous Bugle Call* . Baltimore: JV Music.

Washington, G. (1732-1799). *George Washington's Will, The Papers of George Washington, Retirement Series, 4:485*. Charlottesville: University Press Virginia.

Washington, G. (1776, January 1). General Orders, 1 January 1776. *Founders Online*. National Historical Publications and Records Commission. Retrieved from https://founders.archives.gov/documents/Washington/03-03-02-0001#GEWN-03-03-02-0001-fn-0003

Whitney, J. L. (1993, August). The True Story of Taps. *Blue and Grey Magazine*, pp. 30-33.

William R. Weisberger, W. M. (2002). *Freemasonry on Both Sides of the Atlantic: Essays Concerning the Craft in the British Isles, Europe, the United States, and Mexico.* . Boulder, CO: East European Monographs.

Williams, E. P. (1996, June 14). A Civil Servant Designed Our National Banner: The Unsung Legacy of Francis Hopkinson". The New Constellation . *Newsletter of the National Flag Foundation). Special Edition #7: 8.*

Williams, E. P. (2010, October). Did Francis Hopkinson Design Two Flags? *NAVA New*, 7-9. Archived (PDF) from the original on March 6, 2016. Retrieved from https://www.flagguys.com/pdf/NAVANews_2012_no216.pdf

Wilson, J. W. (1978). *Engineer Memoirs.* Mobile: US Army Corps of Engineers.

Worthington, R. (1938, November). Homecoming. *The American Legion Magazine*, p. 3.

Wrapped in a flag . (2013, March 2). Retrieved from Gettysburg Flag Works: https://www.gettysburgflag.com/blog/wrapped-in-a-flag/

Wylie, N. (2020, November 16). We Are Americans Patriotic Speech by Ronald Regan. [Video]. YouTube. Retrieved from https://www.youtube.com/watch?v=9h7xD4mIcdw

Yagi, J. G. (2019, July 3). The Birth of the 'Stars and Stripes' – How America's Flag Evolved During the War of Independence. University of the Pacific. Retrieved from https://militaryhistorynow.com/2019/07/03/the-birth-of-the-stars-and-stripes-how-americas-flag-evolved-during-the-war-of-independence/

Yenne, B. (2015). *The Complete Book of US Presidents.* . Birmingham, Alabama: Sweet Water Press.

Young, J. R. (2017, June 23). *Ulysses S. Grant Quote on the Mexican-American War - Shot Glass of History.* Retrieved from Shot Glass of History: Delivering a Strong Dose of Historical Rethinking: https://www.shotglassofhistory.com/ulysses-s-grant-quote-mexican-american-war/

Younger, E. F. (1936, November 8). I Chose the Unknown Soldier. *This Week.* Retrieved from https://www.arlingtoncemetery.mil/Blog/Post/11465/A-Humble-Sergeant-Edward-F-Younger-and-the-Unknown-Soldier

Zall, P. M. (1976). *Comical Spirit of Seventy-Six: The Humor of Francis Hopkinson.* San Marino, California: Huntington Library.

Made in the USA
Columbia, SC
03 February 2025

52607713R00163